AGAINST RECOGNITION

AGAINST RECOGNITION

Lois McNay

polity

First published in 2008 by Polity Press

Polity Press
65 Bridge Street
Cambridge CB2 1UR, UK

Polity Press
350 Main Street
Malden, MA 02148, USA

ISBN-13: 978-07456-2931-5
ISBN-13: 978-07456-2932-2 (pb)

A catalogue record for this book is available from the British Library

Typeset in 10.5/12 pt Dante
by Servis Filmsetting Ltd, Manchester
Printed and bound in India by Replika Press PVT Ltd, Kundli, India

For further information on Polity, visit our website www.polity.co.uk

Contents

Acknowledgements

Passages from Chapter 1 first appeared as part of 'Out of the Orrery? Situating Language', *Journal of Political Ideologies*, vol. 8, no. 2, pp:. 139–56 and are reprinted by permission from Taylor and Francis Ltd. A shorter version of Chapter 3 first appeared as 'Having it Both Ways: The Incompatibility of Narrative Identity and Communicative Ethics in Feminist Thought', © *Theory, Culture and Society*, 2003, vol. 20, no. 6, pp:. 1–20 and is reprinted by permission from Sage Publications Ltd.

I would like to thank the fellows of Somerville College and the Department of Politics at Oxford University for granting me the year's leave which enabled me to write this book. I would also like to thank Henriette Dahan-Kalev and Megan Vaughan for their helpful comments on sections of the manuscript at various stages of drafting. I am grateful to Sasha Rosenil, Harriet Bjerrum Nielsen and the other members of the Department of Gender and Women's Studies, University of Oslo, who participated in a day's workshop on agency in June 2006 and whose stimulating and incisive remarks helped me develop my thoughts on certain crucial issues. I would like to thank Desmond King for a small but crucial suggestion and Pedro Ferreira for a small but crucial piece of technical assistance. I am very grateful to the two, now no longer anonymous readers, Andrew Cutrofello and Henrietta Moore, for their perceptive, constructive and generous-spirited reports on my manuscript for Polity. I would especially like to thank Henrietta, who always manages to push me to revise my ideas much more thoroughly than I might otherwise have done. I would not have been able to complete the manuscript when I did without the help of my mother, Marian McNay, who uncomplainingly gave up many days of her time to look after one or other of my children when they were too sick to attend school or nursery. I am deeply indebted to her. Above all, I would like to thank Murray Hunt for the countless ways in which he supports and sustains me. This book is dedicated to him.

For Murray

Introduction: Against Recognition

To be 'against recognition' seems, on the face of it, to be an unsustainable position. The Hegelian idea of the struggle for recognition has provided the foundation for numerous important formulations of an alternative conception of subjectivity to the monological and disembodied accounts that prevail in conventional thought. To be against recognition in this sense would be untenable since it would entail opposition to the crucial insights into the dialogical and non-rational nature of subjectivity that have informed many significant, frequently radical, traditions of thought. The idea of recognition has also acquired renewed significance, in the past decade or so, as a way of denoting the increasingly central role played by identity claims in social and political conflict. It would be difficult to be against recognition in this sense, too, as it would be tantamount to disregarding widespread social transformations that have undeniably had catalysing effects on political movements. It would be unreasonable to be against recognition in a final sense, namely, that to be emphatically for or against something is, in so many respects, non-conducive to intellectual debate. It leads all too easily, as Michel Foucault has observed, to the adoption of polemical attitudes that foreclose the exploration of subtleties and interconnections between differing positions.

This book is not 'against recognition', therefore, in any of the general senses outlined above. It is against recognition, however, in the more specific sense that it is critical of a cluster of loosely related formulations of the idea which have become predominant in the past ten or so years and which are associated, by and large, with what can be called communitarian and communicative traditions of thought. The catalyst for this resurgence of interest in recognition is the essay by Charles Taylor (1994a) on the politics of recognition, although the idea has been present, with varying degrees of prominence, in the work of many of the thinkers considered here for much longer. Nonetheless, it is Taylor's signal essay that has given the idea of the struggle for recognition renewed currency as an interpretative trope for explaining the centrality of identity claims to so many significant social and political struggles. The idea has been developed mainly within the terrain of normative political thought and the adjacent domains of cultural and social theory, but it has also been fruitfully developed in the more distant domain of psychoanalysis. Indeed, as the idea has become increasingly prevalent there have been many fruitful engagements between thinkers across these disciplinary fields. Despite its prominence in debate and the important insights it has generated, I argue that the way in which the idea of recognition has been elaborated by a cluster of thinkers is flawed. My basic argument is as follows. Although the idea of recognition highlights the multifarious ways in which identity claims lie close to the heart of many contemporary social and political movements, it frames these issues in a reductive understanding of power. I focus, in particular, on the ways in which the idea of recognition rests on a simplified understanding of subject formation, identity and agency in the context of social hierarchies, in particular, gender. In the final analysis, many of these difficulties stem from the dual significance that the idea of recognition is accorded as both a descriptive tool and a regulative ideal. The exigencies of sustaining the idea of recognition as a viable normative ideal result in a delimitation of its analytical purchase by disconnecting certain aspects of subject formation from an analysis of power. This disconnection is partly concealed by an ontology of recognition that each thinker sets up and that allows them to naturalize and universalize their particular account of subjectivity and agency. The ultimate irony of these naturalizing and universalizing tendencies is that they undermine the initial impulse that led these thinkers to use the idea of recognition in the first place. Far from resulting in a more embodied, dialogical account of subjectivity, most of the thinkers considered here end up invoking relatively abstract and disembodied conceptions that are closer than they might care to acknowledge to the monological concepts they oppose.

In sum, I am not against recognition in that I do not disagree with the basic claims made about the dialogical nature of subjectivity, identity and agency by thinkers of recognition. I am against recognition, however, in so far as these insights are not sufficiently embedded in a sociological understanding of power relations. The consequent ways in which the idea of recognition is naturalized and universalized foreclose anything but the most limited understanding of identity and agency in the context of the reproduction of inequalities of gender.

THE SUBJECT OF RECOGNITION

The force of the idea of recognition derives from its original Hegelian formulation where selfhood is formed not through a solipsistic process of rational contemplation but through an intense and unending conflict with an 'other'. From Hegel's basic depiction of the struggle for recognition have flowed a multiplicity of theories about the precise nature that this agonistic process of subject formation assumes. In general, recent work on recognition has conceptualized this dialectical subjectivity in ways that are quite distinct from earlier phases of interest in the idea, most notably, the theories of the post-war existential phenomenologists such as Kojève, Merleau Ponty, Sartre, De Beauvoir and Fanon. In many respects, the work of the latter has a more nuanced understanding of the entrenched nature of power relations and, as a consequence, a more pessimistic political outlook than the former. The recent resurgence of interest in the idea of recognition has been fuelled partly by opposition to the conception of the subject that underpins the tradition of liberal thought, on the one hand, and poststructuralism, on the other. The theoretical difficulties with these respective conceptions of the subject have been widely debated and they only briefly need stating. The concept of the subject held to underpin much liberal thought, especially recent Anglo-American philosophy, is essentially the antecedently individuated entity whose rational and autonomous characteristics are, arguably, overstated. In contrast, the subject of poststructural thought is, on the whole, negatively conceived as a relatively passive and fragmented entity in so far as it is understood as an effect of discourse. One of the central difficulties of these divergent concepts of subjectivity, which has been exhaustively documented by feminist thinkers, is that they are analytically limited in terms of understanding aspects of gender identity and inequality. It is this concern to integrate a fuller account of gender and other social differences into a concept of subjectivity that has partly led many thinkers to develop the dialogical idea of recognition. Without wanting to over-schematize, the three features that constitute the basic lineaments of the subject in what could be termed the 'new' recognition paradigm are that it is dialogical, situated and generated through practice.

The fundamental insight that subjectivity is dialogical in nature, that it is created only through interaction with an Other, allows social and political theory to be recast around the insight of the central importance of intersubjective relations, rather than instrumental or strategic ones, to social life. Clearly many liberal thinkers acknowledge the dialogical aspects to subjectivity and social life; it is only extreme forms of liberal thought that posit the subject as an autarkic being. On the whole, however, the relation between self and other is attenuated by the ontological primacy liberalism accords to the rational or prudentially self-interested individual evident, for example, in Rawls's original position. In this respect, the subject of poststructuralist thought has a greater affinity with the subject of recognition in that it is conceived as a fundamentally relational rather than monological entity. Poststructuralism formulates this relational dynamic, however, largely in terms of a general model of the linguistic construction of desire where language is conceived as an impersonal system of signification. On this view, the other is the Symbolic Other, that is to say the objectified other who is the effect of the subject's projections and fantasies. In contrast, thinkers using the idea of recognition tend to conceive of this relational dynamic in terms of a social dialogue with concrete others, independent individuals who exist externally to the subject's projections. On this view, language is conceived not as an abstract system of signification but as a type of practical action that aims at self-expression, communication or mutual understanding. Dialogue is, therefore, oriented towards the realization of some kind of pragmatic, intersubjectively shared goal. This difference between the relational subject of poststructuralism and the dialogic subject of recognition can be restated as the difference between an exclusionary and inclusionary view of the interaction betweens self and other. Poststructuralism views subject formation as taking place through the exclusionary dynamic of the constitutive other. The 'illusion' of stable subjectivity is maintained only through a derogation or denial of the potentially troubling alterity of the other. Theories of recognition tend to stress conversely the inclusive features of subject formation, that is, stable subjectivity is based on the ability to tolerate and embrace the other's difference. A significant implication of the inclusionary recasting of dialogical subjectivity is that it seemingly institutes an inalienable ethical bond to the other at the heart of normative thought.

The proposition that subjectivity is dialogical in nature is closely related to a second characteristic of the subject of recognition, namely, that it is ineluctably situated. The situated nature of subjectivity can be taken to mean many things but, in general, it denotes the way in which our sense of self, our understanding of what is good and what is just, are not trans-historical, universal phenomena but are insepa- rable from specific cultural and social contexts. This view of the situ- ated nature of subjectivity is generally compatible with types of constructivism where identities are understood as performatively constructed, to varying degrees, rather than as having an essential core. This leads to the further claim that the constructive elements of thought on recognition are embedded in and derived from actual social practices. In other words, an explicit connection is posited in theories of recognition between political prescription and social theory both in terms of its normative consequences and also in terms of its tacit pre-understandings. In this regard, thinkers of recognition clearly position themselves in opposition to many Anglo-American political philosophers who assert that ideal thought must necessarily be free-standing. There is a further sense in which subjectivity can be understood as situated that is more closely connected to the idea of the situation, which is central to the work of phenomenologists such as Merleau Ponty, Sartre and Beauvoir (Kruks 2001). On this view, subjectivity is situated in that it cannot be fully understood from the abstract perspective of determining structures, but must also be grasped from the perspective of the lived reality of embodied social relations. Such an interpretative perspective is often formulated in terms of the idea of 'experience', which is widely held to be problem- atic because it seems to refer to some kind of self-evident and authen- tic realm. If, however, this perspective is detached from the recovery of an essential experience and used more as a heuristic tool, it deliv- ers crucial insights into aspects of embodied subjectivity and agency. It is not possible, for example, to fully explain the dialectic of freedom and constraint that is generative of agency without adopting some kind of phenomenal perspective on the intentionality of embodied existence. Action cannot be grasped only from an abstract account of structural contradiction or linguistic indeterminacy but must also be understood through ideas of intention, aim and commitment 'that can also be refused' (Kruks 2001: 12). It is this inseparability of self from situation and the consequent necessity of adopting some kind of inter- pretative or phenomenal perspective that informs, for instance, the emphasis placed by recognition thinkers on language as a form of pragmatic interaction rather than as pure signification.

A third characteristic of the subject of recognition is that it is gen- erated through embodied practice. Subjectivity is not a punctuated phenomenon but the outcome of an ongoing process of engagement with the world. This idea is closely related to the idea of the situation and likewise, it can be traced back to an influential formulation of existential phenomenology, most famously expressed in Beauvoir's claim that one is not born but becomes woman. The idea that subjectivity is produced through practice is, of course, not limited to phenomenology; it has been interpreted in a multiplicity of ways, many of which emphasize the embodied, pre-reflexive and shared dimensions of this generative process. Practices are understood as 'embodied, materially mediated arrays of human activity centrally organized around shared practical understanding' (Schatzki 2001: 2). On this view, subjectivity is neither fully willed nor fully determined. It is neither the outcome of a conscious project of self-fashioning nor is it the effect of the iterative operations of discourse upon the body. It is rather the pre-reflexive realization of embodied dispositions which themselves are the result of the incorporation of the latent tendencies of the world into the body. This emphasis on the embodied and pre-rational dimensions of practice is taken in different directions by thinkers of recognition. Charles Taylor, for example, argues that our deepest moral and ethical judgements are not rational or cognitive but are 'inarticulate' in that they are based in emotional and intuitive responses to the world. Along with thinkers like Axel Honneth, Taylor also argues that many of our actions are motivated not by rational interest but by the often pre-rational but elemental 'moral suffering' that occurs from social misrecognition. Likewise, Jurgen Habermas uses the idea of universal pragmatics to show how daily interaction is practically oriented towards reaching understanding rather than being driven by strategic or instrumental concerns. Like the idea of the situated nature of subjectivity, the emphasis on practice returns recognition thinkers again to some kind of phenomenal perspective which attempts to analyse social existence in terms of latent or explicit self-understanding, intention and aim.

Although the subject of recognition is elaborated according to discernible, shared themes, it is important not to overstate these commonalities. Each thinker develops them in distinct ways, in relation to differing problematics, and in order to reach divergent political conclusions. There is one overarching feature, however, that unites these various configurations of the subject, which is that almost all the thinkers considered here invest the idea of recognition with a strong normative significance. The idea of recognition is regarded not just as a useful analytical tool for unravelling processes of subject formation but is also seen as a potent way of expressing a normative ideal of egalitarian self-realization. The attribution of such a normative force to the idea of recognition is motivated, to some degree, by a concern to overcome the issue of difference which, although enormously important in contemporary thought, has become something of a theoretical impasse. Again, the liberal and poststructural treatment of the idea of difference establishes the parameters of the problem that thinkers of recognition seek to overcome. In liberal theory, cultural, social and ethical differences are treated as the more or less unalterable given of value pluralism. Individuals are understood to have fairly fixed, pre-given beliefs and are regarded, therefore, as relatively impervious to democratic deliberation. On the whole, any response to collective social and normative problems must be based on an appeal to their rational self-interest, rather than to any altruistic capacities, or on an appeal to the intrinsic importance of certain normative ideals. This leads to an emphasis on normatively thin procedural solutions that leave the seemingly irreconcilable differences of value pluralism intact (see Habermas 1998b). In poststructuralism, difference is not so much an unalterable empirical given as it is an insurmountable onto-logical premise of existence. On this view, any attempt to set up defin-itive social or political arrangements runs the risk of excluding and oppressing individuals in unforeseen ways. Like liberalism, this leads poststructural thinkers to posit normatively thin political solutions, although they are formulated not so often as procedural frameworks but more as transient political alliances galvanized around contingent universal aims (e.g. Butler, Laclau and Žižek 2000). Against these two streams of thought, thinkers of recognition argue that if subjects are understood in a different way then difference is no longer reified as an ineliminable obstacle to social and political arrangements based on normatively thick ideas of shared understanding, empathy and agree-ment. The inclusive inflexion that thinkers of recognition give to the dialogical constitution of the subject means that individuals have the capacity, indeed in some cases are predisposed, to empathize with the other rather than being locked in an antagonistic relation with them. The inclusive proclivities of the subject are reinforced through the ideas of its situated and practice-oriented nature which emphasize the underlying shared regularities, assumptions and norms that structure embodied social existence. By highlighting the commonalities of existence in this way, even if they are latent, recog-nition thinkers seek to sketch out potential grounds for shared under-standing and action. On this view, difference is not denied but neither is it hypertrophied. As Kruks puts it: 'the commonalities of embodi-ment point beyond the solipsistic tendencies of . . . subjects each of whom objectifies the other' (Kruks 2001: 33). It is in this respect that recognition has an explicitly dual significance; it is both an analytical tool and a political ideal. The normative solution to the problem of difference proposed by thinkers of recognition is inextricably related to their ontology of the subject.

THE ONTOLOGY OF RECOGNITION

On the face of it, the normative force of the idea of recognition is attractive. It resonates, in particular, with feminist attempts to conceptualize subjectivity and agency beyond the well-known analytical and normative limitations of poststructural and liberal thought. The influential work of Seyla Benhabib and Jessica Benjamin, for example, has drawn out the potential implications of the idea of recognition for an understanding of the gendered aspects of embodied existence. The value of the idea of recognition is not limited to feminist thought; it has also provided a fruitful basis for theories of political engagement that seek to transcend the idea of difference; for example, theories of deliberative democracy. Whilst not wanting to discount the valuable insights of this work, it is the central claim of this book that the normative potency invested in the idea of recognition is also the source of a central weakness. There is too often an unexamined conflation of the normative and analytical functions of the idea of recognition with the effect that the former limits the critical purchase of the latter. The normative 'redemptive' force that resides in the ideal of mutual recognition constrains the way it is used as an analytical tool to explain how power creates unequal identities. In order to render recognition plausible as an ideal of self-realization and equality, sociological barriers to its possible implementation must necessarily be diminished or construed as contingent, secondary effects of power. Thus problematic aspects to the reproduction of subjectivity that pertain to the pervasive and insidious nature of social domination are underplayed. This is achieved through the disconnection of an understanding of subject formation from an analysis of power relations, with the consequence that the idea of recognition fails to grasp some important dimensions to the reproduction of social inequalities.

This problematic conflation of the normative sense of the idea of recognition with its analytical scope is not an incidental effect of the way it is conceptualized but rather a constitutive feature. It stems from the way in which almost all of the thinkers considered here legitimate the idea of recognition through ontological claims. The idea of the struggle for recognition permits each thinker to set up a primal dyad as the origin of social relations and to attribute to this dyad a fundamental function, whether it be communication, self-expression or a constitutive need for acknowledgement. Social relations are then assessed according to the extent to which they realize or distort this primal function. On this view, social relations of power are always a *post hoc* effect, distorting or otherwise, of some antecedent and primordial interpersonal dynamic. Thus, for Habermas, social relations are regarded as imperfect realizations of an orientation to understanding that, in his view, constitutes the telos of linguistically mediated recognition, indeed, of language in general. On Taylor's expressivist version of recognition, social relations are assessed in terms of the extent to which they permit the actualization of authentic ethical identities. The problem with such views is that the extrapolation of the essence of sociality from a primal recognition dynamic results in a simplified understanding of power and its operations with regard to the formation of subjectivity and the construction of oppression. These simplifications manifest themselves in various ways. One major difficulty is that the face-to-face dynamic that is intrinsic to the idea of recognition disconnects inequalities from a socio-structural account of power. Gender oppression, for example, is misunderstood by being construed as, in its essence, a form of interpersonally engendered misrecognition rather than also as systemically generated oppression. This is not to deny that inequalities are created through personal interaction, but, by focusing principally on this mode, the idea of recognition obscures the extent to which identity and subjectivity are penetrated by structural dynamics of power which often operate at one remove from the immediate relations of everyday life.

This disconnection of the phenomenal realm of interaction from the underlying nexus of power relations is compounded by the tendency of many of the thinkers considered here to allocate recognition struggles to a distinct realm – the lifeworld or culture – thereby disconnecting it from what is variously configured as the arena of redistribution, the economy or systems. This book follows a multiplicity of thinkers in arguing that it is important to grasp the increasingly complex ways in which identity and subject formation are interconnected to latent structural dynamics (Fraser 2003; Hennessey 2000; Ray and Sayer 1999; Young 2000). The connection between embodied social reality and social structures is not an extrinsic one, expressed in theories of determination, but is an intrinsic one where impersonal forces shape, in a subtle and often indirect fashion, the felt necessities of daily life. Arguably, this interpenetration of the phenomenal and the structural is an intensifying feature of globalized capital where progressively more areas of social life are subject to systemic forces of regulation and commodification. It is important to examine the interconnections between subjective forms and impersonal forces, partly because, as identity increasingly becomes the focus for neo-liberal modes of social control, the nature of agency and resistance is altered. These processes of capitalist expansion are changing, for example, the nature of gender division and gender oppression, and challenge us to rethink the ideas of agency and change beyond dichotomies of domination and resistance

The ontology of recognition also has simplifying consequences for the conceptualization of agency. One of the ostensible strengths of the idea of recognition is that it has been used to develop an alternative theory of political agency to the strategic or rational models that prevail in conventional thought. In particular, it places an important emphasis upon the crucial role played by intuition, emotions and affect in catalysing action. While these insights are undeniably valuable, they are undercut by the ontology of recognition which both reifies these affectual dimensions as spontaneous, ineffable givens and also unifies them by viewing them as expressions of a primal need for recognition. The naturalized model of agency that this ensures is predicated on a one-way causality in which psychological dynamics determine social patterns of behaviour. This forecloses, *inter alia*, any but the most limited understanding of the way in which social forces might be understood as having conditioning effects upon the psyche. Instead of viewing the need for recognition as an inherent part of human psychology, for example, it might be understood as an ideological construction. In this respect, certain thinkers have argued very persuasively that, far from being authentic indicators of oppression or injustice, recognition claims derive their legitimacy from a certain sentimentalized discourse of suffering (e.g. Brown 1995; Berlant 2000). This rhetoric of personal pain is the internalized effect of a certain type of neo-liberal regulation that depoliticizes oppression by establishing a universal equivalence of individual suffering. In the pervasive morass of sentiment, it becomes difficult to distinguish genuine claims of oppression from less legitimate ones. Some thinkers go further and argue that the politics of recognition is essentially a middle-class phenomenon since it is only privileged groups that have the disposition required to manage a rhetoric of personal suffering and distress to personal advantage (Skeggs 2004c). While such arguments might be overstated, they draw attention to the way in which the desire for recognition might be far from a spontaneous and innate phenomenon but the effect of a certain ideological manipulation of individuals. Such a critical perspective is foregone by thinkers who naturalize the idea of recognition by failing to examine more thoroughly the way in which emotions and other aspects of embodied subjectivity are mediated through social relations of power. Ultimately, then, the idea of recognition finishes by binding action too closely to a single aspect of subjectivity and thereby reduces its diverse logic to an invariant psychological need. A claim of this book is that agency cannot be adequately conceptualized through universal models of recognition. Rather, social theory should seek to untangle, in their singularity, the indirect routes of power that connect specific identity formations to the invisible structures underlying them and that mean that agency has diverse motivations and causes.

BEYOND RECOGNITION

So far I have focused on the negative component of my argument against recognition. I turn now to its constructive component which is based on a how a materialist understanding of subject formation might help develop the insights into embodied identity and agency that thinkers of recognition initiate but fail to elaborate adequately in relation to social hierarchies. In order to do this, I draw on Pierre Bourdieu's idea of habitus that yields a notion of embodied subjectivity which is, in many respects, similar to the dialogical conception proposed by thinkers of recognition but is located more securely within a sociological account of power. A crucial difference is that for Bourdieu, power is coextensive with the process of subject formation, whereas, in the ontology of recognition, it is always secondary to this process, to some degree or other. In other words, the conceptualization of subject formation cannot be defined apart from relations of power. The positing of an intrinsic, rather than extrinsic, connection between subjectivity and power delivers a firmer grounding for understanding aspects of embodied agency in the context of the construction of social inequalities, especially gender.

The choice of the Bourdieusian idea of habitus as a counterpoint to theories of recognition and as the basis for an account of embodied agency and gender may at first seem curious on several counts. Foremost amongst these must be the numerous criticisms that have been made of the determinist tendencies of his thought. The concept of habitus has been criticized for over-predicting the accommodation of individuals to social structures and his idea of agency has been widely dismissed for its narrowly strategic emphasis.[1] Furthermore, although he does not disregard issues connected to

gender identity, his thought on 'masculine domination' is underdeveloped and, in many respects, quite simplistic (McNay 2000: 52–7).
I do not want to underplay any of these difficulties and indeed this
book is not intended as a wholesale resuscitation of Bourdieu's
thought. My interpretation of Bourdieu is an avowedly selective one
that focuses principally on the idea of habitus and the way that this
may extend important insights into the nature of embodied subjectivity and agency that is helpful for a feminist concern with issues of
gender. This reading of Bourdieu places more emphasis on the influence of the phenomenological tradition upon the development of
his central ideas rather than the Durkheimian or Marxist traditions,
although their impact is undeniably very significant. It is not,
however, an entirely idiosyncratic interpretation because increasingly, in his later thought, Bourdieu chose to locate his key concepts
within a phenomenological tradition and this corresponds to an
increased emphasis in his late work on ideas of agency, change, discontinuity and resistance (e.g. Bourdieu 1998, 2000). It is these elements of his thought that are too often neglected by his critics and
which I extend – in a way that admittedly Bourdieu does not in his
work on sexual division – to a theory of embodied agency and
gender.[2]

   The idea of habitus is possibly the most discussed and utilized
concept in Bourdieu's analytical framework of habitus-field-capital.
As is well known, habitus denotes a process through which power
relations are incorporated into the body in the form of durable physical and psychological predispositions. On my reading of Bourdieu,
his idea of habitus is not, contra his critics, a straightforwardly determinist category but is a generative one. It is the catalysing concept in
what I term a relational phenomenology which is derived from
Bourdieu's description of his method as a 'social phenomenology' or
a 'phenomenology of social space' (Bourdieu 1990a: 129). The basic
idea that Bourdieu intends to capture in this self-definition is that an
analysis of embodied subjects in context, defined as the individual's
understanding of her conditions of existence, is crucial to any explanation of social life and, in particular, agency: 'Sociology must include
a sociology of the perception of the social world, that is, a sociology of
the construction of visions of the world which themselves contribute
to the construction of this world' (1990a: 130). If social action is to be
properly understood, then it is important to start from the representations that actors have of the world and the way these inform action
and interaction. These representations cannot be deduced from social
structures. Nor, however, do they encompass social reality in that they
are determined by structures that often operate at one remove from

immediate experience: 'the visible, that which is immediately given, hides the invisible which determines it. One thus forgets that the truth of any interaction is never entirely to be found within the interaction as it avails itself for observation' (Bourdieu 1990a: 126–7). In short, the study of embodied reality must not remain at the level of phenomenal immediacy but must be integrated into a relational analysis of power relations. Expressed in this way, Bourdieu's idea of a relational phenomenology is similar to Weber's idea of verstehen where the initial interpretative move must always be integrated back into objective explanation. What makes Bourdieu's work more helpful for my purposes is that, in contrast to Weber's disembodied and heroic model, the idea of habitus grounds an analysis of subjectivity and agency in the possibilities and constraints of embodied existence.

The phenomenological orientation of habitus yields a concept of subjectivity and agency whose central characteristics are similar to those attributed to the subject by thinkers of recognition, i.e. they are relational, situated and practical entities. Bourdieu would not use the term dialogical because of its problematic implications of an unhindered reciprocity that obscures the extent to which inequalities of power permeate even the most intimate of interactions. Subjectivity is, however, a fundamentally relational phenomenon in that it is constituted through incarnate social interaction. Its relational nature is inseparable from its situation, that is to say, the subject's physical and psychological dispositions are the internalized effects of specific social context – the 'field'. The reason the field escapes being a determinist category, or what Judith Butler (1999) has termed an 'unalterable positivity', is that its internal relations are multidimensional and, as a generative principle, the habitus is able to react back upon the field and alter it, it 'transforms that by which it is determined' (Vandenberghe 1999: 50). Furthermore, as a principle of social differentiation, it is possible for a single habitus to be affected by several fields.[3] Fields of action are interrelated but mutually irreducible and individuals move between fields of action. One of the advantages of the concept of the field, for an analysis of gender division, is that it provides a way of conceptualizing differentiated power relations which escape the dualisms of the public and the private. Given phenomena such as the changing nature of intimacy, the increased entry of women into work and other areas of public life and the restructuring of gender divisions along class, racial and generational lines, feminist analysis requires a more differentiated model of power relations than is available in these dualisms. Finally, habitus construes subjectivity as realized through practice, that is, the pre-reflexive living-through of embodied dispositions which, themselves, are the result of the incorporation of the latent tendencies of the world into the body. Unlike the ontology of recognition, however, power relations are not secondary to the process of subject formation, in the sense that they form its context, rather they are constitutive of the process.

The most important consequence of the intrinsic connection posited by habitus between embodied existence and power is that it prevents Bourdieu's phenomenological approach falling into some of the reifying tendencies that limit the way in which the subject is conceived in recognition. Embodied existence is not understood as some self-evident state or arena of authentic experience. Rather, habitus is an heuristic device that, by focusing on 'the perspective of the perceiving subject', calls attention to certain practical and sentient dimensions in the constitution of subjectivity and agency (1990a: 131). In calling attention to these dimensions it does not, however, attribute any epistemological privilege to them. The standpoint of embodied actors is undoubtedly an important possible starting point for constructing new and expanded knowledge of the world. Yet, the construction of knowledge inevitably also involves trying to locate any situated experiential perspective within a more objective understanding of social structures and systems. To claim that the perspective of embodied actors is limited does not necessarily mean that they are, to some degree, passive dupes or that only sociologists are sufficiently 'reflexive' enough to adopt the distantiated perspective necessary for critique (e.g. Bohman 1999; Kogler 1997). Such a view seems to proceed from a zero-sum position where if actors' critical awareness does not reach certain conclusions based on pre-given epistemological or normative criteria then they cannot be said to be autonomous at all. Reflexive autonomy is not, however, an absolute capacity of individuals for full self-awareness, it is a much more incomplete and intermittent feature of social interaction. To consider reflexivity in relation to social position is, therefore, not to undermine it entirely but rather to explore how the workings of power and symbolic violence both constrain and enable the individual self-realization.

Although I engage with such epistemological issues in passing, my main concern in this book is to use the particular perspective engendered by habitus as a critical tool with which to unpick some of the more problematic entailments of the thematization of embodied subjectivity and agency through the idea of recognition. One set of concerns that I develop throughout the book is how the Bourdieusian idea of embodiment corrects the displacement of issues of class which is a consequence of the inadequate concept of power deployed by thinkers of recognition. Many commentators regard the centrality of class as a weakness in Bourdieu's thought, but in my view, it is the opposite. By bringing class to the fore in an understanding of embodiment, the idea of habitus permits, *inter alia*, a reversal of the reductive causality invoked by so much work on recognition where social forms are expressions of *a priori* psychological dynamics. Against this, habitus suggests that social relations do not just reinforce these prior dynamics but may also be constitutive of them, that is, that certain psychological dynamics may have a class nature, for example, the class aspect of psychosexual dispositions.

Another set of related concerns that I explore through the idea of habitus is the way in which thinkers of recognition regard agency as governed in a fairly straightforward way by identity. One of the problems arising from the limited conception of power deployed by recognition thinkers is that it finishes by binding agency too tightly to identity. On this view, social action is impelled by the individual's primordial desire for recognition. This simplifies the diverse logic of action; its causes and its relation to embodied existence. For different reasons, certain types of cultural feminist theory also finish by viewing action as governed by a single aspect of identity, namely sexuality. I argue that this one-dimensional view of agency is the result of the abstract, discursive model of power that prevails in post-Foucauldian feminist thought of which the exemplar is the influential work of Judith Butler. While sexuality is an important part of our embodied identities, a phenomenological orientation, such as the one expressed in habitus, might reveal that it has fluctuating significance in a more general understanding of our embodied selves as citizens, workers, mothers, consumers, etc. The failure to integrate an account of sexuality with other aspects of embodied identity leads to a narrowly sexualized view of agency and women's social existence in general. To overcome this discursive abstraction, subject formation needs to be conceived, in part, as achieved through a practical and creative engagement with the world, which is driven neither by a univocal impulse to achieve recognition nor by a simple adherence to symbolic laws. It provides a way of explaining how aspects of embodied being have varying significance for self-understanding and have, therefore, a variable impact upon action. In short, it enables a way of thinking about agency where women are regarded primarily as social subjects rather than as just sexual ones. In so far as the idea of habitus expresses a socio-centric understanding of embodied existence, it also suggests a useful way of understanding the emotional and affectual dimensions to action beyond the register of the construction of desire which dominates much post-Foucauldian feminist thought. Habitus understands emotions as engendered through the complex of embodied tendencies, intentional relations with the world and social structures. This disrupts the tendency to explain agency through a naturalized set of emotional dispositions (recognition) or a single dimension of embodied identity (sexuality).

BEYOND OBJECTIVISM

I am not alone, of course, in arguing that the idea of recognition forecloses an adequate account of power and social inequality vis-à-vis an understanding of identity. My position is deeply influenced by these other critiques, especially those of Nancy Fraser and Iris Marion Young. But what distinguishes my position from theirs is that their critique of the subjectivism of the idea of recognition leads them to reject the analytical relevance of a cluster of concepts associated with subjectivity and identity altogether. Against this objectivist move, I draw on the idea of habitus to retain an interpretative understanding of embodied existence that, at the same time, avoids the naturalizing tendencies that they seem to view as inevitable in a phenomenological orientation towards subjectivity. A difficulty with the objectivist analysis adopted by Fraser and Young is that it leads to significant analytical gaps in their work, most especially with regard to formulating alternative understandings of agency. In Fraser's case, for example, the lack of a praxeological account of agency reinforces the unintended dualist tendencies of her distinction between recognition and redistribution. If the ideas of subjectivity and agency are formulated in a sufficiently materialist way, then they help mitigate this dualism by providing categories through which the interpenetration of economic with cultural forces might be conceptualised. The intrinsic connection between experience and power that underlies habitus suggests how economic forces are lived in cultural forms and cultural norms structure economic activity.

The move towards objectivism fuelled by a perhaps too ready conflation of subjectivity with subjectivism is not limited to materialist critiques of recognition but is widespread in much cultural feminist thought. Much of it is related to the influence of Foucault's work which leads to the discursive abstraction of cultural feminist thought discussed above. There is, however, another recent strand of feminist thought, influenced by the work of Hannah Arendt, which argues that the preoccupation of contemporary theory with 'the subject question' limits ways of thinking about freedom ι action (Zerilli 2005: 9). According to Linda Zerilli, for example, tι concern with issues of subjectivity and agency has hampered feminism's ability to think of freedom beyond the assertion of identity. It remains stuck in the assertion of the 'I can' rather than considering the possibilities of the 'I will': 'the paradox of subject formation is installed as a vicious circle of agency at the heart of politics. In that case it would be hard to see how politics could ever be a truly transformative practice that might create something new, forms of life that would be more freedom enabling' (Zerilli 2005: 12; see also Dietz 2002). Zerilli finds much potential in Arendt's future-oriented and radically contingent notion of action to rethink freedom as non-sovereignty. Several recent critiques of recognition also deploy similar notions of indeterminacy and contingency in order to unseat the unified subject at its centre. Kelly Oliver (2001), for example, argues that the basic structure of recognition, namely the distinction between subject and object, replicates a 'pathology of oppression'. It attributes a foundational status to the idea that intersubjective relations are intrinsically antagonistic in so far as subjects invariably see other individuals as objects to be dominated. Against the idea of recognition, then, she posits a politics of attestation based on an open-ended and non-judgemental responsibility for injustices done to others. Likewise, Patchen Markell (2003) claims that the idea of recognition attributes a false sovereignty to subjectivity by underplaying its unfinished and uncertain aspects that reside in the future-oriented dimensions of action. Also using Arendt's idea of action as a creative and indeterminate process, Markell sets out a politics of acknowledgement which establishes an ethical relation to others through an acknowledgement of the finitude of the self, i.e., 'of one's practical limits in the face of an unpredictable and contingent future' (Markell 2003: 38). The renunciation of attitudes of self-certainty leads to renewed possibilities of relating to others based on an acceptance of the unstable and unpredictable nature of social interaction.

From these perspectives, my attempt to explore certain ideas of embodied subjectivity and agency though a relational phenomenology remains caught within a circular and impoverished paradigm of thought. A problem, however, with such ideas of a non-subject-centred ethics is that they tacitly rely on an unqualified objectivism that disregards the phenomenal and social realities of the ontological indeterminacy that they invoke. It may be the case that the future-oriented dimensions of action render subjectivity more fragile and uncertain than is often acknowledged in some theories of recognition. It is one thing, however, to assert an essential temporal indeterminacy as a condition of possibility of action and interaction, but it is another to trace out what this might mean at the level of social relations which, even at their most informal, are ineluctably embedded in entrenched hierarchies of power. Social action and interaction are certainly indeterminate to some degree. If this indeterminacy is to have substantive content, however, it must be thought through in connection to social complexity, understood as the way in which the phenomenal realm of subjectivity is necessarily intertwined with structural relations of power. In other words, the assertion of a foundational indeterminacy does not go very far in unpacking the determinate nature of many dimensions of social existence which pertain, in part, to the insidious operations of power upon embodied subjects. Issues pertaining to freedom exceed the dualism of determinacy and indeterminacy and it is in order to explore just how they do that that it seems theoretically precipitate for feminists to abandon their concern with subjectivity and power. Indeed, in response to these invocations of under-developed ideas of indeterminacy, one of the initial comments made by feminists to the poststructural critique of the subject still seems relevant: 'why is it that just at the moment when so many of us who have been silenced begin to demand the right to name ourselves, to act as subjects rather than objects of history, that just then the concept of subjecthood becomes problematic?' (Harstock 1990: 163).

It is important to retain a subject orientation in thinking about freedom, partly because it goes some way to overcoming an easy elision between ideas of agency, resistance and indeterminacy. In so far as any action is never one of simple mechanical reproduction, indeterminacy is a widespread characteristic of social agency, but this cannot be taken as an automatic guarantor of any resistant status. Indeed, in the light of the diverse nature of an intensified consumerism and of changes in methods of social control, what appears to be a non-conformist or resistant act at one level might, at another level, be its opposite. The force of the idea of habitus is that it goes beyond simplistic dualisms of domination and resistance, invoking instead a phenomenological notion of freedom in constraint or 'regulated liberties'. On this view, change is understood as generated by the interplay of necessity and contingency. Habitus is a principle of 'operative spontaneity', that is to say that it is in a state of permanent revision, but this revision is rarely radical because the new and unexpected is always incorporated upon the basis of previously established, embodied dispositions. This does not amount to a denial of creative agency or vibrancy on the part of oppressed groups and

Bmjo

individuals. It is, however, to recognize the importance of putting the creative dimensions of action in the context of immediate and latent relations of force or meaning that operate in any situation. There is always a 'margin of freedom' in the workings of symbolic power and this is created in the same instant as individuals are aligned to the status quo. It is this space of freedom that gives social life its inherent spontaneity, but whether this spontaneity can form the basis of any meaningful resistance or even a transformative social or political movement is a much broader and more complex question altogether.

The structure and argument of the book is as follows: in the first chapter, I examine the way in which the idea of the struggle for recognition has been used to historicize psychoanalytic explanation by taking it as a way of representing the contingent and open-ended nature of subject formation. These historicizing efforts are problematic in so far as the rendering of the recognition relation as a primal psychological dynamic further entrenches rather than dislodges the ahistorical tendencies of psychoanalysis. Social relations are seen as extrapolations from primal psychic dynamics and this results in a one-dimensional account of agency and a simplified understanding of social inequalities as forms of misrecognition. I focus on the versions of the struggle for recognition in the work of Slavoj Žižek and Jessica Benjamin. The problem with Žižek's Lacanian paradigm of ideological misrecognition is that it empties individual practices and phenomenal variation of any significance except in so far as they are imaginary attempts to fend off the destabilizing implications of unconscious disruption. Thus, far from yielding an historically sensitive account of social relations, Žižek's work is profoundly a-historical, freezing the struggle for recognition perpetually at the point of misrecognition. This has particularly troubling implications for an understanding of agency and change in gender relations. Benjamin's work is opposed to Žižek's in fundamental respects. Her relational, rather than Oedipal, account of the formation of gender identity yields a notion of agency based on the idea of 'over-inclusive' identifications. The force of this formulation of agency is that it is grounded in an attention to variations in practice and in the significance they might have for psychoanalytic thought. The problem in Benjamin's work is that the ontological status she accords the recognition paradigm has problematic entailments for an understanding of social relations, in particular those of gender inequality, which are simplistically construed as interpersonal misrecognition. Any possible account of the way in which social relations do not simply reinforce prior psychic dynamics but may also be constitutive of them is foreclosed.

In the second chapter, I examine the way the idea of the struggle for recognition has been used by thinkers to develop an alternative to political theories grounded in a 'philosophy of the subject'. The idea of recognition enables the monological subject of conventional political thought to be replaced with a dialogical conception. This dialogical conception understands individuals not as isolated beings but as beings who only know themselves through interaction with others. It also emphasizes the embodied, practical and cooperative character of the self–other relation. A further related claim made by thinkers of recognition is that normative thought is not free standing but proceeds from an analysis of existing social relations. I consider the work of Jurgen Habermas and Charles Taylor in the light of these claims and I argue that their formulations of the idea of recognition undermine them. Both theorists conceive of the recognition dynamic as primarily linguistic in nature in that language is the principal medium through which self–other relations are mediated. However, in developing the idea of linguistic mediation, both Taylor and Habermas invoke a purified model of language where power relations are seen as extrinsic or secondary forms of distortion of a primal dyad of recognition. This extirpation of power from language allows both theorists to attribute to the recognition dyad a single primordial function: in Taylor's case, language is conceived as an expressive medium; in Habermas's case, it is a communicative one oriented towards understanding. The setting up of language as prior to, rather than coeval with power undermines their claims to develop normative proposals that proceed from a sociological sensitivity to the situated and embodied nature of self–other interactions. This is not a contingent weakness in their thought but a necessary effect of the normative exigencies of their ideal of recognition. It requires them to set up an ontology where individuals are tacitly predisposed to reach some kind of mutual understanding, but this inevitably rests on a reductive understanding of the operations of power upon embodied subjects.

In the third chapter I examine the work of feminists, such as Selya Benhabib, who seek to overcome the formalism of Habermas's original formulation of communicative recognition and to include a more extensive account of identity and power. Some of the work of feminist Habermasians has focused on the idea of the narrative structure of identity as the key concept through which the concept of recognition can be enlarged. The concept of narrative identity is seen as a way of bridging the gap between the rationalism of

Language (Run)

Habermas's idea of the moral subject and the fragmentation of the subject that arises from poststructural critique. The idea of narrative concedes that identities are socially specific discursive constructions, but, in as much as it invokes ideas of intention and reflexivity, it seems to offer a more substantive idea of agency. My argument is that such attempts to expand discourse ethics fail because there is a fundamental incompatibility between the idea of communicative recognition and the notion of narrative identity that, by and large, feminist Habermasians do not acknowledge. The reason that Habermas adheres to a narrowly rationalist conception of communication, despite the many problems it provokes, is that it is central to upholding his claim that discourse ethics is universal in scope. The revised idea of recognition through narrative does indeed invoke a broader understanding of subjectivity with respect to social differences. However, it loses the rationalist core that is the crucial underpinning to Habermas's claim that communicative interaction is universal. Furthermore, the exigencies of remaining within Habermas's communicatively symmetrical model of recognition result in the deployment of a syncretic and over-generalized idea of narrative identity that does not grasp important aspects of agency in the context of the systemic reproduction of gender inequalities.

In the fourth chapter, I consider the wide-ranging debate between Nancy Fraser and Axel Honneth on recognition and redistribution, which turns on how to characterize the dynamics underlying contemporary social and political conflict. For Honneth, all such conflicts, including those over economic distribution, are variants of a fundamental struggle for recognition which itself is the key to understanding the long-term development of social interaction in capitalist societies. Against this, Fraser argues that struggles for recognition are analytically distinct from conflicts over redistribution. She claims furthermore that the way in which the idea of recognition is generally construed reifies the identity politics it designates. I explore this debate from the perspective of the concept of agency that explicitly or implicitly mobilizes their political paradigms. Despite its explicit social theoretical orientation, Honneth's understanding of modernity as an unfolding recognition order is deeply a-historical and relies on a subjectivist account of agency. He identifies the struggle for recognition as the basic psychological dynamic underlying all significant social relations. This yields an account of the emotional grounds of agency in suffering that is arguably more compelling than the instrumental notions of interest that prevail in conventional sociological accounts of action. However, Honneth's social theory lacks a sufficient explanation of how this underlying impulse is mediated through symbolic and material power relations and he finishes with a naïve spontaneist account of action. This lack of a theory of mediation is compounded in his subsequent thesis on the 'liquefaction of the ego' that, by totalizing the interactive structure of recognition, blurs distinctions between the individual and wider social relations. Honneth cannot therefore explain why individuals should act in anything other than a passively conformist manner. Nancy Fraser offers a powerful materialist reconfiguration of the idea of recognition where to be misrecognized is a form of institutionalized status subordination rather than a psychological injury. She also supplements the idea of a cultural politics of recognition with that of a materialist politics of redistribution. While her critique of Honneth's subjectivism is forceful, her consequent move towards an objectivist style of analysis prevents her from developing a notion of agency which is a presupposed concept in her work. This generates several analytical gaps in her abstract framework, not least of which is that she cannot overcome its tendency towards dualism.

The final chapter considers how the idea of habitus suggests an account of embodied agency that goes beyond some of the limitations of the way it is conceived by both thinkers of recognition and certain feminist theorists. One of the problems arising from the limited conception of power deployed by recognition thinkers is that it finishes by binding agency too tightly to identity. Although feminist theory has a more developed understanding of the impact of power upon subjectivity, it also finishes, albeit by a different route, in yoking agency too closely to identity. I focus on Judith Butler's performative account of agency, which is a paradigm of post-Foucauldian feminist thought, and I argue that it is based on an elevation of one aspect of embodied identity, sexuality, over all others. The concern with sexuality itself is not intrinsically a problem, it is rather the way in which it is conceptualized through an abstract model of power as discourse that has troubling consequences. The objectivist definition of discourse separates an account of sexual identity from other aspects of embodied identity (such as class) and it cannot explain certain political aspects of agency related to self-understanding and practice. The idea of practice that is central to the concept of habitus counters the objectivism of cultural feminist accounts of embodiment, suggesting that agency must be understood not only as a discursively generated capacity but as a lived relation. However, by positing an intrinsic connection between the body and power, the idea of practice avoids some of the essentialist tendencies that hamper some phenomenological treatments of embodiment through the idea of experience. Furthermore, the way in which embodied identity is connected to social structures militates against another tendency of feminist thought, namely the conflation of agency with resistance. By relating agency back to the particular configuration of power relations in a given situation, it is understood as a specific and unevenly realized phenomenon whose meaning can only be derived from the position it occupies in the social order.

1

Recognition and Misrecognition in the Psyche

INTRODUCTION

Recently, certain thinkers have used the idea of the struggle for recognition as part of attempts to historicize psychoanalytic explanation. Taking their inspiration from existential readings of Hegel, the perpetually doomed quest for recognition is seen by some psychoanalytic thinkers as a way of representing the contingent and historically open-ended nature of different aspects of subject formation. In this chapter, I argue that these attempts to historicize psychoanalysis fail in so far as they set up an ontology of recognition that has ahistorical and reductive implications for an understanding of subject formation. The ontology of recognition engenders, one way or another, an understanding of social relations as extrapolations of primal psychic dynamics and this results in a one-dimensional account of agency and change in the context of social inequalities, especially gender.

I focus on the way in which the idea of the struggle for recognition has been used in the work of the Lacanian theorist, Slavoj Žižek, and the object relations theorist and analyst, Jessica Benjamin. In Žižek, the struggle for recognition appears as part of a more general fusion of Hegelian dialectics with Lacanian theory and it represents the impossibility of closure in social identities and practices. All socio-symbolic formations are imaginary misrecognitions in so far as they are predicated on ideas of stability and plenitude that are impossible given the perpetual disruptions of the primal void of the unconscious. This yields, *inter alia*, a view of social relations of gender as expressions of a primal sexual difference whose antagonist structure forbids any kind of reciprocal relation. The problem with this construal of misrecognition as a transcendental structure is that it deprives the variations and divergences in the social realization of gender relations of any theoretical significance except in so far as they only ever confirm, in an explicit or disavowed way, the central impossibility of sexual difference. Thus, far from yielding an historically sensitive account of social relations, Žižek's work is profoundly ahistorical, freezing the struggle for recognition perpetually at the point of misrecognition. This has particularly troubling implications for an understanding of agency and change in gender relations.

In many respects, Benjamin's work is explicitly opposed to Žižek's in that she uses the idea of a struggle for recognition to displace the centrality that the Lacanian model accords to the Oedipus complex in the process of subject formation. She uses the idea of recognition to develop an alternative model of relationally generated subjectivity and also an idea of agency as 'over-inclusive' identifications that is grounded in an attention to phenomenal variations in embodied practices. A consequence of her understanding of recognition as a process rather than structure is that it provides the basis for a more differentiated and dynamic account of feminine agency than is available in conventional psychoanalysis. It also has the potential to accommodate an understanding of the effects of class and race upon the process of subject formation. The problem in Benjamin's work is that the ontological status she accords the idea of recognition has reductive entailments for a sociological account of gender oppression. Gender oppression is simplistically construed as deriving from a distorted recognition dynamic between men and women. Modes of oppression that do not operate according to this dyadic logic are rendered theoretically invisible. So, too, is any idea that social relations do not simply reinforce prior psychic dynamics but may actually be constitutive of them.

IDEOLOGY, INTERPELLATION AND MISRECOGNITION

Žižek's reading of the struggle for recognition stands in the tradition of agonistic interpretations of Hegel that were influentially formulated by the existential phenomenologists in the post-war period, notably, Jean Hyppolite, Alexander Kojève and Jean-Paul Sartre. These readings focus on the moments of contradiction, negation and endlessly deferred transcendence in order to formulate a notion of the human condition as a battle to overcome perpetual inauthentic-ity. In this vein, Žižek reads Hegel as a proleptic Lacanian in so far as the struggle for recognition is held as a metaphor for the impossibility of identity: 'does not Hegel's *Phenomenology of Spirit* tell us . . . of the repeated failure of the subject's endeavour to realize his project in social Substance, to impose his vision on the social universe – the story of how the "big Other", the social substance, again and again thwarts his project and turns it upside-down' (1999a: 76. See also 103). For Žižek, the idea of a coherent, self-reflexive individual is a linguistic illusion that conceals the fundamental void or lack upon which all identity is based. This lack arises from an insurmountable incompatibility between language and the other symbolic forms through which the world is experienced ('The big Other') and primordial reality or the Real ('the Thing'). The radical heterogeneity of the Real ensures that it always remains unknowable because it eludes being definitively captured in language. Reality, in the sense of brute objectivity, can never be recovered because it is always-already symbolized and discursively constituted. The symbolization of reality is, however, never complete because the symbolic never fully succeeds in excluding the disruptive effects of the Real. The Real is the 'rock upon which any attempt at symbolization stumbles' (Žižek 1989: 169). This gap or instability in symbolization gives rise to what, following Derrida, Žižek calls the 'spectre' or that which escapes symbolically structured reality: 'what the spectre conceals is not reality but its "primordially repressed", the irrepresentable X on whose "repression" reality itself is founded' (1994: 21). The spectral presence of the Real is glimpsed in the social world in moments of social upheaval, for example violence or revolution. The Real is the traumatic kernel of social life; a submerged antagonism that poses a perpetual threat to social stability. Class struggle provides an example of the Lacanian Real or 'real of antagonism', in that it is never fully manifest in the social realm but only symbolized indirectly in localized, particular struggles. Even though class struggle is never given directly as a positive entity, it gives rise to ever-new partial symbolizations to which all other social phenomena are linked. It is this non-symbolizable traumatic kernel that finds displaced form in the symbolic practices of the actual.

One of the aims of Žižek's fusion of Hegel with Lacan is to develop a reworked theory of ideology. Ideology is the principal medium which conceals the troubling effects of the Real through the generation of certain types of stable meaning. These attempts, however, always necessarily fail. Like Althusser, Žižek uses the Lacanian paradigm to reinvigorate the theory of ideology pushing it towards a theory of subjective interpellation and away from a 'representation-alist problematic' which construes it as false beliefs and illusion (1989: 21). Ideological beliefs are not false or illusory in so far as they are constitutive of social reality in the sense implied by Marx's notion of commodity fetishism. It follows that ideology critique should not be directed at exposing the 'false content' of ideological messages, but rather should concern itself with what Althusser calls the 'topicality of thought' or the way in which thought is inscribed upon the objective world in order to legitimize relations of domination. By exposing the arbitrary and unstable nature of these 'imaginary' relations, ideology critique aims to highlight the fundamentally 'antagonistic character' of the social realm and to ' "estrange" us to the self evidence of its established identity' (1994: 7). The 'night of the world' that lies at the core of social forms, from the individual to the social, is, therefore, the ultimate guarantor of freedom in so far as it bespeaks the possibility of breaking out of orthodox understandings of who we are and of how it is possible to operate politically.

Žižek sees in Hegel's struggle for recognition a paradigm of the ideological interpellation of the subject. Interpellation is itself a form of recognition: a subject is successfully interpellated when he recognizes him/herself in the symbolic structures of society. In the most general sense, the individuals are fully interpellated when they recognize themselves as bourgeois individuals, that is to say, when they misperceive the impersonal structures of capitalism as requiring their particular input. One of the questions posed by this Althusserian formulation of interpellation is whether or not it tacitly presupposes an anterior subject who is always-already capable of recognizing the interpellating call. Žižek responds to this difficulty by arguing that, rather than being a symptom of a failure in the way the process of interpellation is conceived, the presupposition of a pre-existing subject is in fact a symptom of the profound efficacy of the process. Interpellation is fully achieved precisely at the moment when the individual perceives themselves as too complex a person to be encapsulated in one set of ideological identifications. An individual may identify, to a certain degree, with, say, dominant notions of femininity but she also understands herself as too multifaceted an individual to be subsumed within any particular role or label. It is, however, this very distantiation from symbolic identification that is the marker of successful interpellation: 'an interpellation succeeds precisely when I perceive myself as "not only that" but a "complex person who, among other things, is also that" ' (1999a: 258–9). This idea that the individual is too complex a being to be captured in any one set of identifications is a necessary myth and one that does not refer to the existential texture of experience, which, itself, is an imaginary fiction. From the perspective of Žižek's exhaustive Lacanianism, there can be no subject prior to the moment of interpellation, which is, after all, the moment of entry into language. There is only a lack: subjectivity arises *ex nihilo*, it is 'produced as the void' (1999a: 258).

Interpellation works, then, according to a logic of double dis-avowal. It requires that the individual disavows that he is the product of ideological interpellation but this disavowal is based on a further, unacknowledged, disavowal, namely, that the individual's belief in his autonomy is an illusion: 'such an autonomization is doubly false, since it involves a double disavowal, but also that there is no subject prior to the Institution' (1999a: 258). According to Žižek, this double disavowal is paradigmatically expressed in Hegel's struggle for recognition. In the master–slave dialectic, the master disavows his own corporeal existence by forcing the slave to mediate between himself and the external world. At the same time, in order to be complicit with the illusion of the master's autonomy, the slave must disavow that he acts as the master's body and that this has been imposed on him by the master. He must pretend that he acts as an autonomous agent and the more he does so, the more he misrecognizes the illusory nature of his autonomy. The implica-tion of this image of multilayered and intertwined disavowals is that there is no escaping from ideological interpellation: 'it is not a fact that today, more than ever, we, as individuals, are interpellated without even being aware of it: our identity is constituted for the big Other by a series of digitalized informational . . . files that we are mostly not even aware of, so that interpellations function . . . without any gesture of recognition on the part of the subject con-cerned' (1999a: 259). The bleak conclusion of Žižek's theory of ideo-logical subject formation is that the struggle for recognition is always frozen at the moment of misrecognition: 'our recognition in the call is always a misrecognition, an act of falling into ridicule by boast-fully assuming the place of the addressee which is not really ours' (1999a: 259).

HISTORY, LACK AND THE FORECLOSURE OF PRACTICE

Žižek's reworking of the theory of ideology in terms of a perpetual gap between the Real and the symbolic is intended to demonstrate, *inter alia*, the force of psychoanalysis in grasping the contingent, unfinished and potentially transformable nature of social reality. In his view, psychoanalysis is a powerful tool for the analysis of history, rather than, as is often claimed, the means through which history is reified as an effect of primal psychic dynamics. Indeed, far from freezing history, psychoanalysis provides the basis for a revolutionary reconfiguration of identity and politics. Žižek concedes that his theory of ideological interpellation is undoubtedly monolithic but this represents the nature of globalized capital that has become so pervasive and flexible that it is increasingly difficult to imagine a truly radical alternative to it. In Lacanian terms, capital has become today's Real in that it forms the unacknowledged parameters for contemporary political imagination. Indeed, in failing to recognize the pervasive nature of capital, many theories of radical democracy are profoundly complicit, rather than disruptive of the dominant socioeconomic order. These theories '*never* question the fundamentals of the capitalist market economy and the liberal-democratic political regime; they *never* envisage the possibility of a completely different economico-political regime' (Žižek 2000: 223). In this respect, Žižek claims that, despite not providing a blueprint for political intervention, his theory is far more radical in that it draws attention to the limits of thought and action and the possibility of moving beyond them. The precise lineaments of this new political subject are necessarily vague; however, it involves a yoking together of particular claims with universal aims in order to rupture established norms. The political demands made by excluded groups do not just represent specific injustices but stand in for universal injustices. Against liberal beliefs in neutrality, Žižek argues that universal justice can only be discerned from the perspective of those excluded from it. In a pluralist society, a universal leftwing politics is therefore inescapably agonistic, but, for Žižek, politics is the art of the impossible (1998: 63–78). By unearthing the ahistorical limit of particular modes of thought and being, every historical figuration is revealed as being contingent and therefore susceptible to radical overhaul. It is the 'ahistorical bar' as the internal limit of all symbolization that, in a sense, forms the condition of possibility of historicity. It is in this manner that Žižek regards his thought as revivifying the radical promise of Marxism, that is, by jettisoning its economic essentialism and retaining 'the empty messianic emancipatory promise – the new social order should not be "ontologized", but should remain an elusive democracy *a venir*' (Žižek 1999b: ix).

Despite these claims, there are troubling implications in Žižek's argument that the condition of possibility of history resides in an abstract linguistic structure. There is no denying that Žižek proffers a powerful account of the atavistic effects of fantasy and non-rational

forces upon action, for example, in his work on the function of enjoyment in the rise of regressive nationalisms (Žižek 1991). Nonetheless,
the profoundly ahistorical and formulaic nature of his theory has
insurmountably dismissive implications for an understanding of
social action. As a radically negative entity, the unconscious has no
intrinsic connection to the social realm apart from random and fugitive disruptions; it is, as Nancy Chodorow puts it, a *'sui generis*
autochtonous entity that is apart from culture and the symbolic'
(Chodorow 1995: 93). This conception of the unconscious as a radically discrete entity leads to an aporetic conception of language as
simultaneously monolithic and illusory. On the one hand, it is only
through the symbolic order and not through any other systemic type
of power or any other source of agency that the social realm receives
its shape. All social identity receives its form from the imposition of
symbolic order upon an originary lack and thus language becomes a
pervasive and self-sustaining system. On the other hand, language is
an illusory medium in that all symbolic identities are based on an
imaginary unity, resulting in the devaluation of concrete political
struggles and the fetishization of the unconscious as a source of a
supposedly radical instability. In the absence of any notion of social
or political mediation, Žižek's idea of change remains caught in a
'bad infinity', oscillating between the moments of 'structure and anti-
structure' (Fraser 1997: 163).

Such an insurmountable ahistoricism is certainly the charge that
Judith Butler, amongst others, levels at Žižek when she discerns an
abstract universalism or denial of the contingent operating in his
thought which has problematic implications for an understanding of
counter-hegemonic struggle. By locating the 'traumatic kernel' that
prevents identity closure in the unconscious, Žižek effectively
undermines the social and historical specificity of resistance, rendering it an effect of an unchanging psychic lack. The theory of
radical insufficiency operates according to a self-same dynamic that
explains any and every social disruption, and, as such, it is a 'theoretical fetish that disavows the conditions of its own emergence'
(Butler 2000a: 27). It is the denial or domestication of difference
effected by this abstract logic that has the most problematic implications for an understanding of politics. A closed negative dialectic
operates where an apparent opposition between an identity and its
other is deconstructed to reveal not only the disavowed connection
but also that identity eventually becomes its other. This has particularly worrying implications for Žižek's analysis of fascism, for
instance, which effectively collapses historically specific distinctions
between progressive and regressive political forces (Butler 2000b:

173). As she puts it: 'power which seems to be opposed to the obscene is itself fundamentally reliant on that obscene, and finally *is* the obscene' (Butler 2000c: 276). In sum, Žižek's collapse of domination into resistance blocks an analysis of the specific power relations underlying political struggle.

In order to distinguish her position from that of Žižek, Butler claims that resistance should be understood not as the structural operations of the symbolic order but as a process of cultural ritual: 'as the reiteration of cultural norms, as the habitus, of the body in which structural and social dimensions of meaning are not finally separable' (Butler 2000a: 25). This amounts to conceptualizing the radically unfinished nature of identity not, *pace* Žižek, as the point at which self-representation always founders (the Real) but as the inability of social categories to fully capture the 'mobility and flexibility' of persons (e.g. Riley 2000). No subject or politics of identity emerges without foreclosures, but these must be understood primarily as socially variable rather than as psychically universal.[1] By pointing to the reiterative structure of cultural norms, Butler invokes a notion of embodied social practice to counter Žižek's subjectless model of symbolic reproduction. While she is right to do this, her model of performativity is ultimately unable to sustain this notion of practice because it is based on an equally as abstract or 'negative' paradigm of subject formation as Žižek's (McNay 2000). I make this argument about Butler in more detail in Chapter 5, but suffice to note here that, on this negative paradigm, the subject is understood, in essentially passive terms, as an exogenously imposed effect of language or discourse. This one-dimensional conception of language as a constitutive structure, which forecloses an understanding of language as a type of social action, results in its generalization as a model for all forms of social power. The diversity of social relations is replaced by the overextended metaphor of position within the symbolic or linguistic order. This prioritization of *langue* over *parole* easily slides into a conception of language as a self-enclosed symbolic system detached from any kind of social context and, in particular, from attendant problems of struggles over meaning, power relations and practice. As Nancy Fraser puts it: 'the structuralist abstraction *langue* is troped into a quasi divinity, a normative "symbolic order" whose power to shape identities dwarfs to the point of extinction that of mere historical institutions and practices' (Fraser 1997: 157).

Despite her inability to sustain the idea of practice in her theory of the performative, Butler is right nonetheless to draw attention to the way in which Žižek's disregard of the social context of action is the consequence of his abstract and formulaic paradigm. By construing the Real as a self-identical and invariant principle of non-closure, the specific power dynamics of social formations are occluded; in particular, a series of issues pertaining to the historicity of social structures, of language and of agency are foreclosed. For Lacanians, of course, the criticism that they privilege an abstract and ahistorical model of subject formation over embodied social practices both misses the point and invokes an uncritical phenomenalism. Indeed, in Žižek's view, it is Butler herself who is not 'historicist enough' because her idea of the inability of symbolic categories to capture the complexity of social reality relies on a form of simplistic empiricism that contrasts the 'infinite wealth of reality' to the 'abstract poverty' of thought (Žižek 2000: 216). In the Lacanian triad of the Real, the unconscious and the Symbolic, a perspective on social practices and experience is explicitly redundant. Since all experience is formulated within the symbolic realm, any experience that does not conform to its logic is necessarily deemed anomalous or irrelevant. The most well-known expression of this discounting of the specificity of embodied experience is the Lacanian response to questions about whether the presence or absence of the father makes a difference to subject formation. For Lacanians, the presence of the actual father is superfluous because the phallocentric logic of the symbolic order operates independently of biological or social presence. There are many problems that stem from such an assertion, not least the difficulty that the reproduction of the phallocentric order becomes a monolithic given. It is, however, only from the perspective of a self-perpetuating linguistic system that the variations in social practices do not have any theoretical significance. As Nancy Chodorow puts it: 'evidence cannot oppose this logic, since it is a logic, and Lacanians even have a language for dismissing evidence. Anything given, natural, or "real" is repudiated by definition on the symbolic level' (Chodorow 1989: 124–5). The tacit assumption underlying this repudiation of reality is that the phenomenal realm lacks significance or complexity, indeed, that these qualities are only imputed to it by the workings of the unconscious. By adhering to such an unproblematized view of social experience, Žižek arguably makes himself vulnerable to the same charge that he levels at Butler, namely, a reliance on an uncritical empiricism. By construing practice and experience in such a flattened-out manner, he loses any way of explaining the historicity of social being and also its complex, multidimensional nature that is the effect of its constitution through different types of power. He also loses any way of understanding agency except as a secondary effect of the disjunction between the

Real and the symbolic order rather than as a potential capacity of social subjects. This disjunction may certainly constitute a necessary pre-condition of the emergence of agency, but it is not an account of agency as an act of engagement on the part of individuals in response to a historically specific situation. Indeed, the displacement of agency onto a theory of symbolic indeterminacy forecloses the development of a subject-centred theory of action altogether. For, as Cornelius Castoriadis puts it: 'If "truth" is altogether on the side of the unconscious, and if all "knowledge" is mere deception, what importance can the subject's words have . . . If the person is in fact nothing but *persona*, a mask, and if behind this *persona* he is nobody . . . then surely the best way of leading the subject to the "truth" is in fact to leave him to stew in his own juice?' (Castoriadis 1984: 57).

In sum, the adoption of a perspective on social practices in context need not entail, contra Žižek, a reliance upon an naïve empiricism. On the contrary, a certain relational perspective on social practice may yield more socially sensitive and theoretically differentiated accounts of subject formation, agency and change than can be derived from Lacanian resources. In the next section, I draw out the differences that an attention to practice might yield through a consideration of Bourdieu's idea of habitus. In certain respects, there are strong resonances between the work of Žižek and Bourdieu, most notably in that the idea of misrecognition is central to their respective conceptions of ideological inculcation. Furthermore, in Bourdieu, like Žižek, the moment of misrecognition is arguably hypotrophized to the extent that both their understandings of domination, particularly in gender, are overstated. The difference, however, is that, rather than being conceived as a universal linguistic structure, Bourdieu's idea of misrecognition is attached to a notion of embodied practice through the idea of habitus. Although he does not sufficiently develop certain implications of this idea of embodied practice, it nonetheless acts, in theory, as a corrective to the determinist tendencies of his thought.

MISRECOGNITION AND PRACTICE

For Bourdieu, like Žižek and unlike the way it is understood by the other thinkers examined in this book, the idea of recognition has no normative content and, indeed, it cannot be dissociated from an idea of misrecognition or the process whereby individuals are accommodated to their own oppression. On Bourdieu's account, recognition and misrecognition are understood as the specific effects of the habitus or the way in which relations of power profoundly shape an individual's embodied existence in the world. The process whereby social structures are incorporated into individual being is, in part, exogenously imposed through the unequal distribution of material and symbolic resources (economic, social and cultural capital). But it is also, in part, self-imposed through the internalization of symbolic violence or the 'doxa' of hegemonic visions of the world. In other words, the oppressed are often complicit with their oppression. 'Symbolic violence is exercised only through an act of knowledge and practical recognition which takes place below the level of the consciousness and will and which gives all its manifestations – injunctions, suggestions, seduction, threats, reproaches, orders or calls to order – their "hypnotic power" ' (2001: 42). In *Distinction*, for example, Bourdieu has famously shown how an individual's class position is not just an objective location within an abstract structure but is a mode of embodied being, an orientation to the world that is lived out unconsciously in daily practices. Habitus invokes, therefore, the way in which the particularity and immediacy of everyday life is suffused with generality. Individual experiences are infused with regularity and uniformity in so far as they are a product of social institutions. Immediate corporeal being contains within it the latent marks of abstract social structure. It is this process of incorporation that ensures that individuals misrecognize their oppression because the arbitrary nature of class and gender divisions is naturalized by being lived as a profoundly felt set of dispositions and behaviour. Recognition is 'an alienated cognition that looks at the world through categories the world imposes, and apprehends the social world as a natural world' (1990c: 140–1).

On the face of it, then, Bourdieu, like Žižek, posits misrecognition as the condition of possibility of subject formation. A difficulty with this position is that, if misrecognition is generalized as the universal structure of subjectivity, it becomes unclear whether individuals are able to act in an autonomous, creative or resistant manner at all. Indeed, this is certainly a limitation of both Žižek's and Bourdieu's account of the formation of sexual identities which both see it, ultimately, as a relatively uncontested process of masculine domination. The difference between the two thinkers is, however, that whereas for Žižek, misrecognition is conceived as a universal structure of the psyche, for Bourdieu, the idea of misrecognition is strongly attached to an idea of practice through the concept of habitus. The idea of practice certainly implies that oppression is deeply rooted in psychological and physical dispositions. Practice is the result of the habitus that is itself the incorporation of temporal structures or the regularities and tendencies of the world into the body. The living-through of these embodied tendencies serves to endlessly sediment naturalized social hierarchies. At the same time, however, the idea of practice is also generative of a notion of agency in that it necessarily has a future-oriented or anticipatory dimension. In so far as the living-through of embodied tendencies involves encounters with unanticipated or unknown social factors, it is also the source of potential creativity and innovation in daily life. In other words, for Bourdieu, practices do not belong to the realm of insignificant empirical variation as they do for Žižek; instead, they constitute an objective, although often unrealized, potentiality for social change. Indeed, even when practices reinforce rather than disrupt deeper social tendencies they are not theoretically insignificant because they show how social reproduction is never an act of symbolic ventriloquism but rather a dynamic process of interpretation. The most famous example Bourdieu gives of this is his critique of structural anthropology's static analysis of gift giving, which, by ignoring its temporal dimensions, misunderstands how it operates as a social exchange (Bourdieu 2000: 56).

One of the most significant theoretical implications, then, of a perspective on embodied practice is that it injects some social content into the process of subject formation which, on a Lacanian perspective, is an abstract process of symbolic imposition. A perspective on practice potentially brings types of social interaction, that are not necessarily strongly symbolically marked, back into the analytical frame. As Vered Amit has noted: 'some of the most common avenues for forming a sense of fellowship, of belonging and social connection are realized through modest daily practices that are often not strongly marked by symbolic categorical identities' such as 'people and relationships known loosely as friends, neighbours, workmates, companions in a variety of leisure, parenting, schooling, political activities' (Amit and Rapport 2002: 64, 165). This need not imply an uncritical celebration of the varied texture of daily life; instead, it displaces the dominance of the symbolic model of power and brings other types of social relation such as class, back into view. For Christina Steedman, for example, the indifference of Lacanian psychoanalysis to variations in social experience renders it, in many cases, incapable of understanding the conditions of working-class existence. Steedman queries how it is possible for the myth of patriarchy to operate when a father is rendered vulnerable by social relations, when his position in a household is not supported by recognition of social status and power outside. What can be learnt about the father from the 'relatively unimportant and powerless man, who cannot present the case for patriarchy embodied in his own person' (Steedman 1986: 79). The Lacanian response that patriarchy is a phallocentric order that permeates and structures all social relations and is not dependent for its efficacy on the literal presence or absence of the father in the family leaves unaddressed the question of how children practically learn about the 'rule of the father'. Do children in families without fathers learn about patriarchy later than seems psychologically plausible, or do they learn about it through the mother as passive agent of the law? These questions remain unanswered in Lacanian theory because social relations are conflated with a phallocentric linguistic order which seems to perpetuate itself intact regardless of the operations of other social forces such as class.

In his work on gender inequality, Bourdieu does not consider these issues either, and, as a result, it is simplistic and overstated. However, the notion of practice embedded in the idea of habitus has interesting implications for an understanding of reproduction and change within gender identity. It shifts the burden away from understanding sexual difference not just as abstract symbolic designations but also as partially negotiated processes of social interaction. Likewise, agency is understood not in terms of a structural principle of unconscious displacement but as an interpretative process whose infinitesimal realizations in practice may form the potential for wider social change. In sketching out these implications for an understanding of gender, it is certainly important to avoid a celebration of everyday practices but it is also equally as important to avoid, *pace* Žižek, a symbolic over-determination where change is either impossible or cataclysmic. It is these issues that are considered in the next section.

THERE IS NO SEXUAL RELATION

The logic of double disavowal that Žižek discerns in the master–slave dialectic is also the constitutive dynamic in the 'patriarchal matrix' of relations between men and women. Woman is posited as a secondary, lesser being than Man. However, this secondary status has necessarily to be disavowed: she must act as if she is autonomous, as if she has actively chosen the role of submissive, compassionate servitude. A consequence of this logic of disavowal is that it is never possible for women to escape their sexual interpellation through an assertion of independence because this simply reinforces the primordial illusion of feminine autonomy. In a way that resonates with the idea of femininity as a masquerade, Žižek asserts that it is far more subversive for women to openly avow, rather than deny, that they are an hysterical imitation of male subjectivity: 'perhaps the ultimate feminist statement is to proclaim openly: "I do not exist in myself, I am merely the Other's fantasy embodied" ' (1999a: 258).

The self-defeating structure of feminine interpellation is repeated in the masochistic structure of contemporary gender relations. In the essay 'Courtly Love, or Woman as Thing' (1999c), Žižek argues that courtly love, far from being an outmoded relation between the sexes, in fact captures the libidinal economy of the modern 'masochist couple'. A defining characteristic of the Lady in courtly love is that she is a cold, indifferent partner who subjects the Knight to 'senseless, outrageous, impossible, arbitrary, capricious ordeals' (1999c: 151). The Lady is an uncanny, monstrous character with whom no relationship of empathy is possible. The conventional idealization of the Lady as spiritual guide is in fact a secondary phenomenon; it is a narcissistic projection on the part of the Knight designed to conceal the traumatic otherness of the Lady. A further masochistic feature of courtly love is its rigid theatricality; its dependence on strict adherence to codes of etiquette and performance. Unlike the unbounded and destructive power exerted by the sadist, the masochist (the Knight) is in fact he who initiates the contract with the Lady authorizing her to humiliate him. The masochist, therefore, stages his own servitude: 'the masochist constantly maintains a kind of reflective distance; he never really gives way to his feelings or fully abandons himself to the game; in the midst of the game, he can suddenly assume the stance of a stage director, giving precise instructions . . . *without thereby in the least "destroying the illusion"* ' (1999c: 153). The game only breaks down when the dominant partner (the Lady) is sickened by the role accorded to her of the 'object-instrument' in the masochist's scenario.

In Žižek's view, masochism exemplifies the paradoxes of the symbolic order and the impossibility of desire. The fascination of the Lady is not that she is inaccessible but precisely that she has been made inaccessible by the Knight because he cannot confront the impossibility of what he seeks. The Lady-Thing functions as a 'black-hole' around which the desire of the knight is structured. The only way to reach the Lady as Desire is through a logic of 'anamorphosis', that is to say, indirectly, partially, through processes of sublimation which always ensure that the Thing itself remains inaccessible: 'The Object, therefore, is literally something that is created – whose place is encircled – through a network of detours, approximations and near-misses' (1999c: 156). The very agency that impels us to search for enjoyment also compels us to renounce it. This paradox, or the 'detour of desire', exemplifies the way sexual difference is a Real which resists symbolization: 'the sexual relationship is condemned to remain an asymmetrical non-relationship in which the Other, our partner, prior to being a subject, is a Thing, an "inhuman partner"' (1999c: 168). For Žižek, it also exemplifies the impossibility of utopian scenarios of symmetrical relationships between men and women envisaged by certain types of feminism. His contentious claim is that, by opposing patriarchal domination, feminism undermines the 'fantasy support' of women's feminine identity (1999c: 168). For Žižek, then, the desire for recognition has the paradigmatic structure of all desire – it can never be fulfilled. The struggle for recognition is frozen at the moment of misrecognition expressed in the perpetual impossibility of relations between men and women.

It is this interpretation of all social relations of gender as manifold expressions of the psychic impossibility of sexual difference that starkly illustrates the difficulties with Žižek's disregard of practice. If autonomous agency is always an effect of a more insidious ideological interpellation and existential variety is, therefore, a type of social imaginary, then any of the tentative changes in the lived practice of contemporary gender relations are dismissed as insignificant *per se*: 'the dimension of subjectivity that eludes symbolic identification is *not* the imaginary wealth/texture of experiences which allows me to assume an illusory distance towards my symbolic identity: the Lacanian "barred subject" (s) is "empty" not in the sense of some psychologico-existential "experience of a void" but, rather, in the sense of a dimension of self-relating negativity which a priori eludes the domain of *vecu*, of lived experience' (1999a: 259). On this view, agency is conceived of as a property of structures rather than of individuals. It is the effect of the work of the unconscious which itself is an expression of the primal dislocation between the psychic and socio-symbolic orders. This symbolic abstraction, however, tells us very little about change within gender relations, other than pointing to an unchanging phantasmatic structure which is constitutive of all desire and to a self-same principle of radical indeterminacy. It says nothing about the social causes of change in gender relations, about the specific nature or scope of these changes, about why it is that changes are discontinuous and uneven or about the new forms of autonomy and dependence arising from such transformations. For Žižek, for example, given the general impossibility of symbolization, heterosexual norms are no more fixed or stable than 'perverse' sexual identities: 'it is . . . on account of the gap which forever persists between the real of sexual difference and the determinate forms of heterosexual symbolic norms that we have the multitude of "perverse" forms of sexuality' (1999a: 273). In these Lacanian terms, every type of identity is 'outside' the norm. The problem with this position is that it disregards a host of issues connected to the political analysis of power relations and different types of intervention. The radical instability of symbolized sexual identity does not address, for example, the issue of discrimination which, in many respects, renders heterosexual identity a more stable subject position than homosexual identity. Nor, for example, does his position shed much light on how the ultimately negative dynamic of psychic disruption may be sublimated or transmogrified into a more positive force underlying the emergence of new social identities (e.g. Nielsen 2004). How it is that, within the constraints of a prevailing social order, individuals may respond to problems and difficulties through the institution of new practices. In the case of gender identity, it cannot explain why women as historical subjects are not crushed by the constraints of a phallocentric order but have been able to act autonomously within its interstices. Individuals must partly respond in an open and innovative fashion to social complexity if they are to create meaningful and coherent existences from the contingent flux of the world. Such a substantive model of agency cannot easily be derived from a view of subjectification as introjection of the symbolic law.

To criticize Žižek in this way is not necessarily to reinstate an uncritical phenomenalism, nor is it to deny the role that unconscious and irrational forces play in motivating action. Lacanian theorists frequently argue that the force of the category of the unconscious is that it highlights the extent to which social identities are never easily assumed, that the motivations for action are never straightforward (Rose 1986). However, one might question whether it is necessary to adhere to a Lacanian concept of the unconscious as a primal lack that is orthogonal to social systems in order to be able to explain the irrational aspects and ambivalences in different types of socialization. By reconceptualizing the unconscious so that its connection to the social realm is not a purely arbitrary and disruptive one, a space can be opened up for a more substantive understanding of agency other than as an imaginary suturing of a primal void.[2] The forcing of diverse practices into a monolithic framework of sexual difference obscures not only cultural variation in the way gender norms are worked through but also similarities between men and women. In

Nancy Chodorow's (1995) work on the 'power of feelings', for example, the relationship between the unconscious, language and individual experience is reconfigured to suggest a porous interpenetration between the three realms and thereby highlights, *inter alia*, the significance of individual practice for a psychoanalytic understanding of subject formation. Subject formation is not achieved through symbolically imposed meaning, rather the creation of meaning comes from within and without. Subjects are formed by being positioned within matrixes of meaning that are specific to a given socio-cultural system but their own experiences or psychobiographies determine the way in which these meanings are taken up and assume particular significance for the individual. On this view, gender identity cannot be explained through the monolithic framework of symbolically prescribed sexual difference; rather it emerges from the dynamic fusion of personal and cultural meaning. Gender identity is thus, in an important sense, an individual creation: 'when I claim that gender is inevitably personal as well as cultural, I mean not only that people create individualized cultural or linguistic versions of meaning by drawing on the cultural or linguistic categories at hand. Rather, perception and the creation of meaning are psychologically constituted' (Chodorow 1999: 71). It is not just that individuals actively interpret cultural and linguistic meanings but that they also have the potential to create new meanings that may run counter to hegemonic cultural categories. Furthermore, generalizing from the clinical encounter, Chodorow postulates that the inner creation of meaning is never simply a response to early childhood and past events but also builds on the events and interactions of the more immediate present. The causal priority that psychoanalysis usually attributes to the past in the creation of meaning is displaced, giving equal significance to the contingencies of present interactions in this process (Chodorow 1999: 35–65).

The idea of 'emergent meaning', like the protensive dimensions of practice in the Bourdieusian habitus, reverses the determinism of the past that is a consequence of the essentially retroactive structure of Lacanian subjectivity and gives renewed significance to an account of agency. Whereas Žižek's thematization of the 'dark night of the soul' always refers backwards to a primal lack, the idea of emergent meaning embedded in practice is essentially forward looking, giving autonomy to the significance of the present in relation to the past. This sheds a new light on the potential significance of shifts within the practice of contemporary gender relations. Harriet Bjerrum Nielsen (2004) has argued, for example, that over the past thirty years, young women have created and taken up new subject positions that were not available to previous generations of women. The newness of this 'relational individualism' resides in a heightened reflexivity where young women have 'worked through' rather than directly challenged (as their mother's generation did) the norms of conventional femininity in order to establish altered subject positions vis-à-vis gender and sexuality. Its newness also resides in the fact that these subject positions are not reducible to gender. While the extent to which this relational individualism dislodges conventional gender divisions may be more unclear, these new practices cannot be dismissed if change in gender relations is to be understood; in Nielsen and Rudberg's words: 'change will probably occur as the result of infinitesimal displacements of social and cultural conditions that will easily escape attention unless we focus on them' (Nielson and Rudberg 1994: 6). The consequence of Žižek's dismissal of historical variation as insignificant in relation to the central impossibility of the Real is that it occludes any perspective on these myriad, ordinary types of agency and confines an understanding of change to an aporia of radical rupture or stasis.

In sum, Žižek's reworking of ideology as misrecognition may escape the limitations of the obviously negative and unidirectional concepts of false consciousness. However, its reliance on an abstract notion of the symbolic order disconnected from any idea of practice means that he is unable to fully explain these more 'positive' aspects of ideology which may enable individuals to articulate their wants and needs by coalescing with others possibly to express organized dissent. Žižek's paradigm is undoubtedly conceptually sophisticated and rightly problematizes the commonsensical certainties and appearance of unity of everyday experience in order to expose the troubling and unconscious investments – 'passionate attachments' – that individuals maintain in their own subordination. Yet, the essentially abstract understanding of a linguistically formulated desire that is central to his idea of interpellation as misrecognition is disconnected from the social context and results in the reification of identity and agency. In a rather intemperate critique of structuralism, E. P. Thompson used the term 'orrery' to describe the monolithic and self-perpetuating concept of language that undergirds Althusser's theory of ideology. The structuralist account of ideological interpellation is, in Thompson's view, an abstract 'system of closure' in which 'human practice is reified, and "man is in some way developed by the development of structure"' (Thompson 1995: 137). Despite his attempts to render a theory of interpellation more open by drawing on the destabilizing implications of Lacan's idea of the unconscious, Žižek's idea of ideological misrecognition also ultimately fails to escape from the orrery. Social power is conflated with linguistic violence and the symbolic order is conceived as an abstract and self-sustaining system – as the agent through which desire is both incited and thwarted. This view of the symbolic realm as an arbitrary monolith bearing little relation to experience is connected, by Michael Rustin, to the cultural experience of communism. The Lacanian view of the subject as an illusory effect of the symbolic order and as having insatiable desires deriving from its originary lack is a plausible view of the self in an authoritarian society where 'all desire is socially repressed and deadened' (Rustin 1995: 236). Such a view, where 'ideological misrepresentation and delusion have taken over', becomes implausible when it is generalized from the specific context of a post-totalitarian society to stand as a universal theory of subject formation. The invariant principle of unconscious disruption does not provide a sufficiently nuanced account of the varying modalities of agency and change and it is thus hard to see how Žižek sustains the claim that his work is intended to facilitate a radical reconfiguration of social agency that breaks from the traditional terms of structure and agency (Laclau 1989: xv).

RECOGNITION AND THE OTHER

Žižek's psychoanalytic rendering of the struggle for recognition runs counter, in many respects, to the ways in which it has been used by other thinkers in the past decade or so. Whereas he highlights the idea of perpetual misrecognition as the paradigmatic symptom of a primal lack, most other thinkers use the idea of recognition to explore potentially new forms of accommodation between self and other. Jessica Benjamin's work falls into this second camp of thought and, like other types of object relations theory, is directed at overcoming the more general theoretical limitations of Lacanian and Oedipal forms of psychoanalysis (see Chodorow 1989). The key aim of Benjamin's recent work is to derive a theory of gendered agency and intersubjectivity from the idea of the struggle for recognition. Like other feminist thinkers, Benjamin believes that a meaningful account of women's agency cannot be derived from Lacan's work because its phallocentric emphasis takes masculinity as the active, defining principle and femininity as its passive and empty other. At the same time, Benjamin distances herself from a tendency in some types of object relations theory which bases an account of female agency on a sentimentalized conception of motherhood. In Benjamin's view, the centrality of the mother in object relations theory is the inverse of the centrality of the phallus in Lacan in that it takes maternal identification as primary and masculinity comes into being as 'not mother' (Benjamin 1998: xvi). In both cases, inter-subjective dynamics are conceptualized in a skewed and etiolated fashion. Benjamin uses the idea of the struggle for recognition, there-fore, to elaborate a more differentiated understanding of intersub-jectivity and thereby to develop a fuller account of gender identity and agency. The psychoanalytical preoccupation with intra-psychic dynamics leads, by and large, to an overwhelmingly 'egological' view of subject formation and individuality that is untethered from any but the most minimal idea of social interaction. On the occasions when an idea of intersubjectivity is used, the other is conceived pri-marily as an object for the self or an internal fantasy – the Symbolic Other – rather than as an independent, exterior being – the external other. Benjamin claims that psychoanalysis can be historicized if the external other is made more central to its accounts of subject forma-tion or, in other words, if intersubjectivity is understood as a socially situated rather than exclusively psychic dynamic. In contrast, then, to Žižek's dismissal of social practices as expressions of a funda-mental type of ideological misrecognition, Benjamin accords a central significance to these variations in practice in that they are the underpinnings of a substantive account of psychic agency.

The failure to go beyond a narrow egological conception of the other as a symbolic entity is not limited to psychoanalysis but also, in Benjamin's view, characterizes other types of feminist and social thought. It is particularly evident, for example, in the false dichotomy between 'inclusionary' and 'exclusionary' views of inter-subjectivity that are a defining feature of the debate over modernity and postmodernity. The proponents of modernity – exemplified in the communicative theories of thinkers such as Jurgen Habermas and Seyla Benhabib – generally rely on an inclusionary paradigm that is skewed towards the subject's capacity to empathize with the other and to accommodate their demands. This paradigm tends to disregard the non-assimilable features of the other as an external entity and, as a consequence, it underplays issues of asymmetry, misunderstanding and domination in intersubjective relations. In short, subjects are tacitly predisposed towards reaching agreement, mutual acknowledgement and consensus. The centrality of the moment of negation in the dialectic of recognition is discounted and so too is the consequent liability of the other 'not to survive, the inevitable failure of recognition' (Benjamin 1998: 93). In contrast, in the exclusionary paradigm of so-called postmodern theorists, of which Foucault is often taken as an exemplar, the subject remains locked in a zero-sum logic where the troubling alterity of the other has to be perpetually disavowed to maintain the coherence and autonomy of the self. The trouble with this exclusionary dynamic is that it underestimates the subject's capacity to sustain a more positive relation with the other and often leads to a problematic fetishization of non-identity which fails to interrogate its own investment as a fixed position (Benjamin 1998: 103; McNay 2000: 102–9). Despite their apparent opposition, both the inclusionary and exclusionary views share the same conceptual error of conceiving of the other primarily as the symbolic Other of the subject's fantasy rather than also as a particular, external individual.

By developing an account of the struggle for recognition as a formative and dynamic process rather than as, *pace* Žižek, an ahistorical linguistic structure, Benjamin hopes to conceptualize the other more fully as both symbolic and external being. To this end, she synthesizes Hegel's struggle for recognition with a relational understanding of early child development. Like Žižek, Benjamin follows Kojève's existential reading of Hegel where the paradox of recognition is unending and insoluble. The individual is perpetually riven by the conflict between her desire for the freely given recognition from the other, on the one side, and her longing to extort this recognition through domination, even annihilation, on the other. Unlike Žižek, however, this conflict is not reified as an insurmountable condition of existence; for Benjamin there is a potential resolution that flows from her replacement of a structural with a processual account of subject formation through recognition. It is the existential acceptance of the insolubility of this conflict that constitutes its only possible resolution. 'From the standpoint of intersubjective theory, the ideal "resolution" of the paradox of recognition is that it continue as a *constant tension* between recognizing the other and asserting the self' (Benjamin 1995: 38). To facilitate the resolution of the Hegelian struggle, Benjamin adds Winnicott's developmental account of subject formation, in particular, his idea that the other must be grasped as both the object of fantasy and an external being. It is only by comprehending the twofold significance of the other as object of fantasy and external being that the full complexity of the self's dependency upon another is revealed. Benjamin draws this out further by claiming that it is only on the basis of the self's acceptance of the other as an external being that viable intersubjective relations can be established. Such relations are based on the idea of a 'mimetic resonance' in which two separate minds are felt to be present, rather than on the idea of projective identification where the other is felt to embody part of the self (Benjamin 1998: 80). Orthodox psychoanalysis never really confronts the subject with an outside object or an exterior intervention into its projections and identifications and, thus, the subject remains caught within 'nothing other than introjective-projective "web-spinning" ' (Benjamin 1998: 90).

Recognition of the Other as an independent being whose relation to the subject is in excess of any projection and is, therefore, indeterminate brings to the fore intersubjective moments of confrontation and negativity where the subject has to relinquish its fantasies of omnipotence. This confrontation is potentially destructive of intersubjective relations because of the liability of the other not to survive. In developmental terms, the child reaches a point where she attempts to negate the autonomy of the other (i.e. the parent) through the assertion of her will. Problems arise if the other does not 'survive' the child's acts, where the failure to survive might take the form either of punitive retaliation or of passive submission. Both of these responses block the possibility of the child developing feeling for, and acceptance of, the other. The child's thwarted feelings of frustration and anger may be internalized as pathological effects: 'the self thus limited in its contact with externality remains in the thrall of idealization and repudiation, of identifications and projections' (Benjamin 1998: 91). The subject's fantasy of omnipotence can only be constructively dismantled by the other's survival of the attempts to negate him. The compensation for the destruction of this 'closed energy system' is that it is only the external other who can be loved (Benjamin 1998: 91–2).

This reworked account of the relationship with the other leads to a view of psychological agency expressed in the concept of 'splitting' that denotes the mechanism by which the individual is capable of holding in tension ambivalent and conflicting emotional states. The idea of splitting as an 'active, ongoing process of psychic defence' yields an idea of 'psychic agency' where the self has the ability to sustain ambiguous emotional states (Benjamin 1998: 88). Most significantly, the concept of splitting underpins Benjamin's idea of over-inclusive identifications, which she uses as the basis of an account of gendered agency, as the ownership of both active and passive elements in the self. The idea of over-inclusiveness replaces the more usual psychoanalytic separation of these active and passive elements along the lines of masculine and feminine identifications. The paradigm of this gender exclusivity is Oedipus where, in order for a child to assume adult gender identity, it must break its primal attachment to the mother – who represents narcissism and fantasy – in order to identify with the father who represents reality and maturity. In place of this idealization–denigration paradigm, Benjamin argues that, in their pre-Oedipal period, girls and boys are not only attached to the powerful and loving figure of the mother but also make strong identifications with the loving father. Indeed children are capable of making many 'polymorphous' identifications with significant figures at this stage and these enable them to recognize that it is possible to assume a variety of gendered positions 'particularly enhancing "complementarity" rather than the kind of exclusivity which results in the triumph of one gender position over another' (Frosh 1999: 235). Furthermore, these multiple identifications are not just characteristic of early development but are also retrievable post-Oedipus. They are recoverable if the essential ambivalence of the self's relationship to the other is accepted rather than it being skewed into idealization or denigration. 'Multiple identifications forge the basis for gender identities which themselves are multiple and fluid' (Frosh 1999: 235). Recognition, on this dynamic, processual view, means not some impossible transcendence of negation but rather acceptance of its 'strain', of both its creative and destructive elements (Benjamin 1998: 105). It is the ability to accept authorship of this ambivalence that constitutes psychic agency. One of the most important implications for feminists of Benjamin's theory of over-inclusive identifications is that it sketches out the grounds for a theory of women's agency that escapes the double bind of Lacanian negativity, on the one side, and of romanticized motherhood, on the other.

NEGATIVITY AND THE DETOURS OF DESIRE

It is clear that understanding the struggle for recognition as a differentiated process rather than as an invariant structure has significant implications for historicising psychoanalytic explanation.[3] By conceiving of the other as both an exterior subject as well as a symbolic projection, the process of intersubjective identity formation is, in principle, opened up to historical variation (Benjamin 1998: xix, 98–99). Rather than reifying polarized sexual difference as an inevitable feature of psychic formation, Benjamin's notion of over-inclusive identifications reveals this polarization to be an effect of socially instituted forms of gender inequality. The multifarious and non-exclusive identifications denoted in the idea of over-inclusiveness attest to the complexity of lived experience and to its significance for a theoretical account of identity formation.

According significance to varieties of experience in this way contrasts with Žižek's Lacanian view where the realm of phenomenal experience is considered noteworthy only to the extent that it confirms the abstract dynamics of identity formation. Benjamin's relational model posits selfhood as the product of complex social and psychological interactions rather than as a symbolically ascribed position, and this yields an important distinction between the individual gendered self and hegemonic gender identity. Although gender is an important part of self-awareness, selfhood cannot be subsumed by gender identity in the way that it is in Lacanian thought, where subjectivity is sexuality. This distinction between what Chodorow has called gender personality and gender identity is crucial for allowing existential variation into otherwise over-sexualized accounts of subject formation. As Chodorow puts it: ' qualities of self or self in relation . . . and a generically constructed sense of self that is not necessarily tied to a sense of gender become more important than unconsciously or consciously experienced gender identity and cognition and assessment of gender difference' (Chodorow 1989: 122). It follows that the according of theoretical importance to the phenomenal realm permits the possibility of conceptualizing the idea of gender salience, that is, that gender and sexuality have variable significance for different dimensions of women's lives. This, in turn, generates a more dynamic account of women's agency than is available in a Lacanian account where it is both over-sexualized and defined by negativity. In theory, Benjamin's reworking of the recognition paradigm loosens the connection between women's agency and sexuality; women can be understood as social rather than just sexual subjects. In short, its emphasis on the specificity of interactions of recognition introduces, in theory, an understanding of the effects of other social structures such as class and race into a psychological account of subject formation.

The historicizing potential of Benjamin's model of recognition is undercut, however, by being tied to the contentious ontological assertion that a primal dyad lies at the origins of social relations. This ontology of recognition sets up a causal chain where psychic dynamics are projected outwards onto social relations. On this view, power relations are always a *post hoc* effect, distorting or otherwise, of some antecedent and primordial interpersonal dynamic. The problem with this extrapolation of the essence of sociality from a primal recognition dynamic is that it results in a simplified understanding of power and its operations with regard to the formation of subjectivity and the construction of oppression. The ontology of recognition understands the source of inequalities as generated through an interpersonal dynamic of struggle, but this face-to-face dynamic is disconnected from a socio-structural account of power. Gender oppression, for example, is misunderstood by being construed as, in its essence, a form of interpersonally engendered misrecognition rather than also as systemically generated oppression. This is not to deny that inequalities are created through personal interaction, but, by focusing principally on this mode, the idea of recognition obscures the extent to which identity and subjectivity are penetrated by structural dynamics of power which often operate at one remove from the immediate relations of everyday life. It also hinders the conceptualization of a countervailing causality where social and economic forces might determine the shape of the psyche. In the final analysis, Benjamin's configuration of the recognition dynamic remains too wedded to an interpersonal model of power relations to be able to adequately capture the complex and variable ways in which hierarchical identities are constructed.

Some of these theoretical limitations in Benjamin's use of the idea of recognition arise from the dual status she imputes it as an analytical tool and normative category. Recognition encompasses both the process of subject formation and also another, third perspective, that of intersubjective recognition itself. It denotes, on the one hand, the process of struggle where the self battles with its desires for omnipotence and contact, with its incompatible urges to destroy and engage with the other. It gestures towards an ideal, on the other hand, namely, a state of healthy intersubjective relations reached when the self is able to manage these conflicting feelings and to recognize the other as both an object of desire and also as a subject in her own right. The difficulty is that the second normative conception of recognition becomes implicitly conflated with the analysis of how intersubjectivity operates concretely. This leads Benjamin to significantly underplay the moments of negativity and the extent of destructive feelings for the other in intersubjectivity. Negativity becomes an incidental but not intrinsic part of the self–other dynamic and, arguably, this invokes an implausibly sanitized view of subjectivity. In short, the normative 'redemptive' force that resides in the ideal of mutual recognition retroactively limits the sociological analysis of the way in which power structures unequal identities. The stress placed on recognition as vehicle of self-realization and mutual acknowledgement between the subject and its other disregards problematic aspects of subjectivity, simplifies the relation between identity and agency and underplays the pervasive nature of relations of domination. The insights generated by the idea of recognition into the situated and dialogical nature of subjectivity are undercut by its status as a regulative ideal. Its understanding of

subject formation is disconnected from an analysis of power relations and, as a consequence, it fails to grasp some important dimensions to the reproduction of social inequalities.

The effects of this unexamined conflation of the normative and
descriptive functions of Benjamin's idea of recognition have been
commented on by several thinkers, including Judith Butler (Butler
2004; see also Scott 1993; Weir 1996). Butler is undoubtedly sympa-
thetic to Benjamin's use of the idea of over-inclusiveness to criticize
the Lacanian privileging of the phallus which both confines femininity to a perpetual negativity and construes homosexual desire in
the one-dimensional terms of the failure of Oedipus. In Butler's
view, however, the therapeutic ideal of recognition simplifies intersubjective relations by domesticating difference; as she puts it, 'any
therapeutic norm that bases itself on overcoming destructiveness
seems to base itself on impossible premises' (Butler 2004: 147). This
simplification takes place through Benjamin's containment of the
complexities of desire in the reciprocal structure of a primary dyad.
The idea that genuine recognition occurs when the other is neither
rejected nor idealized relies on a conception of the self–other relation
where each remains at the centre of the other's desire. For Butler,
however, the relation between desire and its objects is engendered
through far more complex, impacted and asymmetrical relations.
The entanglements of heterosexual and homosexual desire, for
example, cannot be captured in a dyadic logic of mutual exclusion
or reciprocity: 'if desire works through relays that are not always
easy to trace, then who I am for the Other will be . . . at risk of displacement. Can one find the Other whom one loves apart from all
the Others who have come to lodge at the site of that Other? . . . is
part of what it means to "recognize" the Other, to recognize that he
or she comes, of necessity, with a history which does not have
oneself at its centre' (Butler 2004: 146). Benjamin certainly complicates the status of the other by distinguishing between external
being and symbolic projection but she still unifies these meanings in
a single individual who is involved in a reciprocal relation with
another individual. This uncomplicated mutuality throws into question Benjamin's claim to have unseated the egological emphasis of
mainstream psychoanalysis. She may have overthrown a certain
radically unsituated conception of the subject but, arguably, its egological tendencies remain intact in the reciprocal dynamic that operates between the two discrete and unified beings of the recognition
dyad. Ultimately then, Benjamin's concept of recognition upholds a
notion of sovereign subjectivity in so far as it imputes an implausible degree of reflexivity and unity to the subject who is capable of

holding in tension its split or contradictory desires. The moment of inclusion remains the controlling trope in the struggle for recognition: 'if we assume that the self exists and then it splits, we assume that the ontological status of the self is self-sufficient before it undergoes its splitting . . . But this is not to understand the ontological primacy of relationality itself and its consequences for thinking the self in its necessary . . . disunity' (Butler 2004: 150).

Benjamin responds to these criticisms by claiming that Butler works with a one-dimensional concept of the subject and of the type of relations that it is capable of sustaining with the other. Ultimately, Butler's critique of the unified subject collapses distinctions between subjectivity, selfhood and identity. Subjectivity is considered only as sexual identity and is therefore construed as a relatively passive entity. In eschewing any idea of selfhood, Butler cannot explain the active dimensions of subjectivity that Benjamin denotes in the idea of psychic agency. The one-dimensionality of Butler's conception of the subject is evident in her etiolated account of the exclusionary relation with the other. The excluded other can only be the Symbolic other of the subject's fantasy and not the external and autonomous being who constitutes the concrete other because the latter cannot be excluded in the same way as the former. In psychic terms, the idea of exclusion is an illusion since it can only really mean to relocate psychically. The irreducibility of the external other to inner life opens the possibility of the self maintaining a more complex position towards the other, characterized by ambivalence rather than exclusion. This ability to sustain psychic tension is not ultimately, *pace* Butler, a form of harmonious inclusion; rather it involves the self's capacity to hold conflicting feelings: 'Difference, hate, failure of love can be surmounted not because the self is unified, but because it can tolerate being divided' (Benjamin 1998: 105). This interpretative perspective escapes Butler because subject formation is understood through an abstract symbolic logic where exclusion and negativity are formal positions associated with the indeterminacy of meaning. This symbolic abstraction bypasses the phenomenal reality of negativity, it 'does not speak to the concretes – fear, pain, loss – that generally drive disintegration and therefore make integration look like a good thing' (1998: 104). In short, it is only by considering the other as both a psychic and concrete entity that a rounded view of agency and intersubjectivity comes into view.[4]

The central difficulty with Benjamin's work therefore lies not so much in its alleged resuscitation of a 'sovereign' subject but in the extent to which the ontology of recognition reifies the social processes through which gender identity is constructed. Benjamin is well aware of the dangers of falling back into an over-unified notion of subjectivity and, in a certain sense, the charge that Butler levels at her is the effect of her own problematic fetishization of underdeveloped ideas of indeterminacy and non-identity which *de facto* outlaws any attempt to explain the coherence of the subject. If there is therefore a reappearance of a putative sovereign subject in Benjamin's thought, it is not the origin of the theoretical difficulties considered above but one of the effects of a more pervasive reductionism where social relations are misrecognized by being viewed through the lens of psychic dynamics. In this respect, Butler's abstract linguistic account of subject formation also remains vulnerable to the charge that it forecloses an adequate understanding of the social specificity of the process of subject formation (see Chapter 5). In the following sections, I show how Benjamin's ontologization of the recognition dyad has problematic implications for an understanding of the social relations of gender oppression. Ultimately, the essentially individualist and psychological sense in which Benjamin construes the terms recognition and misrecognition cannot capture the systemic and historically variable ways in which oppression is constructed. The struggle for recognition is ultimately conceived as a free-floating archetype whose fundamental dynamic is superimposed onto all subsequent social relations. This sets up a one-way causality from psyche to society which undercuts Benjamin's claim that her version of the struggle for recognition is sensitive to socio-cultural variation.

RECOGNITION AND THE HISTORICAL OTHER

Prior to the issue of whether it provides an adequate understanding of gender inequality, there is the question of whether the idea of recognition is not a theoretically dubious way of depicting the relational aspects of human development. Although Benjamin rightly calls attention to the difficulties of explaining subject formation through Oedipus, she does not query the universal, ontological status she accords the recognition dynamic in this role. The struggle for recognition is regarded not just as one particular dynamic within intersubjective relations but as the foundational and determining dynamic. There are compelling reasons to regard this as a tendentious theoretical imposition on Benjamin's part; indeed, as Joan Scott puts it: 'Benjamin is offering a counter-myth of the Oedipal one that is as radically unverifiable as the theoretical fiction of parricide. Hers is a theory of intersubjective relations, not a way of establishing specific subjectivities' (Scott 1993: 442–3). In the first place, it is questionable whether it is appropriate to typify the parent–child dyad as a struggle for recognition. The extreme dependency of the child upon the parent is not analogous to the dynamic between two independent adults seeking recognition from each other even when they occupy asymmetrical social positions. Furthermore, the mutuality imputed to the parent–child dyad obscures the sense in which the child can really be understood to have the cognitive capacity implied in the Hegelian idea of recognition. As Alison Weir puts it, 'Benjamin makes the mistake of assuming that an intersubjective theory of self-development requires . . . the assumption that . . . human beings are born ready-made subjects with the capacity to recognize themselves and others as subjects' (Weir 1996: 87). Other ways of modelling the primal bond between mother and child acknowledge the asymmetry of capability and power more explicitly. Jean Laplanche, for example, uses the notion of 'primal seduction' to capture the infant's helplessness and inability to comprehend the enigmatic world of the parent (Laplanche 1999). Rather than categorize the relation between infant and parent as intersubjective, Cynthia Willett describes it as one of 'subjectless sociality'. Sociality occurs before the infant is a subject and, therefore, before the onset of intersubjectivity and is better understood as akin to dance or music rather than in linguistic and cognitive terms (Willett 1995: 18). In short, the transposition of the dialectic of recognition onto the parent–child dyad can only make sense through a tendentious and retroactive imputation of self-consciousness to the child. As Peter Osborne puts it: 'To render Benjamin's position consistent with its own Hegelian categories we need to view the earliest phase . . . as *unconsciously* and only *retrospectively* "intersubjective"' (Osborne 1995: 100).

It is not just that the idea of the struggle for recognition is a questionable depiction of human development, but also it undermines Benjamin's aim to introduce an element of historicity into psychoanalytic theory. Her ontology of recognition forecloses an account of the mediating work of power relations, thereby establishing a short circuit between psyche and society where the latter seems to derive its shape and logic almost entirely from the former. Social relations are regarded as extrapolations from a primal dyad of recognition and are thereby simplified and deprived of social specificity. This reductionism, albeit unintended, is most evident in the final chapter of *The Bonds of Love*, where Benjamin locates the origins of a rationalized, patriarchal society in the skewed logic of misrecognized gender differences. On this view, rationalization is an unmediated expression of male rationality: 'rationality which social theorists since Weber

have seen as the hallmark of modernity . . . is in fact a male rationality' (Benjamin 1988: 184). The imposition of a principal of male dominance across all social realms has the effect of denying women's
agency: 'regardless of woman's increasing participation in the public,
productive sphere of society, it remains . . . "a man's world". The
presence of women has no effect on its rules and processes' (1988:
187). It is in such overstated claims that the limitations of understanding oppression through an undifferentiated idea of recognition
become most apparent. It is not that there is not some connection
between the rationalization of the lifeworld and a certain instrumental masculine disposition. The problem is that, without any theory of
the mediating work of differentiated power relations, the idea of a
rationalized masculinity becomes a ubiquitous principle of sexual
division that is monolithically imposed onto the social realm in a way
that belies the complexities of social subordination. The simplistic
account of gender domination that is an entailment of extrapolating
from Benjamin's recognition paradigm has been criticized by feminists, most especially for what is held to be her rejection of a concept
of autonomy as an expression of a masculine will to power:
'autonomous individuality derives from the male posture in differentiation; that is from the repudiation of the primary experience of
nurturance and identity with the mother' (1988: 188). In her early
work, Benjamin argues that for feminist politics to progress, it must
break down the logic which polarizes and sexualizes the distinction
between transcendence and immanence or between the desire for
autonomy and the recognition of one's dependence upon others.
While Benjamin is right to criticize the idea of autonomy as a her-
metic state of self-sufficiency, her reformulation of the concept
through a notion of the nuturing maternal bond is problematic.
Rather than mediating the sexual dualism of autonomy and dependence, she reinstates it by associating her renewed notion of individuation so closely with a sentimentalized conception of motherhood
(Johnson 1988: 22). Benjamin's later work on over-inclusive identifications certainly corrects this residual sexual dualism by defining
autonomy as the relinquishment by both men and women of their
investments in conventional notions of masculinity and femininity.
However, the idea of over-inclusivity is still governed by the emphasis inherent to the idea of recognition upon face-to-face interaction
that leads to a one-dimensional understanding of gender as principally a form of personal identity.

This filtering of gender through the narrow prism of interpersonally generated identity cannot explain how, in late-capitalist societies,
gender inequalities are often created through structural oppression

rather than direct domination, that is to say, at an impersonal level, through processes such as the systemic organization of the workforce. For materialists, gender has a logical priority over sexual identity because, as Stevi Jackson says, 'from a materialist feminist perspective, it is not difference which produces hierarchy but hierarchy which gives rise to socially significant differences' (Jackson 1999: 129). It is not that a materialist perspective would necessarily demur from Benjamin's claim that gender inequalities are deeply rooted in the psyche; it is, however, that it would locate its origins in a wider range of dynamics than the struggle for recognition. All accounts of heterosexuality recognize the inequality between men and women but they do not posit that this inequality is evenly produced across all social practices in the way implied by Benjamin's analysis. Theorists such as Bob Connell, for example, have suggested that there are many different types of hegemonic and subordinate masculinities and femininities and it is important to distinguish them analytically in order to understand the complex dynamics of social hierarchies (Connell 1987; see also Chodorow 1995: 94–5). By tracing all oppression back to the same psychological dynamic, the idea of recognition retroactively attributes a false unity to social existence. Heterosexuality, for example, is not simply a psychically generated identity, it is also produced through structures and institutions, most obviously marriage, the family and the domestic division of labour. This allows for a more complex analysis of the dynamics of oppression. Psychoanalysis, by and large, locates individuals in the universalist terms of 'men' or 'women', 'boys' or 'girls', whereas a sociological analysis of gender inequalities might differentiate these subject positions further (see Chodorow 1989: 129). On the latter view, it is often women's role as wives and not necessarily their role as mothers that is the key to their subordination (Johnson 1988; Delphy 1984). The definition of wife is not simply that of 'married woman' but is construed in more specific terms as diminished access, relative to men, to economic and symbolic resources. Thus, Miriam Johnson understands the socially subordinate role of wife as arising from economic dependence and the accompanying psychological characteristics such as deference that it inculcates, whereas Christine Delphy defines a wife as someone whose paid and unpaid labour is appropriated by the male head of household. A consequence of construing the role of wife in socially specific rather than psychological terms is that it can be seen that women are constituted as 'wives' in social practices beyond the family, both in terms of the types of segregated work women perform (e.g. nursing and other caring professions) or in terms of the expectations of certain professional jobs

(Adkins 1995). As Jo VanEvery says: 'gender is not culturally produced elsewhere and influential on the domestic division of labour . . . but is culturally produced (at least partly) through the domestic division of labour' (VanEvery 1996: 45–6).

The misrecognition of the social relations of oppression that flows from the ontology of recognition is evident also in Benjamin's discussion of racial segregation. In *The Shadow of the Other*, Benjamin seeks to demonstrate the historical sensitivity of the recognition paradigm by using it to explain the ending of apartheid in South Africa. On Benjamin's view, the ending of apartheid in South Africa represents the break-up of an exclusionary view of the Other (Benjamin 1998: 98–99). On the most schematic level, one could hardly disagree with Benjamin's depiction of the underlying psychic dynamics of apartheid. The very generality of the analysis, however, highlights precisely why the struggle for recognition remains such an inappropriate paradigm for capturing the particular dynamics of oppression. It effaces the specificities of the situation: it romanticizes the oppressed black majority as the Macro subject of the Other, it effaces the violence of the struggle, it skates over the schisms and struggles for power between the ANC and other political groups, it passes over the doubts about the efficacy of the strategy of Truth and Reconciliation (e.g. Norval 1998). Indeed, any other number of successful struggles against oppression, for example, the Velvet revolutions in Eastern Europe during the 1980s could be described in precisely the same terms as the disintegration of an exclusionary view of the other. The limitations of representing socially constructed inequalities as misrecognition are powerfully illustrated in Fanon's critique of the struggle for recognition in *Black Skin, White Masks*. Fanon's basic point is that the Hegelian dialectic has no relevance for the colonial context because the overwhelming power inequalities annihilate any sense of mutuality that the idea of recognition presumes. Fanon describes how the colonial subject is sealed into the 'crushing object-hood' of blackness by the gaze of the colonial oppressor. It is not the struggle for recognition that forms the subjectivity of the colonial subject but social subordination. The black man suffers from a 'situational' not a psychological neurosis (Fanon 1952: 60). His status as other derives not from misunderstanding but from historically entrenched processes of overdetermination, where he is not free to be anything other than black: 'The Martinican is a man crucified. The environment that has shaped him (but that he has not shaped) has horribly drawn and quartered him' (Fanon 1952: 216). The 'governing fiction' of the colonial situation is, therefore, 'not personal but social' (1952: 215). Fanon powerfully exposes the analytical inadequacy of an individualist model of power for explaining the dynamics of social oppression. By reading social struggles through an eternally recurrent struggle for recognition, the cultural specificity of oppression, the 'uniqueness of racial alienation' is effaced (Oliver 2001: 38).

Despite Benjamin's claims for its historical relevance, the essentially interpersonal model of power inherent in the ontology of recognition cannot be satisfactorily generalized outwards to explain the logic of power relations in terms of what Gayatri Spivak has called a model of social indirection. There are types of systemic oppression that operate at one remove from the immediacy of social life, for example the structuring of the labour market and gender division of labour. Such forms of systemic oppression operate in ways that are often distinct from the logic of interpersonal relations of recognition. To fail to situate gender identity within the context of other systems of power is to risk falling into a form of culturalism or 'associational mode' of thinking where all social inequalities are considered primarily as issues of recognition and identity formation and not as systemically perpetuated forms of discrimination. By understanding gender only as a mode of personal identity, the recognition dyad reifies the complexities of social interaction. This is not to deny that gender inequalities are reproduced, in part, through interpersonal interaction. It is does, however, throw into relief the problematic foreclosures of Benjamin's idea of recognition which, by failing to connect the phenomenal level of interaction and identity formation to underlying power relations, misunderstands how hierarchical gender relations are reproduced in late capitalist society.

PSYCHIC INJURIES OF CLASS

The view of social relations as extrapolations of a fundamental struggle for recognition tacitly invokes a causal chain that flows from the psyche to society. If a more mediated understanding of power relations is adopted then it becomes possible to reverse this causality so that psychic dynamics may be understood, in some cases, as the effects of the internalization of social relations of oppression rather than their cause. Perhaps one of the most significant consequences of this reversal is that it allows the impact of class relations upon subject formation to come into view. From this perspective, recognition may be understood not as an innate psychic dynamic but as the effect of certain types of economic and social deprivation. In *Landscape for a Good Woman*, Carolyn Steedman (1986) explores the impact that social deprivation has upon the psyche. Through an account of her own relationship with her mother, she explores how, in circumstances of dispossession, the affectual dynamics of the mother–child relationship are often dictated by economic calculations. She claims that the effects of poverty on working-class women like her mother were such that having children was regarded as a form of traffic with the future. In the absence of any other resources or power, working-class women realized that their reproductive capacity was an object that they might use to acquire security in the form of marriage. In these circumstances, children often came to understand themselves as 'items of expenditure, investments and as objects of exchange' (Steedman 1986: 69). Thus, the sense of disregard she felt emanating from her mother towards herself was because, as an object of exchange, she had failed to realize her value; having children had not brought her mother the material security she craved.

It is undoubtedly possible to describe the affectless relationship between Steedman and her mother in terms of withheld recognition where economic deprivation destructively skews the primal dynamic between mother and child. But this would be to miss Steedman's point, which is to throw that causality into question; it is social circumstances which shape the psyche rather than simply reinforcing its primal dynamics. In recasting recognition as a socioeconomic rather than a psychological category, Steedman draws attention to the specific class dynamics of the mother–child relation which cannot be adequately captured in the idea of recognition.[5] Indeed, her work resonates with other feminist accounts whose documentation of the emotional impact of deeply internalized class differences complicates the treatment of motherhood as a psychologically undifferentiated and universal role (e.g. Lawler 2000; Reay 2000). More generally, this work on class as a psycho-affectual structure throws into question the way in which the granting of an ontological status to the recognition dynamic sets it apart from and prior to other power relations. Ultimately, for Steedman, the determining primacy given to the psyche is evidence of the inherent class bias of psychoanalytic schema which either efface or paternalistically misconstrue the structures of feeling that arise from class oppression. The original psychoanalytic corpus is evidentially based in middle-class case studies which are usually extended to the working classes through the imposition of a certain model of the bourgeois family. From this top-down perspective, the working class is seen as the passive object of transmission processes. However, once a working-class perspective is reconstructed, a new light is shed on the validity of the psychoanalytic interpretation. Envy, for example, is seen from a psychoanalytic viewpoint, as a kind of 'infant original' sin. However, from the perspective of those who are socially deprived, it is mundanely explicable, not as a pathology, but as a coherent response to political and social exclusions (see Lawler 1999). As Steedman puts it: 'From a social viewpoint it is possible to see the most extraordinary and transparent political paternalism attaching itself to the general use of the notion in psychoanalysis' (Steedman 1986: 112). It is not necessary to accept Steedman's claim about the inherent class bias of the evidential foundations of psychoanalysis in order to acknowledge the more general difficulty that it deals with social forces of subject formation only as relatively epiphenomenal vis-à-vis what are too often conceived as prior psychic dynamics. In Benjamin's understanding of recognition, for example, autonomy is defined primarily as an affective state, as the capacity to reconcile oneself to conflicting and coextensive feelings of love and hate within one's self and within the other. On this view, subjects are intersubjectively related through the dimension of affect: shared feeling and emotion are the primary mediating force: 'recognition is always and only affective recognition' (Weir 1996: 75). By defining autonomy in such affectual terms, Benjamin does not recognize that recognition might in fact be a psychic disposition induced by social circumstances. For Habermas, for instance, autonomy is socially created in that it is primarily a cognitive state in so far as it is linked to the role that social norms play in the demand for, and the creation of, relationships based on recognition.

Reversing the casual dynamic that Benjamin's ontology of recognition posits between psyche and society institutes an expanded understanding of the causes and possibilities for change in gender relations. The struggle for recognition locates both the causes of, and resistance to, gender inequality in psychological relations. It is certainly the case that changes within social practices and relations often need to be accompanied by a 'psychological readiness' if their emancipatory potential is to be realized (Rudberg and Nielsen 2005: 128). However, on Benjamin's account, psychic agency is generated through the satisfactory psychological resolution of the struggle for recognition rather than it being a possible consequence of changes in material and social circumstances. In other words, psychic change necessarily precedes social transformation. Because of this, Benjamin fails to see, for example, that aspects of the rationalization of the social world do not lead unequivocally to the domination of women but have resulted also in the creation of complex new forms of autonomy and dependence. The decline in the birth rate in industrialized countries, the increasing divorce rate, the entry of women into paid

employment and the slow erosion of the glass ceiling in some professions all attest to a fragility in the institutional reproduction of heterosexuality which could provide the basis for greater emancipation
for women. These complexities in the reproduction of gender hierarchies are obscured if its institutional reproduction is subsumed into
questions of psycho-sexual identity. Ultimately, the explanatory privilege accorded to the recognition dyad undercuts Benjamin's claim to
want to provide a psychological account of subject formation that
takes account of social and historical variation. To be sure, Benjamin's
relational framework is more amenable to these variations than
Žižek's hyperstructuralist paradigm. She contests the unrelenting
phallocentricity of his Lacanian version of the struggle for recognition
theory with her notion of an over-inclusive post-Oedipal state which
yields a more positive account of the subject positions available for
men and women between the poles of masculinity and femininity.
However, while her recognition dynamic dislodges a monolithic
phallocentrism, it still cannot yield a satisfactory account of how
social forces, like those of class, can profoundly shape the psyche. The
superordination of the idea of recognition as the fundamental psychic
structure means that all social relations are read through a sexualized
dyad of affect. This is problematic because, although many forms of
power are eroticized, structures of class and race oppression cannot
be read as versions of sexual identity formed in the struggle for recognition without denying them complexity and specificity. It would be
to misrepresent the nature of many oppressions which have a logic
that is irreducible to such an interpersonal dynamic.[6]

CONCLUSION

Ultimately, the attempts by Žižek and Benjamin to use the idea of
recognition to historicize psychoanalytical explanation fail in certain
central respects. Žižek claims that the radical lack that is constitutive
of the human condition is itself historicizing in that it ensures the
fragility and contingency of every symbolic constellation. The difficulty with this formulation is that he dismisses any appeal to variations and divergences in social practice as theoretically insignificant
vis-à-vis his view of human relations as necessarily based in psychic
misrecognition. This leaves him, *inter alia*, with a construal of sexual
difference that is transcendental and therefore ahistorical. It is a
central claim of this book that an appeal to embodied practice need
not necessarily invoke an uncritical phenomenalism and also that it

is central to any nuanced understanding of agency and change within gender relations. In sum, the complexity and instability of social and symbolic formations can be better understood without recourse to the ahistorical formulation of the unconscious as autochthonous and radical lack.

In important respects, Benjamin's theory of over-inclusive identification yields a more dynamic and subtle account of gendered agency for both men and women than is available in the Lacanian paradigm. Her formulation of recognition as an interactive process rather than invariant structure dislodges the central role accorded to sexual difference in an Oedipal account of development and replaces it with an attention to the variation that arises in the social realization of gender roles. In principle, this relational dynamic could be extended beyond gender to encompass other relations of power such as race and class. However, the considerable potential of Benjamin's socialization of key psychoanalytic concepts is undercut by her ontological construal of the struggle for recognition. The dynamics of gender oppression are simplified by being depicted as extrapolations from a primal dyad of recognition and a determining force is imputed to the psyche that forecloses an understanding of the way in which hierarchies of power are internalized as psychic dispositions.

A possible response to the claims I make above is that it is psychoanalysis itself, rather than the idea of recognition that is fundamentally ahistorical. This argument has much force, especially with regard to Lacanian versions of psychoanalytic theory. However, in the subsequent chapters, I explore how, even within versions of the struggle for recognition that explicitly attend to social and political diversity, there are also ahistorical and psychologically reductive tendencies in the account of subject formation. These tendencies are undoubtedly related to the normative force which most of these thinkers attribute to the idea of recognition and which requires them to set up an ontology that tacitly inclines subjects towards mutual understanding of some kind or another.

2

The Politics of Recognition

INTRODUCTION

In political theory, the idea of the struggle for recognition has been used to develop an alternative to normative thought grounded in what has been called the 'philosophy of the subject'. Above all, the idea of recognition has been elaborated in such a way as to replace the monological conception of the subject in liberal political philosophy with a dialogical conception. This dialogical conception understands individuals not as isolated or antecedently individuated beings but as beings who only know themselves through interaction with others. It emphasizes, therefore, the embodied, practical and cooperative character of the self–other relation. A normative consequence of this adoption of the idea of recognition is that it highlights the centrality of intersubjective relations to social life and thereby enshrines a primordial ethical bond with the other at the heart of political prescription. Two of the most notable proponents of the idea of recognition in political theory are Charles Taylor and Jürgen Habermas. Both thinkers use the idea to develop a series of interrelated ontological, sociological and normative claims about the inescapably dialogical texture of social life. In doing so, both proceed from the assumption that normative political thought is not 'free standing' but is inextricably bound up with an understanding and critique of existing social relations.[1] Political thought must constantly interrogate its sociological implications both in terms of its normative consequences and its often tacitly held pre-understandings of society. For Taylor, the politics of recognition is driven by a deep-seated need

on the part of individuals and groups to have a publicly acknowledged stable and authentic identity that, *inter alia*, serves to situate
them in overarching moral horizons. For Habermas, a fully implemented politics of recognition is a fundamental pre-condition for his
democratic ideal of a communicative ethics. Although Taylor and
Habermas start from the same presumption of the dialogical nature
of subjectivity and identity, they, of course, reach different political
conclusions which have been well documented in their sporadic
engagement with the work of the other over the years.

Despite these political differences, I argue that there is a latent similarity in the way that both thinkers formulate the idea of recognition
and that this similarity is, ultimately, the cause of difficulties in their
normative theories. Like Jessica Benjamin, both theorists posit that
the struggle for recognition is constitutive of subjectivity and identity
but, unlike Benjamin, both emphasize the role that language plays as
the primary medium through which self–other relations are mediated. However, in developing the idea of linguistic mediation, both
Taylor and Habermas invoke a purified model of language where
relations of power are seen as extrinsic or secondary forms of distortion of a primal dyad of recognition. This extirpation of power from
language allows both theorists to attribute to the recognition dyad a
single primordial function; in Taylor's case, language is conceived as
an expressive medium, in Habermas's case, it is a communicative one
oriented towards understanding. The setting up of language as prior
to, rather than coeval with, power undermines their claims to
develop normative proposals that proceed from a sociological sensitivity to the situated and embodied nature of self–other interactions.
This is not a contingent weakness in their thought but a necessary
effect of the normative exigencies of their ideal of recognition. It
requires them to set up an ontology where individuals are tacitly predisposed to reach some kind of mutual understanding, but this
inevitably rests on a reductive understanding of the operations of
power upon embodied subjects.

In order to make my argument about the untenability of these
purified linguistic ontologies of recognition, I draw in part on
Bourdieu's concept of linguistic habitus. This encapsulates an alternative conception of language as a social institution, one of whose
principal effects is a form of symbolic violence. In other words,
contra Taylor and Habermas, language is understood as coeval with
power rather than antecedent to it. On this view, language cannot be
attributed a single essential function, whether it be communication
or self-expression, rather it is a complex medium where expression
and understanding are inextricably bound up with the modes of

symbolic violence that determine embodied existence. In the final analysis, the opposition of Bourdieu to Habermas and Taylor raises questions about the relation between normative political theory and critical social theory. It could be argued that to criticize the emancipatory force of the idea of recognition from the standpoint of social relations of power is to fall back into a form of cynical empiricism that undermines normative thought by reducing it to what Arendt has called the 'social question'. I argue that this need not be the case and that normative thought can only develop in the context of continuous sociological self-critique. Moreover, such critique need not forego the possibility that the idea of recognition may be invested with some delimited normative force. It does, however, throw into question the claims that Taylor and Habermas make about the universal relevance of their normative theories.

TAYLOR ON RECOGNITION

Charles Taylor's influential essay 'The Politics of Recognition' is probably the main catalyst for the renewal of interest in the idea of the struggle for recognition as a way of explaining the rise of identity politics *post* 1968. Taylor's principal concern in this essay is to demonstrate how the discourse of recognition is a way of framing claims about the individual that are distinct to the rise of modernity. The idea of the recognition of the individual starts to gain currency with the transition from hierarchical status-bound societies organized around a principle of honour to egalitarian, democratic societies organized around a principle of dignity. It receives a powerful formulation in the work of Romantic writers such as Rousseau and Herder, who connect it to the idea of dignity and the realization of authentic selfhood understood as 'my own original way of being', distinct from socially imposed social roles (Taylor 1994a: 32). A crucial feature of the rise of a discourse of recognition is that it draws attention to the fundamentally dialogical process through which individuality is established. In Taylor's view, the ontological status of interaction in the formation of identity has been underplayed within Western philosophy which, apart from the Hegelian tradition, adheres, on the whole, to a monological conception of the subject as antecedently individuated (Mulhall and Swift 1992: 41). A dialogical conception of subjectivity proposes that identity does not arise spontaneously from within isolated individuals but is the result of interaction with significant others: 'the development of an ideal of inwardly generated identity gives a new importance to recognition. My own identity crucially depends on my dialogical relations with others' (Taylor 1994a: 34).

When claims for recognition become the basis for political movements, as they have done increasingly in the post WWII era, they potentially run into conflict with prevailing liberal systems of individual rights. The universal aspect of a politics of recognition, that every individual should be accorded equal dignity and an identical set of rights and immunities, potentially clashes with its differentiating aspect that might require that certain groups and individuals be given distinct forms of recognition in order to enable them to achieve expression of their authentic identity. Taylor considers some of the implications of this equality–difference clash in his well-known discussion of the Meech Lake Accord, which implemented certain measures aimed at preserving Quebec as a distinct francophone community (1994a: 51–61). He concludes that, if the paramount nature of individual rights is sufficiently safeguarded, there may be exceptional cases when it is legitimate to accord special collective rights to groups in order to ensure their 'survival' as a culture. In Taylor's view, the survival of a given culture may become a political imperative if its values and practices provide a unique and irreplaceable evaluative framework from within which individuals derive meaningful conceptions of selfhood. He rejects, however, the relativist stance that could be a consequence of an uncritical affirmation of difference where equal recognition is automatically accorded to all cultures and lifestyles, regardless of their values and practices. Taylor argues that the worth of any given culture needs to be assessed through a cross-cultural dialogue that proceeds in a manner similar to that suggested in Gadamer's 'fusion of horizons'. The presumption of equal worth would be the starting point, but not the guaranteed conclusion of such a cross-cultural dialogue. The process of critical exchange should reveal new standards and values that enrich and expand previously held values and, ultimately, provide new grounds on which the presumption of equal worth can be validated or not (1994a: 66–7). It is this idea of 'epistemic gain' that Taylor claims prevents his idea of cultural exchange falling into an uncritical relativism, on the one side, and an abstract proceduralism, on the other.

THE PROBLEM OF ESSENTIALISM

Taylor's essay on recognition has been very influential and has sparked extensive debate. A substantial part of this debate has focused on the problematic implications of his understanding of identities as integral and authentic, which is a key theme not just in his thought on recognition but throughout his oeuvre (e.g. Novotony 1998; Tempelman 1999). The basic claim is that his formulation of individual and group identity is essentialist in so far as it underplays the complexities and instabilities intrinsic to the processes through which social identities are formed. There are different versions of this criticism but many connect this essentialism to the narrow cultural model of identity that underpins Taylor's thematization of recognition. Sasja Tempelman (1999), for example, has argued that Taylor's formulation of multicultural movements as driven by a need for recognition effaces the very different and often more expedient ways in which social and political identities are constructed. The privileging of cohesive cultural identity ignores other types of group membership that may be non-exclusive, accommodate high degrees of internal differentiation and of individual autonomy, for example ideas of civic cosmopolitanism. Thus, Tempelman supplements Taylor's 'primordial' model of cultural identity with two other possible modes, the civic and the universal. Likewise, Susan Wolf (1994) argues that the complex and diverse processes through which social and political identities are formed cannot be grasped through a single model of cultural recognition. The limitations of the paradigm are particularly glaring when it comes to issues of recognition pertaining to women. Claims made by feminist movements around gender identity cannot be considered parallel to claims made by, say, an ethnic or religious group for cultural survival. The problem for women is not a straightforward one of the lack of recognition or the issue of cultural survival as a group. Gender identity is recognized but often in a way that devalues women's skill and activities. The question then becomes not the assertion of gender identity, but its deconstruction, so that women (and men) can be recognized as individuals rather than as representatives of a group (Wolf 1994: 76–7). Taylor's single model of cultural recognition not only wrongly attributes an isomorphic structure to different political and social movements but also fails to distinguish between the different audiences or agents who bestow recognition. Fiona Williams, for example, argues how recognition can occur on multiple levels. In the case of black and migrant women's struggle for representation in the EU, she shows that achieving recognition on a trans-national level automatically invoked struggles at the local and national level (Williams 2003: 132). Seeking representation for black and migrant women at the level of the EU is complicated, not least because the institutional modes of dealing with migration and gender are distinct and often divergent.

In so far as it imputes a false unity to diverse struggles for recognition, Taylor's paradigm is also normalizing. His spontaneous, bottom-upwards model of identity formation obscures the possible disciplinary and normalizing effects that may be inherent to the maintenance of a cohesive model of individual and group identity: 'a politics of recognition that neglects such differences, transformations and internal disputes only affirms the authority of those already in power' (Tempelman 1999: 22–3). Anthony Appiah makes such a point when he declares that Taylor's emphasis on an 'ethics of authenticity' not only underplays the extent to which all identities are internally riven and contested but, in suggesting that there is an essential core to identity, ignores the extent to which 'there is no bright line' between a politics of recognition and a 'politics of compulsion' (Appiah 1994: 163). In a similar vein, Quentin Skinner claims that Taylor's work reinstates a kind of theistic Hegelianism that, at the limit, can result in intolerance and coercion (Skinner 1991). As Stephen White puts it, 'Skinner's critique buttresses the default judgement of many liberals today . . .: too much talk of ontology is bad for a pluralistic society' (White 2000: 43). Acts of recognition may indeed create a coherent and legitimate identity for groups that have hitherto been internally divided. However, the act of recognition itself may itself be a normalizing gesture with oppressive implications. Michael Warner argues, for example, that the recognition of same-sex marriage normalizes a certain 'acceptable' image of gay relationships whilst marginalizing those who choose not to live within the confines of institutionalized coupledom (Warner 1999: 96. See also Povinelli 2002).

In as much as Taylor's idea of recognition is held to reify identity, some critics have argued that it should be abandoned as a way of addressing political and social conflict. Nancy Fraser argues, for example, that not only does Taylor's idea of recognition de-historicize social and political struggle but it misrepresents conflict over systemic types of maldistribution of resources and exclusion as struggles about the misrecognition of integral identities. Likewise, Iris Marion Young argues that the problem with the recognition paradigm is that it rests on a conception of identity as a substance rather than as a relation. If identity is understood in relational terms then the problematic idea of a politics based in recognition claims can be bypassed in favour of the idea of a politics of difference. The idea of recognition may be retained to denote very specific cultural movements against stereotypical representation but, in general, identity claims are better understood as being part of larger claims for political and social inclusion or economic redistribution: 'where there are problems of lack of recognition . . . these are usually tied to questions of control over resources, exclusion from benefits of politic influence or economic participation, strategic power, or segregation from opportunities' (Young 2000: 105).

The difficulty with such critiques is that the claim that Taylor's idea of recognition reifies identity is often overstated and disregards explicit anti-essentialist elements in his work. The criticism of essentialism certainly raises important difficulties in Taylor's work but, as I argue in the next section, it does not go to the heart of the problem with his recognition model of identity formation. This is partly because Taylor himself is aware of the problems of essentialism and his dialogical account of subject formation is intended to be anti-essentialist in important respects. Taylor certainly makes ontological claims about identity but they form part of an anti-essentialist or what Stephen K. White has called a 'weak' ontology that does not commit individuals to any particular patterns of behaviour or types of identity. Indeed, one of the central difficulties with the work of commentators who reject the idea of recognition for its alleged essentialism is that it often leads them to abandon the concepts of subjectivity and identity *per se* and to move towards an objectivist mode of analysis that cannot address important aspects of political agency. Arguably, one of the advantages of Taylor's recognition model is that it connects the modern concern with identity to the emergence of a new type of political agency. In contrast, the move to objectivism made by Young and Fraser, amongst others, leads to a less dynamic analytical model that seems closer to a theory of structural causation and leaves certain crucial issues surrounding the motivations for action unaddressed (see Chapter 4).

The critique of Taylor's essentialism can also lead to the assertion of a countervailing anti-essentialism which itself is a reconfigured expression of the objectivist move away from ideas of identity and subjectivity *per se*.[2] Patchen Markell (2003), for example, rightly criticizes Taylor for his problematic conflation of individual with group identity. His account of the relation between individual and moral community is one where tension and conflict have been eradicated. The self-same unity and reflexivity that Taylor questions in monological concepts of the subject are covertly transferred to the moral speech community which unproblematically provides all the resources that the individual requires for self-realization. According to Markell, this idea of the individual's inescapable orientation towards moral horizons has the consequence of tacitly reinstalling a 'sovereign' account of agency. There is no dissonance between the individual and community; collective values are a resource for agency and, in a circular logic, they are reconfirmed in action:

The first of these moves, from monologue to dialogue, shatters the pretense that one might achieve sovereign agency in isolation: but the second move, from dialogue to community, reinstates the aspiration to sovereignty in a different form, casting sovereign agency now not as a matter of radically free choice, but as a matter of acting in accordance with who, by virtue of one's membership in a larger whole, one always already is (Markell 2003: 57).

The potential notions of contingency and uncertainty that may be implied in a dialogical account of subject formation are closed off by Taylor's view of interaction as normatively unified. In Markell's view, this is a problem not limited to Taylor's thought but is characteristic of the recognition model of subject formation in general. The necessarily open-ended and contingent nature of interaction, foreclosed in the recognition paradigm, signifies the radical temporal indeterminacy that is one of the sources of human finitude: 'language itself is an ongoing activity, open to the future . . . linguistic agency is constitutively risky' (Markell 2003: 56). Markell argues that this idea of the temporal indeterminacy that is the condition of possibility of action forms the basis for a 'politics of acknowledgment' intended as an alternative to the idea of recognition. An ethical relation to others can be established through an acknowledgement of the finitude of the self understood as a 'matter of one's practical limits in the face of an unpredictable and contingent future' (Markell 2003: 38). The renunciation of attitudes of self-certainty leads to renewed possibilities of relating to others based on an acceptance of the unstable and unpredictable nature of social interaction. The difficulty with Markell's idea of acknowledgement is, however, that it asserts a counter-veiling indeterminacy whose precise connection to agency and social relations remains vague. It is undoubtedly the case, *pace* Markell, that the future-oriented dimensions of action render interaction more fragile and uncertain than is acknowledged in certain theories of recognition. It is one thing, however, to assert an essential temporal indeterminacy as a condition of possibility of agency and another to trace out what this might mean at the level of social interaction which, even at its most informal, is ineluctably embedded in entrenched relations of power.[3] In other words, the assertion of a foundational indeterminacy does not go very far in unpacking the determinate nature of many dimensions of social existence which pertain, in part, to the insidious operations of power upon embodied subjects. Indeed, in many respects, the apodictic radical potential that Markell invests in the temporally open-ended nature of human action is not far removed from a much-noted problem characteristic of poststructural thought where the idea of indeterminacy becomes valorized as good in itself. It is true that Taylor's work on recognition does not go very far in connecting the determinate features of social existence to underlying structures of power but, against a fetishized indeterminacy, it has the virtue of recognizing the importance of notions of coherence, unity and meaning to an agent's own ability to act in the world.

The difficulties, then, in Taylor's formulation of the idea of recognition exceed the way it is often framed as an opposition between essentialism and anti-essentialism, between determinacy and indeterminacy. Indeed, as we will see in the next section, Taylor explicitly tries to incorporate ideas of indeterminacy into his idea of recognition. There is no denying that the trope of authenticity has problematic implications but these are not, in principle, insurmountable. Taylor's claim that identity is dialogically constructed does not in itself preclude a historical and social specificity, as some commentators who have generalized his work to the political terrain have recognized (e.g. Hobson 2003). The difficulties in Taylor's idea of recognition, then, pertain more to the way in which Taylor's linguistic version of the recognition model of subject formation is divorced from an account of power. On this view, power relations are secondary to the formation of identity in language, instead of being regarded as coeval with it. This detachment of language from power allows Taylor to isolate the expressive function of language as its primal *modus operandi* and, as a consequence, to foreclose an analysis of how self-expression is constitutively shaped by power relations. A comparison with Bourdieu's idea of language as a mode of symbolic domination will make these shortcomings in Taylor's formulation of the dialogical constitution of identity apparent.

DIALOGIC ACTION AND HABITUS

Taylor's idea of the dialogical subject is developed as a counter to the 'utter inadequacy of the monological subject of representations' that dominates the 'epistemological tradition' of Western thought (Taylor 1999: 36). The main features of the monological conception of the subject are that it is monadic, disembodied and rational. Against this, Taylor claims that individuals are formed through interaction with others and that their relation to the world is embodied, emotional and pre-reflexive. On the monological view of the subject, action is understood largely in terms of an intellectual orientation where individuals make explicit representations of the world, of their place within it and of their aims. While Taylor would not deny that this characterizes certain aspects of action, on his dialogical view, action is primarily practical, that is to say that it emerges from an intuitive, pre-reflexive relation with the world that exceeds the individual's understanding: 'It [action] flows from an understanding which is largely inarticulate. This understanding is more fundamental in two ways: first, it is always there, whereas sometimes we frame representations and sometimes we do not, and, second, the representations we do make are only comprehensible against the background provided by this inarticulate understanding' (Taylor 1999: 34).

In so far as it is inarticulate, dialogic action is not to be understood as interaction between two essentially independent beings because this is to frame dialogue in monological terms. Dialogical interaction implies that, from the outset, the agent understands herself as part of a wider commonality or 'we'. The principle medium of the dialogical constitution of the self is language; individuals, on Taylor's view, are linguistic animals. Language is principally an expressive medium rather than a representational or designative instrument with which to grasp and control the world. As such, it is comprised of multiple and overlapping webs of meaning into which individuals are thrown and through which they realize ways of being in the world. The realization of identity in language is never an act of self-mastery because it is not possible for the individual to fully grasp the webs of meaning in which they are immersed. But equally, and in contrast to post-structuralist views of language, the individual is not simply a passive effect of the operations of language. There is always an active, creative element to the process that flows from the spontaneous and open-ended nature of linguistic interaction: 'reshaping it without dominating it, or being able to oversee it, means that we never fully know what we are doing to it; we develop language without knowing fully what we are making it into' (Taylor 1985: 232).

It is this idea of the dialogical, inarticulate nature of action that undercuts the potentially essentialist implications of Taylor's expressivist conception of language as the medium through which we disclose what we already are. The revelation of self within language is always incomplete and partial because the individual is never able to fully comprehend the background web of assumptions that inform self-understanding. Furthermore, the self that is expressed in language is a collective rather than an individual creation. Self-expression is not simply an act of disclosure, it has performative dimensions; it is the act of expressing an emotion in language that brings that emotion into being: 'for us language-animals our language is constitutive of our emotions, not just because *de facto* we have articulated some of them, but also *de jure* as the medium in which all our emotions, articulate and inarticulate, are experienced' (1985: 74). It is not just that the expression of inchoate feelings in language transforms them into interpretable emotions, but also that the very act of articulation allows us to reflect and refine our emotions so that the experience of them is transformed. It does not bring into being a pre-given object, rather it transforms its object: 'formulation or reformulation does not leave its object unchanged. To give a certain articulation is to shape our sense of what we desire or what we hold important in a certain way (Taylor 1985: 28). It is this process of reflection, a kind of dialectical interaction between inchoate feelings and their expression within language, that renders individuals 'self-interpreting' beings. The anti-essentialist implications of Taylor's formulation of linguistic expression are reinforced by his adherence to the Gadamerian method of a 'fusion of horizons' which eschews any easy reconciliation between the competing claims to recognition of different individuals and groups. There is no endpoint in the struggle for recognition; it is rather an ongoing, unfinished conversation that must ceaselessly renew itself (Taylor 1994b: 230).

These anti-essentialist elements and moments of sustained uncertainty in Taylor's work constitute what Stephen K. White calls a 'weak ontology'. A weak ontology makes fundamental claims about the nature of being in the world but recognizes that these claims are contestable. Against strong ontologies, these claims do not establish incontrovertible truths and political-ethico certainties, rather they provide individuals with a cognitive and affective orientation in the world. A weak ontology is affirmative while simultaneously drawing attention to its limits. Despite their contestability, it is nonetheless important to engage in making such claims if the grounds for a sufficiently reflective ethical and political life are to be established. Typically, against liberal conceptions of the 'teflon' subject, weak ontologies draw attention to the embeddedness of the subject by establishing 'figurations of human being in terms of certain existential realities, most notably language, mortality, or finitude, natality, and the articulation of "sources of the self"' (White 2000: 9). They also have strongly aesthetic and affective dimensions which emphasize being in the world as a creative and tentative process of cultivation rather than as the enactment of certain ontological certainties.

If White is right to see in Taylor's thought a weak ontology then it draws attention to the rather one-sided reading of him as reinstalling an essentialist concept of the subject. Indeed, the difficulty with Taylor's idea of recognition is not that it isn't sufficiently indeterminate, rather it fails to give adequate consideration to the determinate aspects of social existence. In other words, his linguistic model of identity formation is not grounded in a sufficient theory of power relations. Taylor's ontology of recognition is based in a problematic linguistic abstraction that sets up expression as the primal function of language antecedent to social relations. Power remains an exogeneous factor that comes to operate *post hoc* upon the recognition dynamic rather than being seen as intrinsic to it. The theoretical difficulties that this generates can be illustrated through a comparison with Bourdieu's idea of linguistic habitus.

The comparison with Bourdieu comes from Taylor himself, who sees an affinity between his idea of dialogical action and the process, denoted by habitus, where collective norms are internalized by the individual and form the pre-reflexive basis for action. For Taylor, the motivational basis for action is never purely individual but the result of a shared understanding of the world which is, more often than not, implicit and practical in nature. There are different types of dialogical action. There are actions that require coordination with (an) other(s), such as playing a game of hockey. But there are also actions, such as ballroom dancing or flowing conversation, that go beyond coordination and are based instead on a common 'rhythmizing' where agency cannot be attributed to a single individual. This rhythmizing type of action occurs not only in face-to-face encounters but also at a collective level in, for example, religious and political movements which create a sense of shared purpose despite the geographical dispersion of its members. An action is dialogical in this strong sense when 'it is effected by an integrated, non-individual agent. This means that for those involved in it, its identity as this kind of action essentially depends on the agency being shared. These actions are constituted as such by a shared understanding among those who make up the common agent' (Taylor 1999: 36). Taylor regards Bourdieu's idea of habitus as similarly pitted against individualist accounts of subjectivity and agency. Habitus yields an account of practical action whose origin is not in freely willed decisions made by the individual but in the values and norms of the collective that the individual has mostly unconsciously internalized. Just as, for Taylor, the orientation towards particular moral horizons is rooted in an emotional rather than cognitive response to the world, so too, for Bourdieu, the process of internalization is pre-reflexive and corporeal in nature. Collective values and norms are not something that are consciously learned but are spontaneously absorbed in the form of the physical and emotional dispositions of the habitus, that is to say, the individual's embodied orientation towards the world. What is missing, however, from Taylor's interpretation of habitus is that, for

Bourdieu, it is inseparable from an account of the way in which social inequalities are reproduced and naturalized by being internalized in the body. Thus, what Taylor designates as collective norms or evaluative horizons, Bourdieu would regard as the 'doxa' imposed by a dominant group in order to legitimate its own authority. On Bourdieu's view, norms are not collective resources but are inseparable from the reproduction of class, race and gender inequalities. In this regard, Bourdieu's idea of habitus is closer to Foucault's work on discipline than it is to Taylor's idea of dialogical action. From the perspective of habitus, the central problem with Taylor's account of expression in language is that it is based on a tacit separation of the abstract capacity for expression from socially realized forms of expression. Such a separation is untenable because language is coeval with power; it is, first and foremost, a social institution. It has no prior abstract existence that is subsequently distorted by its social conditions of use. Far from being extrinsic to it, the social conditions of its usage overdetermine the expressive functions of language.

Whereas for Taylor, identity is formed in the organic, expressive medium of language, for Bourdieu it is formed through symbolic violence. Language is a form of symbolic power, it is a medium through which individuals are accommodated to social hierarchies in a process that is neither forced or freely assumed. 'All symbolic domination presupposes, on the part of those who submit to it, a form of complicity which is neither passive submission to external constraint nor a free adherence to values . . . it is inscribed, in a practical state, in dispositions which are impalpably inculcated, through a long and slow process of acquisition, by the sanctions of the linguistic market' (Bourdieu 1991: 50–1). Habitus is the concept that expresses how symbolic violence shapes embodied being in the most profound and insidious ways. It follows from this that linguistic habitus is defined as a propensity to speak in a certain way and to say certain determinate things rather than others. This involves 'both the linguistic capacity to generate an infinite number of grammatically correct discourses, and the social capacity to use this competence adequately in a determinate situation' (1991: 37). These capacities and propensities are not abstract potentials but are lived as physical and psychological dispositions. As such, they are inseparable from the position that an individual occupies within a social formation; in other words, linguistic capacities are shaped by class, gender and race relations. An individual's linguistic competence is formed primarily within specific familial dynamics and then, depending on the place the family occupies within social relations, the value of this competence is reinforced or undermined by a series of subsequent encounters with other 'linguistic markets' (for example, the education system, the workplace, etc). Thus linguistic competence is coextensive with social competence understood as a practical, intuitive sense of knowing one's place and worth within the social world: 'This linguistic sense of place governs the degree of constraint which a given field will bring to bear on the production of discourse, imposing silence or a hyper-controlled language on some people while allowing others the liberties of a language that is securely established' (1991: 82). Knowing one's place within the social order is not a conscious knowledge but is expressed at a practical, intuitive level, in certain types of linguistic 'distinction' such as ease in speaking in certain situations and certain registers of discourse ('relaxation in tension') or lack of distinction such as a tendency to hypercorrection and euphemization in speaking. Thus Bourdieu claims that 'language is a body technique, and specifically linguistic, especially phonetic, competence is a dimension of bodily hexis in which one's whole relation to the social world, and one's whole socially informed relation to the world, are expressed' (1991: 86).

NATURALIZATION OF POWER

It is not that Taylor doesn't acknowledge that there are obstacles to the expression of self in language that pertain to social position. These constraints on the 'spaces of common action' opened up by language are regarded, however, as extrinsic to rather than inherent in linguistic expression and they are naturalized by being detached from an account of power (Taylor 1999: 37). One way in which these constraints are naturalized is through being individualized, that is by being presented as idiosyncratic patterns of behaviour as, for example, in Taylor's account of strong evaluations. Identity formation in language involves not just the disclosure of individual motivations and desires but also the assessment of how worthy and valuable these are, i.e., 'strong evaluations'. Language in its expressive mode discloses new moral horizons towards which the individual orients herself: 'Strong evaluation is not just a condition of articulacy about preferences, but also about the quality of life, the kind of beings we are or want to be' (1985: 26). As articulate beings, the potential for strong evaluation is always present and is the reason why we can be depicted as responsible agents: 'Because this self-resolution is something we do, when we do it, we can be called responsible for ourselves; and because it is within limits always up to us to do it, even when we do not . . . we can be called responsible in another sense for ourselves, whether we undertake this radical evaluation or not' (1985: 42). Taylor concedes, however, that this process of evaluation is by no means assured. There are many reasons that individuals may not be responsible agents – that is, fail to have a sufficiently coherent understanding of self with regard to moral norms – such as 'habit, fear or weakness'. There is no suggestion, on Taylor's part, that habit, fear or weakness may be borne out of deprivation, exclusion or oppression. There is no suggestion that expressive competence may be linked to structurally generated inequalities such as gender. There are numerous feminist studies, for example, that show that there are pervasive gender differences in communicative competence and others that argue that there is a 'powerless language' characteristic of 'low status' social groups (Coates 1993: 139). It is not necessary to subscribe to the overstated view that less privileged individuals are entirely dominated in language to recognize that these differences are not superficial stylistic or purely individual ones but are expressive of inequalities in the distribution of social resources. Furthermore, there is no suggestion by Taylor that collective norms may not be just free-floating resources that are communicated *via* the neutral medium of language but are, in fact, hegemonic and contested values that are mediated through specific linguistic markets.

Taylor's exhortation that an authentic life should assume a coherent narrative structure rests on a similarly normative view of language as basically an untrammelled medium of self-expression. It overlooks entirely the ways in which narratives function as modes of ideological closure and also as forms of symbolic domination (see Chapter 3). Where inequalities are touched upon, Taylor considers them in terms of the face-to-face dynamic of the recognition dyad (Taylor 1999: 38–9). By localizing inequality in this way, it is reduced to an interpersonal rather than structural dynamic. Taylor cannot see how the dyad of recognition is always asymmetrical from the outset, in the manner suggested, for example, by Paul Gilroy's use of the struggle between master and slave to depict slavery as a constitutive feature of modernity (Gilroy 1993). If these connections between the visible and the invisible are not made then social inequalities are made to appear arbitrary rather than being related to systemic inequalities. It is not enough to understand the situated nature of existence in terms of immediate embodied context. To avoid a myopic, flattened-out concept of social difference, embodied context must, in turn, be linked to systemic social divisions. As Rosemary Hennessey puts it: 'Even after we situate the speaker historically, there remains the question of how we understand history – in terms of local contexts or . . . in terms of a systemic vision of social life, a perspective that connects the circulation of knowledges in local situations to the broader social relations in which they are embedded' (Hennessey 1995: 144–5). Taylor's formulation of the struggle for recognition as one of expression in language is a metaphysical fiction because there is no symmetrical encounter at the outset. The dyad is always situated and, as such, is always marked, to greater or lesser degrees, by the 'invisible, silent violence' of symbolic domination. As Bourdieu puts it: 'The relation between two people may be such that one of them has only to appear in order to impose on the other, without even having to want to, let alone formulate any command, a definition of the situation and of himself . . . which is all the more absolute and undisputed for not having to be stated' (1991: 52). It is only by making power extrinsic to, rather than coextensive with, language that Taylor's central intellectual concern can be limited to the understanding of what it means to be an authentic human being. If, however, he were to develop his idea of language as a social institution further, he would then be forced to modify the focus of his inquiry towards how individuals can express themselves through and despite social inequalities.

The naturalization of power that is a feature of Taylor's account of the formation of the subject within language also extends to his wider political analyses. Like other liberals and communitarians, Taylor's concept of civil society tends to be emptied of any power relations which are understood, by and large, to be features of the state and its institutions. This leads him, in his discussion of the politics of recognition, to an aporetic political solution characterized by legal paternalism, on the one side, and a naïvely spontaneous account of individual autonomy, on the other. This, in essence, is Habermas's charge against him. Taylor's dilemma, where claims for cultural recognition may require the enactment of collective rights that conflict with individual rights protecting freedom and autonomy, is, in Habermas's view, false. It rests on an inadequately generalized account of power that misunderstands the nature of both state intervention and individual autonomy. On the one hand, Taylor questions the extent to which the legal system can deal adequately with issues of injustice relating to cultural difference by upholding a system of disembodied individual rights. On the other hand, despite this scepticism, he relies on a form of legal intervention to solve the problem of the protection of cultural minorities. Habermas argues that this idea of legally protected autonomy, whether individual or collective, is one-sided because it is paternalistic. If recognition is seen primarily as legal or political action then it risks becoming a normalizing intervention that 'perceptibly restrict[s] the capacities of the presumed beneficiaries to shape their lives autonomously' (1994: 208–9). This 'reflexively generated discrimination' is one of the major problems with the way social welfare rights have been implemented in Western Europe in that their top-down logic has often reinforced dependency and clientelism rather than promoting individual autonomy. Many of the social welfare programmes implemented to assist women, for example, have had ambivalent consequences such as reinforcing through 'negative-feedback loops' the 'feminization of poverty': 'a materialization of law directed at the real discrimination directed against women has had the opposite effect' (Habermas 1996: 422). The flip side to this paternalism is that Taylor fails to see that individuals are not just subject to the law as private persons but are themselves also 'authors of the laws'. His view of recognition leaves private autonomy untheorized as the 'inevitable' pluralism that forms the backdrop to legal and political intervention. Against Taylor, Habermas asserts that autonomy is not a self-evident quality that arises spontaneously in the socio-cultural realm and is then protected through a system of rights. Rather, public and private autonomy of the individual are co-original. They are simultaneously constructed and protected through the communicatively regulated interaction of discrete processes of legal, political and social recognition.[4]

It could be argued that the criticism of Taylor for his inadequate conceptualization of power fails to appreciate the normative implications of his theory of recognition. On such a view, it might be the case that Taylor is inattentive to the pervasive nature of inequalities of power, but this should not necessarily impinge upon his attempt to set up recognition as a regulative ideal. The fact that inequalities of power constrain the ways in which individuals are able to express themselves is not an objection in itself to the utopian claim that all individuals have a right to a self-ascribed and publicly esteemed identity. The difficulty is, however, that normative claims cannot be separated so stringently from sociological analysis. Taylor himself recognizes this interconnection but, nonetheless, he slides into a conflation of the descriptive and normative senses of the idea of recognition. The effect of this conflation is that the emancipatory force of the idea of recognition tacitly circumscribes its analytical function, resulting in a misrecognition of the social conditions of existence. It is this disconnection from the actuality of social inequalities that throws into question the validity of Taylor's idea of recognition. The value of an ideal must inevitably be limited if the passage from the 'is' to the 'ought' seems improbable. I will consider this issue of the intertwinement of norms and power in the final section of this chapter. I now turn to Habermas's communicative formulation of the idea of recognition, which is explicitly predicated on a dialectical connection between critical and normative thought. It is certainly the case that Habermas's idea of communicative recognition is grounded in a more rigorous and extensive social theory than Taylor's. However, in order to shore up his claim about the universal scope of discourse ethics, Habermas also disconnects his account of linguistic communication from an account of power. Like Taylor, his social theory ultimately rests in a problematic ontology of recognition where a primal function of communication is set up as the origin of social relations.

RECOGNITION AND THE POSTCONVENTIONAL SUBJECT

Habermas, like Taylor, posits that subjectivity is formed through a linguistically mediated process of recognition but, unlike Taylor, language is conceived as principally a communicative, rather than an expressive medium. Habermas argues that the idea of recognition through communication serves to ground a theory of subject formation in an exhaustive social theory and also delivers more robust accounts of autonomy and intersubjectivity. Although Taylor makes similar claims about his dialogic theory of identity constitution, his adherence to a linguistic expressivism remains, on Habermas's account, caught within the 'philosophy of the subject'. The understanding of language as an expressive medium renders individuals primarily self-referential beings who are united through being situated in the same cultural and moral horizons. The self is dialogic in so far as its sources lie in shared webs of interlocution. For Habermas this is a weak concept of intersubjectivity, in two respects. At the level of immediate interaction, individuals are bound to each other only in so far as they recognize the other as engaged in a similar project of self-expression. This is essentially a Romantic conception of the unifying achievements of the Spirit of Language: 'the organic life of the linguistic totality . . . asserts itself within all these differentiations as the *superordinated* universal' (1991: 217). At the supra individual level, individuals are bound together by shared values and norms. The existence of such pre-given consensus is not only a problematic sociological presupposition but ultimately it places the unifying force of the community above the individual. As Habermas puts it: 'I- and We- perspectives are supposed to complement one another, but in Taylor's work the latter then take precedence after all' (1991: 217).

Against Taylor's privileging of the community over the individual, Habermas argues that the idea of language as communication posits self, other and the universal as equi-primordial. The process of reaching understanding is simultaneously constitutive of the individual's identity, his bond to the other and of overarching regulative social norms. This allows Habermas to link the process of identity formation to a critical social theory rather than subsuming the process under a problematic organic conception of community.[5] The communicative view of recognition yields a critical and differentiated account of the dialogical aspects of social life and a pragmatic concept of action oriented to reaching understanding. The expressivist view cannot explain this collective logic to social action because it tends towards a balkanized conception of society where groups and individuals are bound together by competing identity claims. For Habermas, the dialogic reproduction of identity and, indeed, the normative orientation of the lifeworld are always threatened by the distorting effects of money and power. This is why his communicative ideal of discourse ethics is based on processes of rational reconstruction as a way of undoing the warped effects that inequalities of power have upon our identities and self-understanding.

A particular disadvantage, in Habermas's view, with Taylor's organic model of language is that it downplays the extent to which individuals may adopt a critical relation to the communal and social norms and values. His theory of recognition can only explain individuals within a conventional normative context but it cannot account for the postconventional normativism that prevails in late modernity where individuals are increasingly likely to be critically independent rather than conformist. A reconfigured notion of recognition as communication can explain this putative critical independence because it presumes the absolute autonomy of each individual who has the power to negate the validity claims of the other: 'consensus achieved through communication depends both on the idealizing supposition that an identity in linguistic meanings already prevails and also on the power of negation and the autonomy of unique, non-substitutable subjects – from whom intersubjective consent to criticize validity claims has to be obtained anew in each case' (1991: 217). Habermas develops this idea of the emancipatory potential of postconventional society using the work of George Herbert Mead on 'progressive individuation'. The issue that faces Habermas is, in many respects, similar to that faced by classical sociologists such as Durkheim and Parsons who sought to explain how modernity reconciles the conflicting tendencies towards the intensification of individualization, on the one hand, and the emergence of more complex forms of interdependence and solidarity, on the other. Habermas argues that they are not able to produce a satisfactory answer to how these conflicting tendencies are reconciled because they do not have an adequate account of subject formation. For these thinkers, individuation is an effect of social differentiation but this is a determinist explanation which can account only for the multiplication of different social roles and not for the rise of the individual as a singular and complex being (Habermas 1992: 150). This dilemma is potentially solved by using Mead's well-known distinction between the 'I' and the 'me', which is at the centre of his idea of progressive individualism and which offers an intersubjective account of socialization where the orientation towards others is compatible with increased levels of individuation and autonomy. Linguistic communication with an other enables the self to take a distantiated relation towards itself, i.e., it understand itself as a 'me' rather than as an 'I'. The 'me' is the source of both a knowing or epistemic relation to the self and an acting or practical relation (1992: 178). It is in the practical relation that the subject monitors or controls his/her own behaviour: 'The "me" of the *practical* relation-to-self is no longer the seat of an originary or reflected self-*consciousness* but an agency of self-*control*' (1992: 179). This me is what Mead refers to as the generalized other and involves the internalization of behavioural expectations of one's social surroundings and the regulation of one's behaviour accordingly. In this sense, the 'me' is conservative in that it moves the individual towards conformity through the development of conventional moral consciousness. However, this practical me is constitutive of a practical 'I' who is the source of spontaneous disruption to conformity: 'as the onrush of impulses that are subjected to control and as the source of innovations that break up and renew conventionally rigidified controls' (1992: 179–80). At the conventional stage of morality, the I is permanently held in check by the me. Taylor's superordination of community over individual correlates with this conventional subject who internalizes prevailing social norms. At the postconventional stage of morality, however, the stage at which individuals are required to be critical of norms, the relation between I and me is reversed. This is because the self is oriented to a larger, more complex society whose values are highly differentiated and mediated through communicative structures which require that everyone can take up the perspective of everyone else: 'it (the self) now comes upon itself as the alter ego of all others in every community – specifically, as a free will in moral self reflection and as a fully individuated being in existential self reflection' (1992: 187). Thus, the postconventional subject acquires the capacity for autonomous thought and for self-realization as a unique and irreplaceable being: 'The idealizing supposition of a universalistic form of life, in which everyone can take up the perspective of everyone else and can count on reciprocal recognition by everybody, makes it possible for individuated beings to exist within a community – individualism as the flip side of universalism' (1992: 186). Habermas's communicative account of recognition can explain, then, what Taylor's expressivist account cannot, namely, how the postconventional individual may have a meaningful existence while adopting a critical distance to established norms.

It is this idea that individuation arises, not in opposition to socialization, but as a result of its progressive implementation that Habermas uses as the basis of the claim that communicative ethics is rooted in a respect for individual autonomy and difference. In this respect, the idea is central to a rebuttal by Habermas of the numerous criticisms of his theory of communicative ethics that its rationalist bias does not give sufficient consideration to questions of social difference, particularly issues connected to identity politics (see e.g. Meehan 1995). Against these claims, Habermas argues that far from overlooking difference, communicative ethics can only proceed on the basis of full recognition of the autonomy and irreplaceability of each individual: 'Among the universal and unavoidable presuppositions of action oriented to reaching understanding is the presupposition that the speaker qua actor lays claim to recognition both as an autonomous will and as an individuated being' (Habermas 1992: 191). The claims that individuals make for recognition of their unique identities form the ethical grounds for communicative deliberation. Communicative debate, that is, disputation over moral norms, could not take place unless others in the debate had already recognized the speaker as a unique and autonomous being. Recognition claims must be fully realized, therefore, within all the communicative structures of social life before any debate about overarching normative constraints can proceed: 'The speaker certainly could not count on the acceptance of his speech acts if he did not already presuppose that the addressee took him seriously as someone who could orient his action with validity claims. The one must have recognized the other as an accountable actor whenever he expects him to take a position with "yes" or "no" to his speech act offers. In communicative action everyone thus recognizes in the other his own autonomy' (1992: 190). Thus, far from effacing difference, the linguistic structure of communicative ethics enshrines a respect for individual difference as its ethical starting point: 'I should be recognized as an individual person who cannot be replaced in taking responsibility for my own life history' (1992: 144).

It may be that Habermas's communicative reformulation of recognition overcomes certain limitations of Taylor's expressivist rendering of the relation between self and society, for example, the localization of politics and the tendency to moral relativism. However, the claim that a theory of communicative individuation explains postconventional normativism and also enshrines a politics of recognition at the heart of discourse ethics rests on a tendentious purification of language which sets up a series of equally as implausible dualisms. These dualisms, of which the separation between I and me is an exemplar, revolve basically around the disassociation of speech acts from embodied context. They permeate Habermas's thought and, ultimately, undermine his claim that communicative ethics can accommodate an understanding of individual difference. Issues connected to the politics of identity are incorporated only in a highly circumscribed manner where they are understood as some kind of epistemic input into communicative debate. If, however, communication is understood, *pace* Bourdieu, as inseparable from embodied context, then Habermas's formalized conceptions of identity claims and deliberative debate are undermined.

PURIFICATION OF LANGUAGE

The separation of language from its embodied context that pervades the dualisms of Habermas's thought finds its paradigmatic expression in his formal definition of speech acts which lie at the heart of his theory of universal pragmatics.[6] His assertion that the telos of language is orientation towards understanding arises from this definition that the universal core of speech acts resides in the raising of validity claims. In everyday interaction, these validity claims are often implicit and unexplored, but in the ideal speech situation they have to be made explicit and expressed in a rational manner. In order to allow this rationally motivating core to speech acts to be fully realized, Habermas sets up a series of conditions governing discourse ethics about the nature of speech and equality between participants. Central to these conditions is the separation of the illocutionary from the perlocutionary dimensions of speech acts. The illocutionary dimensions of speech acts enact what they are saying in the moment of saying whereas, from the perlocutionary dimensions, certain effects follow, rather than being synchronous with, the act of speech. The intersubjective binding effects of speech acts, that is, the commitments that speakers and hearers make and reciprocally recognize when they enter into communication, are necessarily illocutionary. The communicative situation is based upon 'the unreserved and sincere pursuit of illocutionary aims' (1992: 80). Perlocutionary effects must not be present in discourse ethics because they belong to the 'latently strategic' use of language and involve some form of concealment in the sense that their consequences are deferred rather than instantaneous. Illocutionarily strong speech acts are the means by which the sincerity of participants is assured and the original telos of language as reaching understanding is realized. Not only should the perlocutionary effects of speech acts be minimized in the communicative situation but also, on Habermas's view, they are secondary or parasitic to illocutionary effects: 'The latently strategic use of language is parasitic because it only functions when at least one side assumes that language is being used with an orientation toward reaching understanding. Whoever acts strategically in this way must violate the sincerity condition of communicative action inconspicuously' (1992: 82). Thus, Habermas infers that for the analysis of commitments, it is justifiable to consider only 'those linguistically mediated interactions in which all participants pursue illocutionary aims, and only illocutionary aims, with their speech acts' (in Thompson 1984: 295).

The idea that speech can be purified of its rhetorical and figurative aspects in order to minimize unintended perlocutionary effects and to render it a transparent medium for sincere communication has been widely criticized as untenable from many different perspectives on language (e.g. Butler 1999; Culler 1985; Wood 1985). The establishment of a hierarchy between the illocutionary and perlocutionary functions of speech rests on an implausible separation of what are, in fact, inextricably intertwined elements in linguistic interaction. The telling of a joke, for example, may have both an illocutionary aim (perhaps to make myself understood) and a perlocutionary one (entertaining an audience). Furthermore, if it is the aim of entertainment which is being pursued, why should this be relegated to a secondary form of communication as Habermas suggests? As John Thompson concludes: 'It is difficult to avoid the impression that Habermas's theory of communicative action is based upon a delimitation of the object domain which excludes, in an arbitrary or implausible way, every kind of communication that might prove a counter-example to his case' (Thompson 1984: 296). In a similar vein, Jonathan Culler argues that the illocutionary and perlocutionary aspects of speech cannot be held apart so rigorously and, even if they could, they do not correspond to the distinction between communicative and strategic action, so that establishing the priority of illocutionary over the perlocutionary does not advance Habermas's argument about the primacy of communicative action (Culler 1985: 136). Culler concludes that Habermas's claim that reaching understanding is the inherent telos of speech is one of the least justified aspects of his theory of communicative action. Indeed, in most cases of speech, it is more plausible to assume that its inherent telos is not reaching understanding but rather that something significant is being said: 'the presumption of all interpretive activity, that there is some point to what seems to need interpretation, even if the point is an absence of point' (Culler 1985: 139). The requirement that sincerity is the overriding characteristic of the orientation towards understanding can only plausibly be understood as a 'special feature of particular situations rather than a universal norm' (Culler 1985: 140). Habermas is only able to maintain the insistence on sincerity by outlawing as derivative all other types of communicative activity that do not privilege the illocutionary elements of speech.

The purification of communication to a putative illocutionary essence is not only problematic from a linguistic perspective but is also the result of an abstraction of speech from embodied context and, more generally, of language from power. For Bourdieu, for example, Habermas's claim that illocutionary force is a property of speech acts is the result of an internalist approach to language which ignores its status as a social institution. Bourdieu claims that illocutionary force is, in fact, a delegated force or power originating in the social context of the speech act: 'By trying to understand the power of linguistic manifestations linguistically, by looking in language for the principle underlying the logic and effectiveness of the language of institution, one forgets that authority comes to language from outside . . . Language at most *represents* this authority, manifests and symbolizes it' (1991: 109). The illocutionary efficacy of a speech act is, then, the effect of a set of interdependent conditions which constitute social rituals. The 'social magic' of a given illocutionary speech act depends on it being uttered in a legitimate situation, uttered according to legitimate forms and, above all, uttered by a person legitimately entitled to do so (1991: 113). The extent to which the illocutionary force of speech acts is dependent on their social conditions of utterance can be illustrated by disputes over whether women priests have sufficient authority to utter the liturgy or Austin's example of a passer-by who christens a ship 'Mr Stalin'.

The problem is that, for Bourdieu, language and power are inseparable whereas, for Habermas, power must be extrinsic to language for him to assert that its original telos is orientation towards understanding. Habermas claims that the problem with Taylor's expressivist model of recognition is that it disconnects an account of identity formation from an adequate social theory. He can neither explain the distorting effects of power upon the interactive processes through which identities are constructed, nor can he provide an adequate response to how these distortions might be transcended. Despite his claims to operate with a more comprehensive theory of power relations, however, the idea of communicative action rests on the same untenable separation of language from power as Taylor's work. Both the expressive and communicative versions of recognition regard power as essentially extrinsic to linguistic interaction. The disassociation of language from power allows Habermas to set up an account of subject formation as a linguistic process divorced from embodied situation. Subjectivity emerges from a primal linguistic dyad centred around untrammelled and symmetrical communication. The operations of power that distort communicative interactions follow *ex posteriori*, they are secondary and contingent to a linguistically mediated 'intact intersubjectivity . . . marked by free, reciprocal recognition' (Habermas 1992: 145). This purification of language 'has the practical effect of removing from relations of communication the power relations which are implemented within them in a transfigured form' (Bourdieu 1991: 257). There is no recognition in Habermas's model that the subject's entry into language is a simultaneous entry into power relations, in so far as language and power are coeval rather than sequentially ordered. As we will see in the next section, this separation enables Habermas to achieve, *inter alia*, a domestication of the subjects of discourse by conceiving of them as purely linguistic rather than embodied beings. Although this is a problematic strategy, it is crucial for Habermas to be able to maintain the assertion of the universal relevance of his idea of communicative ethics

DELIBERATION: LINGUISTIC AND SOCIAL COMPETENCE

It is certainly the case that Habermas recognizes the distorting effects of power upon communicative structures and, accordingly, he sets out procedures to ensure equality between participants in discussion. Each participant must have an equal chance to initiate and continue communication. Each must have a chance to make assertions, recommendations and explanations, and to challenge justifications. All participants must have equal chances to express their wishes, feelings and intentions. Finally, the speaker must act as if in contexts of action there is an equal distribution of chances to order and to resist orders, to be accountable for one's conduct and to demand accountability from others (see Benhabib 1986: 285; Thompson and Held 1982: 124). These procedures seem ineffectual, however, if power is not understood as a *post hoc* distortion of pure understanding but, *pace* Bourdieu, as ineluctably inscribed upon bodies and embedded in the structure of speech. The formation of the habitus takes place 'without passing through language or consciousness' and therefore there are significant forms of power and inequality that operate below the scope of Habermas rules governing discourse: 'ways of looking, sitting, standing, keeping silent, or even of speaking . . . are full of injunctions that are powerful and hard to resist precisely because they are silent, insidious, insistent and insinuating' (1991: 51). The theory of universal pragmatics divorces the formal ability to produce speech acts from the social conditions in which they are always produced and thus treats interlocutors in the ideal speech situation as disembodied linguistic beings. It thus fails to appreciate fully the subtle forms of symbolic domination whereby the capacity to produce a comprehensible speech act by no means ensures that a particular subject's speech acts will be listened to or understood: 'the competence adequate to produce sentences that are likely to be understood may be quite inadequate to produce sentences that are likely to be listened to, likely to be recognized as acceptable in all situations in which there is occasion to speak' (Bourdieu 1991: 55). The divorcing of linguistic from social competence cannot regulate, for example, the operation of prejudices which, in subtle and insidious ways, incline individuals to hear some speakers and some arguments rather than others. Although the rules of deliberation ensure formal equality between participants in Habermas's communicative ethics, prejudice escapes regulation in this manner because it operates at a prior, embodied level. As Lynne Sanders puts it: 'Prejudice and privilege do not emerge in deliberative settings as bad reasons, and they are not countered by good arguments . . . one cannot counter a pernicious group dynamic with a good reason' (Sanders 1997: 353–4).

On such a view of speech acts as expressions of somatized power relations, the neutral language of rational discourse is in fact the imposed discourse of the cultural elite which has been naturalized through processes of social inculcation (1991: 62–4). The apparently neutral status of a certain discourse conceals the gap that always exists between the universal recognition of a language as legitimate and the much more limited competence or authority to operate within this language. Habermas cannot address this structural disparity because he takes competence within rational discourse as a universal given rather than as a skill whose acquisition is closely connected to position within social order. Agreement may not be the result of the most rational argument prevailing but of the tacit operation of symbolic forms of distinction which are themselves expressions of social privilege. In 'linguistic markets', language rarely functions as a pure instrument of neutral communication; rather, it more often functions as a tool through which symbolic profits are consciously or unconsciously pursued (Bourdieu 1991: 67). Any given linguistic market is governed by its own immanent rules which establish the value of linguistic expressions. All speakers within the market operate with a sense of the probable value of their own linguistic productions and with an orientation towards maximizing their profits. This sense is not a form of rational calculation but is a tacit social sense which expresses itself in forms of linguistic adjustment to render one's speech socially acceptable. The inseparability of language and power denoted in the idea of linguistic habitus draws attention to the tacit, embodied cues that render communication successful. Indeed, as Culler puts it: 'we would not be very competent if we invariably approached language with the presumption that it is always true, truthful, right and serious' (Culler 1985: 143). In locating the essence of communication in the rational justification of validity claims, Habermas not only disregards a crucial dimension in the reproduction of social inequalities but he also fails to adequately address the potentially anti-democratic implications of his own idea of deliberation. The insistence on a certain type of disembodied, rational deliberation potentially compounds rather than challenges the under-representation of disadvantaged groups, in Sander's words: 'learning to deliberate . . . might be inseparable from indoctrination in familiar routes of hierarchy and deference' (Sanders 1997: 362).

A possible response to such criticisms is that these issues of exclusion, marginality and inequality should be resolved prior to the commencement of communicative debate through a fully implemented politics of recognition. This is, indeed, the thrust of Habermas's progressive individuation argument where the recognition of difference forms an absolute prerequisite to normative deliberation. The same difficulty of a linguistic abstraction from embodied existence raises itself here, however, and is evident in a series of tendentious dualisms that Habermas makes. Although intersubjectively generated claims for recognition precede communicative debate, they themselves cannot be the subject of such debate because they represent particularist ethical claims that do not have universal moral relevance. This relegation of recognition claims to a stage prior to normative deliberation rests on a problematic and much-criticized distinction made by Habermas between the just and the good. Not only is it questionable to confine the politics of identity to the realm of particularist ethics but it is also debatable whether it is possible to sustain such a rigorous separation of issues of the just from issues of the good. Numerous critics have argued that the just and the good are inextricably intertwined sets of beliefs and it is therefore implausible to expect individuals to bracket off their deeply held ethical views when it comes to disputation over universal norms of justice. Taylor, for example, criticizes Habermas's formalist concept of morality on these grounds. An individual's self-understanding and conceptions of the good are continuous with their understanding of broader questions of morality and justice rather than standing on one side or the other of an artificial division between the particular and the universal. Taylor claims that, in the face of radical doubt about why one should prefer a proceduralist mode of deliberation over other forms of disputation, Habermas cannot really provide a satisfactory answer. His answer that communicatively reached understanding is based on the basic structure of speech is too formalist to persuade someone who would prefer to reach their desired goal 'at the cost of being slightly inconsistent' (Taylor 1991: 31). The only compelling answer to the communicative sceptic, according to Taylor, is one that necessarily makes reference to a substantialist conception of human nature in order to justify the primacy of rational understanding over all other purposes: 'I must be able to show why it is that I attach a value to rational understanding so great that it should be preferred to all other purposes' (Taylor 1991: 31).

Habermas is able to maintain this stringent separation between the good and the just, in part, on the basis of a linguistic abstraction from embodied existence that renders identity little more than a formalizable set of propositions. It enables him to empty identity claims of any emotional content and consider them not as expressions of the suffering that emerges from misrecognition but in a formalistic way as 'epistemic inputs' into the deliberative process. Through this linguistic rendering of identity, he can ignore fundamental issues such as how it is possible to persuade individuals with deeply held grievances and convictions to abandon them at the threshold of deliberative debate. As Newey puts it: 'The requirement that the conceptions of the good be treated as epistemic inputs prejudices both the deliberative framework's ability to model political negotiations and the willingness of rational individuals to make themselves a party to it' (Newey 2001: 168). It is this idea of identity, emptied of any embodied, affectual or non-rational content, that not only underpins the separation of the good from the just but also enables Habermas to maintain the distinction between conventional and postconventional rationality. Taylor's understanding of the emotional and inarticulate nature of the bond that embeds the self in moral horizons suggests that, at any given point, an individual's set of beliefs is a mixture of rationalism and intuition. In order to maintain the absolute separation between the conventional and postconventional, Habermas ignores this co-extensivity of reason with emotion. He rationalizes Mead's work by installing a sharp division between the 'I' and 'me' where the former becomes the communicatively mediated capacity to recognize the alterity of others. For Mead, however, 'taking the role of the other' is never a purely intellectual or self-conscious exercise but can describe a number of emphatic and pre-reflexive exchanges (Aboulafia 1999: 163). There are numerous other accounts of intersubjective recognition that suggest that understanding the other is never purely a linguistically mediated act of communication but involves an admixture of intellectual, imaginative and emotional impulses, for example Ricoeur's idea of analogical apperception (McNay 2000: 98–102). Thus, although Habermas may be right to claim that Taylor effaces a critical dimension in the subject's relation to communal values and norms, his idea of the postconventional subject rests on an exaggerated break with the preceding conventional subject where the autonomous, intellectual 'I' is separated too distinctly from the conformist, pre-reflexive 'me'. The linguistic abstraction from embodied context ultimately allows Habermas to set up a moral psychology where individuals are *a priori* pre-disposed to communicative debate. In sum, the postulation that subjects are formed through a process of communicatively mediated recognition expediently forecloses a cluster of issues connected to embodied power relations.

REFLEXIVITY AND NORMS

To emphasize the inseparability of language and power through the idea of embodiment is not tantamount to denying the possibility of reflexive agency. It is the denial of individual reflexivity that some critics have claimed is the inevitable consequence of Bourdieu's theory of embodied speech acts which is tied too closely to ritualized and institutionalized utterances and ignores the more informal and indeterminate uses of speech (e.g. Butler 1999; Thompson 1991: 10).[7] In defence of Habermas, James Bohman argues, for example, that Bourdieu's conflation of linguistic with social competence reduces speech to its narrowly strategic functions. He thereby forecloses an account of agency based on the reflexive capacity of individuals to reflect on the conditions under which they act and speak. By failing to attribute the capacity for practical reflection to actors: 'the possibility of innovation and transformation becomes improbable and dependent on external social conditions' (Bohman 1999: 141). The force of the Habermasian idea of communication is that it is a second-order form of discourse that transcends the first order, strategic use of speech. The reflective functions of language can be used both in the disputation of norms and also in scrutinizing the form and style of discursive deliberation with the aim of transforming it if it proves to be exclusionary. Communicative reason is thus capable of challenging the basis on which any antecedent consensus has been established. In Bohman's view, Bourdieu 'one-sidedly emphasizes the suppression of modes of expression through relations of power, rather than the way public institutions could promote voice through open and fair procedures of public justification' (Bohman 1999: 148).

It is undeniable that there are difficulties with Bourdieu's understanding of reflexive agency but these pertain mainly to his emphasis on individuals as strategic actors rather than to the idea of the embodied context of speech acts (see Chapter 4). Indeed, the criticism that the emphasis on embodiment denies 'ordinary' individuals the capacity for reflexive thought seems to proceed from a false opposition where if actors' critical awareness does not reach certain conclusions based on pre-given epistemological or normative criteria then they cannot be said to be autonomous at all. It is certainly from such a zero-sum logic that Habermasian critiques of Bourdieu often proceed, invoking what Richard Flathmann calls a 'biblical' view of autonomous agency where 'knowing the truth is a necessary or at least a sufficient condition of freedom'. It is undeniable that 'knowing the truth can contribute towards one's freedom' but it does not mean to say that agents are not autonomous if this knowledge does not reach 'established or envisioned criteria of correctness' (Flathmann 2003: 9). It is such notions of untrammelled reflexivity which form the underpinnings of Habermas's theory of communicative competence that are justifiably problematized in Bourdieu's insistence on the inescapably embodied nature of speech acts. The idea of linguistic habitus highlights how speech is always an indeterminate ensemble of motivations and effects and cannot be reduced to a putative essence of the communicative disputation of validity claims. Habermas claims that speech acts inevitably raise at least one of three types of validity claim: objective rightness, normative truthfulness and subjective truthfulness. It is hard to see, however, how these claims can be detached so definitively from an individual's intuitive understanding of themselves and their embodied situation in the world, particularly the ones pertaining to normative and subjective truthfulness. It is Habermas's communicative version of recognition that permits this linguistic abstraction and allows him to set up a notion of linguistic reflexivity based on an implausibly exhaustive degree of self-understanding. Indeed, as Ricoeur argues in his medi-ation of Habermas's debate with Gadamer, the choice that the former presents between the possibility of critical distantiation and uncriti-cal belonging is a false one. The possibility of critical reflexivity is always immanent in the interpretative process that embeds individ-uals within a particular cultural or social order (Ricoeur 1981).

Habermas's requirement of sincerity through the privileging of the illocutionary elements of speech over the perlocutionary ones under-pins his untenable account of self-reflexivity. It locks the account of reflexivity into a zero-sum logic where understanding can be acquired only on the basis of complete self-transparency or not at all. Anything less than absolute sincerity on the part of participants exposes the deliberative process to the distortions of strategic interests. Yet this zero-sum logic forecloses the possibility that efficacious political deliberation and agency can emerge from linguistic processes that are much more 'impure' and indeterminate. One of the exclusions that Habermas's privileging of the illocutionary excludes is, for example, the unforeseen types of resistant political agency outlined by Judith Butler's rethinking of the perlocutionary effects of speech. It is the very instability of language that the communicative themes of reci-procity and reflexivity try to contain that forms an important political resource. Speech is always, to some degree, out of control, rendering it susceptible to processes of unauthorized appropriation and, hence, resignification. This instability is connected to the perlocutionary effects of speech, in that the process of temporal deferral, where the original conditions of utterance cannot be indefinitely sustained, points to the possibility of the intentionality of the utterance going awry and producing unintended effects of subversion and counter-discourse. The open temporality of speech results in a dissemination of effects beyond the control of the speaking subject that leads to the possibility of counter-hegemonic processes of resignification. For example, the subversion of forms of 'hate speech' by the very groups against whom they are directed. Similarly, Bourdieu's emphasis on the embodied context of speech acts does not foreclose the possibility of reflexive knowledge and agency. Embodiment is not a one-sided process where the somatization of power relations ensures the blind conformity of individuals to social structures. It is also an active process of self-realization, of 'living through' the tendencies of the world that have been incorporated into the body. These anticipatory and future-oriented dimensions of embodied practice mean that indi-viduals are always potentially in the position of having to respond creatively to unforeseen events and to process the new knowledge that is generated through these interactions. It follows that linguistic exchanges will always potentially have a spontaneous and uncertain dimension that can be generative of new knowledges and critical self-understanding. Indeed, the basic insight of Bourdieu's idea of relational phenomenology is that important insights into social existence can only be gleaned from the reflexive self-understanding of actors. This critical understanding can never, however, take the form of a purified, communicatively mediated reflexivity; it is always necessarily partial, incomplete and subject to permanent revision.

The issue of reflexivity is clearly connected to the more general question of the possibility of normative critique. In this respect, a response to the criticism that Taylor and Habermas pay insufficient attention to language as a medium of symbolic power is that their ideas of recognition are intended as regulative ideals. The idea of recognition serves as an ultimate horizon which, even though it can never be fully realized, provides a standard against which empirical struggles over identity can be evaluated. Habermas frequently marshals this defence for discourses ethics which, he claims, is an ultimate standard towards which our behaviour should be oriented even if, in reality, it can never be attained: 'No prospect of such forms of life can be given to us, not even in the abstract, this side of prophetic teachings' (1992: 146).[8] Likewise, Taylor claims that the idea that the authentic life should be structured as a narrative quest is a transcendental condition of selfhood that can never be exhausted by actuality: 'the issue of our condition can never be exhausted for us by what we *are*, because we are always also changing and *becoming*' (Taylor 1989: 46–7). On this view, to criticize normative thought through reference to existing power relations is to deny the contingency and creativity of freedom by reducing it to what Hannah Arendt calls the 'social question'. Yet, at the same time, both Habermas and Taylor claim that their ideals are not abstract utopias but are immanent in, and derived from, everyday social practices. The social question cannot be left behind entirely because there is an intrinsic connection between the 'is' and the 'ought'.

The question of the normative status of the idea of recognition raises the more general issue of the nature of the relation between political and social theory. If social theory is about the analysis of how power relations permeate social practices and political theory is about the regulation of these relations, then the two share common territory and are mutually implicated. While the two are not reducible to each other, it becomes difficult, at the limit, to establish a precise border between the two domains. As Wendy Brown says: 'If politics is in culture and culture is relentlessly political, what denotes the boundary between political theory and anthropological or other kinds of cultural theory . . . what other than anxiety about loss of identity and place, animates the drawing of a line . . . between theories of culture and theories of politics, between social or political economic theory and political theory?' (Brown 2004: 107–8). There is obviously then a crucial, albeit indeterminate, connection between social and political thought which both Taylor and Habermas acknowledge. In *Between Facts and Norms*, Habermas discusses the way in which supposedly neutral paradigms of law are tacitly upheld by latent background assumptions about society. The implication of his argument, as Thomas McCarthy points out, holds *ceteris paribus* for political theorists too: 'such understandings, images, or models of society, which are always at work, though usually only tacitly, in normative theorizing, have to become an explicit theme if political theorists hope to avoid exalting intuitive preunderstandings of their social contexts into universal ideals' (McCarthy 2004: 166). Yet although both Taylor and Habermas accept that political thought can never be free-standing, both ultimately deploy the normative status of the idea of recognition to circumvent an examination of the implications that a perspective on social power might have for their theories. This is, ultimately, because it would undermine the claims each makes for the universal normative relevance of their version of subject formation in recognition. Habermas's idea of recognition as communication allows him to achieve a series of questionable linguistic reductions, starting with the assertion that orientation towards understanding is a universal constant within human communication. This allows him to further delimit understanding to the narrowly cognitive idea of the disputation of validity claims that is allegedly presupposed in all significant speech acts. Speech acts are then further purified by being conceptualized as the utterances of disembodied beings. If this radical separation between language and power, between speech acts and social context is thrown into question, in the manner suggested by Bourdieu's idea of linguistic habitus, then the universal scope of Habermas's work is also undermined. The implications of such a critique for Taylor's idea of recognition as expression are less serious in so far as it is a weaker form of transcendental thought than Habermas's. Nonetheless, his failure to understand recognition claims in the context of structured social inequalities also throws into question some of the more tacitly universal aspects of this thought. Without a more systematic account of power, for example, it becomes unclear on what basis Taylor would adjudicate between competing claims for recognition. He concedes that not all claims to recognition should be automatically upheld. Rather, they should be assessed through a process of cross-cultural critical dialogue which seeks to provide an expanded understanding of the grounds on which the presumption of equal worth can be validated or not. Yet the evaluative criteria upon which such a 'fusion of horizons' would proceed remain unclear. In *Voice, Trust, and Memory*, Melissa Williams argues, for example, that it is only by comparing social groups along the related dimensions of contemporary inequality and past discrimination that judgements can be made about the relative merits of different recognition claims (Williams 1998: 176–202). Without such criteria, which are relatively objective and empirically measurable, it is hard to see how Taylor would stop his method of 'epistemic gain' sliding into the kind of relativism of which he is rightly critical. Ultimately then, his unmediated linguistic expressivism detaches his normative idea of recognition from the objective context that would give his theory some analytical bite.

It is too easy, then, to argue that the criticism of ideal thought from a non-ideal sociological perspective on power is tantamount to falling back into a resigned pragmatism that undermines the basis for normative theory altogether. If the idea of recognition is posited on a fundamental misunderstanding of the conditions of social existence then it is necessary to scrutinize its validity as a regulative ideal. Furthermore, if it presupposes narrow or untenable notions of subjectivity and identity, then it is also legitimate to question its desirability, in so far as, if it were to be realized, it might result in conformist social orders (Duttman 2000: 156–7; Foucault 1988: 18). To criticize normative political theory in terms of its sociological preunderstandings is not necessarily to forestall it. It is rather to continue the dialectical engagement between the two areas of thought and, in using each to expose the limits of the other, to provide renewed grounds for critical debate. Political theory can only develop in tandem with a continuous sociological self-critique that, as McCarthy puts it, is oriented to uncovering the exclusions that it makes: 'the search for a genuinely inclusive theory of justice is a never ending, constantly renewed effort to rethink supposedly universal basic norms and reshape their practical and institutional embodiments to include, what, in their limited historical forms, they unjustly exclude.' (McCarthy 2004: 163).

CONCLUSION

Thinkers of radical difference and so-called agonistic theories of democracy frequently criticize ideas of deliberative democracy on the grounds that the reasonable and open-minded attitudes adopted by participants in debate are not borne out by the actuality of political discussion. Given the volatile and biased nature of actual political debate, it is reasonable to enquire of deliberative democrats where these required attitudes should come from (Dryzek 2005: 221). In the case of Taylor and Habermas, it is clear that these attitudes are generated by their respective ontologies of recognition that tacitly predispose individuals towards cooperative and open-minded debate. It is not that individuals are not capable of deliberating in such a manner, but the exclusively linguistic construal of identity enables Habermas and Taylor to downplay the dimensions of embodied existence that are often the source of deep division and hostility in political debate. The conceptual inadequacies of both paradigms, when it comes to the treatment of issues connected to gender, are illustrative of these expedient foreclosures. For both thinkers, linguistically mediated recognition is conceived in such a way that there is little friction between its sociological and normative senses; it becomes what Duttman has called 'presupposition and result' (Duttman 2000: 140–1). One of the costs of this harmonious circularity is that their normative ideals of recognition seem naïve and slightly tangential with regard to both political practice and other types of political theory. This linguistic abstraction ultimately undermines one of the animating impulses of their thought. In different ways, both Taylor's and Habermas's versions of recognition are reliant upon disembodied concepts of subjectivity which are not that far removed from the monological philosophy of the subject to which they are both opposed.

3

Narrative and Recognition

INTRODUCTION

It is undeniable that Habermas's communicative formulation of the idea of recognition has been an important catalyst in highlighting the significance of intersubjective relations in social life. His work has been intellectually conducive to many feminists in that its dialogical accounts of agency and rationality provide renewed grounds for emancipatory social critique in the face of the deconstructive arguments of neo-Nietzschean poststructuralist thinkers. The difficulty, however, for feminists, is that the rationalist bias of his ontology of recognition and the restrictive definition of communication it invokes preclude anything but the most limited understanding of social differences, in particular those pertaining to gender. In this respect, Seyla Benhabib has been in the forefront of feminist attempts to modify discourse ethics so that it encompasses a more adequate understanding of embodied social identity. Along with several other thinkers, Benhabib's recent work has focused on the idea of the narrative structure of identity as the key concept through which the scope of discourse ethics can be enlarged. Narrative identity is seen as a way of bridging the gap between the abstraction of Habermas's idea of the communicative subject, on the one side, and the fragmentation of the subject which arises from the poststructural critique, on the other. The idea of the narrated self as an individual creation replaces the disembodied subject of discourse ethics with a particularized notion of subjectivity. At the same time, the notion of dynamic coherence that it invokes circumvents the dispersion of the subject that is a frequent consequence of the poststructural emphasis on difference. In this respect, the idea of narrative identity is presented as an alternative to performative accounts of agency that prevail in post-Foucauldian work on gender. The idea of narrative shares the latter's presumption that gender identity is discursively constructed and culturally variable, but, in as much as it invokes ideas of intention and reflexivity, it seems to offer a more substantive idea of agency than the abstract notion of discursive construction.

I argue in this chapter that the feminist attempt to enlarge discourse ethics with the idea of narrative identity is contradictory and, ultimately, fails. This is because there is a fundamental incompatibility between the communicative formulation of recognition and the notion of narrative which, by and large, feminist Habermasians have failed to acknowledge. The reason that Habermas adheres to a narrowly rationalist conception of communication, despite the many problems it provokes, is that it is central to upholding his claim that discourse ethics is universal in scope. The feminist reformulation of the idea of recognition around the notion of narrative does indeed entail an enlarged understanding of the formation of subjectivity in the context of inequalities of power. It loses, however, the rationalist core that is the crucial underpinning to Habermas's claim that communicative interaction is universal. In sum, my argument is that Habermasian feminists cannot have it both ways; they cannot extend the idea of communicative ethics to include a broader account of difference and identity and still retain the universal status that Habermas declares for his theory.

It is not just that in their narrative reconfiguration of discourse ethics feminists move closer to an ethical relativism than they would care to concede. The exigencies of remaining within Habermas's communicatively symmetrical model of recognition also compromise their understanding of the extent to which subjectivity assumes a narrative structure. Ultimately, feminist Habermasians rely on a syncretic and over-generalized idea of narrative identity that does not grasp important aspects of subjectivity and agency in the context of the systemic reproduction of gender inequalities. The normative 'redemptive' force that feminist Habermasians invest in the idea of narrative retroactively limits their sociological analysis of the role narratives play in social life. The stress these thinkers place on the inherent unity and meaningfulness of narrative structures underplays problematic aspects of subjectivity such as its discontinuous nature and also disregards the role narratives may play in sustaining relations of domination. Furthermore, the narrative version of recognition relies on a limited notion of intersubjectivity understood as a form of immediate co-presence that forecloses an understanding of the systemic ways in which gender inequalities are maintained in late capitalist society.

PERFORMATIVE AND PRAGMATIC AGENCY

The turn to Habermas's thought amongst feminists is part of a more general reaction to what are regarded as the limitations of poststructural theory, most notably the way in which it is held to undermine a coherent foundation for feminist critique. The appeal of Habermas's theory of communication for feminists is twofold. First, in terms of social analysis, his recovery of an intersubjective rationality that structures interaction in the lifeworld provides a theoretical lens through which to examine many of the activities conventionally undertaken by women that have been disregarded in mainstream sociology. In place of the heroic model of action that governs, say, Weberian sociology, Habermas's notion of interaction oriented towards understanding provides a more appropriate model for understanding the logic of nurture and care that defines so many of the social functions that women assume. Second, Habermas's redefinition of rationality along communicative, rather than legislative lines initiates an ethic based on an openness to the other or 'reversibility' of perspectives and establishes a universal foundation for social critique. The idea of communicative rationality provides a powerful tool with which to think about the ethical potential embedded in the intersubjective relations that shape social life and yields an alternative to the anti-foundationalism of poststructural thought. While poststructural theory shares with feminism a critique of the disembodied masculinism of classical philosophy, it is problematic in so far as it is understood to be reliant on an aestheticized, Nietzschean individualism which is antipathetic to the values and aims of feminist critique.

The feminist criticisms of poststructural theory are, of course, well known and have been rehearsed frequently in the modern–postmodern debate (e.g. Fraser and Nicholson 1990). An exchange between Judith Butler and Selya Benhabib on the concept of agency encapsulates some of the issues at stake (Benhabib et al. 1995). In Benhabib's view, the poststructural view of the unified subject as a discursive effect is far too abstract to provide an adequate account of agency. Agency is regarded as a property of language conceived as an abstract structure, rather than as pragmatically oriented speech between individuals. The possibility of linguistic agency in Derrida, for example, is linked to the reiterative structure of language itself. When this essentially structural account of agency is generalized, as it is in Butler's idea of 'performative resignification', it is unable to answer the question 'how does anyone know, that such resignification and reinterpretation have taken place?' (Benhabib 1999: 340; Osborne and Segal 1994). This conception of agency as an abstract potential connected to the reiterative structure of speech does not adequately address ideas of intention, reflexivity and attendant notions of validity against which the political legitimacy of a given speech act can be assessed. In other words, the idea of instability within meaning systems provides a necessary but not sufficient condition for understanding agency (McNay 2000: 44–5). Benhabib concludes that, by sidestepping these issues of agency and validity, Butler's idea of performativity is no more than a 'doing without the doer' and individuals 'no more than the sum total of the gendered expressions we perform' (Benhabib et al. 1995: 21). In contrast, for Habermas, the surplus of meaning that forms the condition of possibility of agency is not a purely structural property of language but must be understood as the product of pragmatic communication or 'language-in-use': 'this "more" in language comes about through the communicative competence of social actors in generating situational interpretations of their lifeworld through communicative acts oriented to validity claims' (Benhabib 1999: 339–40).

In response to these criticisms, Butler argues that Benhabib fails to grasp the poststructural critique of the subject by misunderstanding the nature of the relation that it proposes between agency and power. The idea that the agent is an effect of the reiterative structure of language does not deny a doer of actions, but rather throws into question unproblematic notions of intention and motivation as the source of all action. In her view, intention does not precede action in any simple, causal sense, but is an effect of the subject's prior inscription within language. Actions do not 'reflect the power of an individual's will or intention', but rather 'draw upon and reengage conventions which have gained their power precisely through a *sedimented iterability*' (Benhabib et al. 1995: 134). The coherent, rational subject does not exist, therefore, in some pure sense prior to action, but emerges through time as an effect of the repeated reworking of sedimented linguistic conventions. In short, the agent is neither entirely determined by language nor, however, does she use language, in a fully willed fashion, as an instrument of self-expression. As Butler has repeatedly pointed out, gender performativity does not denote a freely assumed performance or masquerade. Rather, it evokes a dialectic of freedom and constraint where the subject is constituted through subjection and invested simultaneously with the capacity for autonomous action: 'there is no opposition to power which is not itself part of the very workings of power, that agency is implicated in what it opposes, that "emancipation" will never be the transcendence of power as such' (Benhabib et al. 1995: 137). By misinterpreting the idea of the performative, Benhabib seems to be reinstalling a simplified referential relation between the subject and language where the latter is understood as a transparent medium in which individuals express themselves. For Butler, agency is not a transcendental category but must be regarded as a contingent and fragile possibility opened up in the midst of constituting discursive relations (Benhabib et al. 1995: 139). The 'heroic' view of agency propounded by Benhabib ultimately invokes a 'de-situated transcendentalized self' which is uncomfortably close to the disembedded, disembodied tendencies of the philosophy of consciousness against which much feminist thought, Benhabib's included, has been directed.

In response to Butler's trenchant remarks, Benhabib concedes that her reading of the idea of performativity as failing to address the 'doer' behind the deed has voluntarist implications. Acknowledging the force of Butler's thought on the performative construction of gender, Benhabib maintains, nonetheless, that a primarily discursive understanding of the subject does not distinguish sufficiently between different modes of subject formation; between, for example, 'subjectivity, selfhood and agency' (Benhabib et al. 1995: 108). The primacy accorded to linguistic processes of signification does not differentiate between structural processes and dynamics of socialization and individuation, on the one side, and historical processes of signification and meaning constitution, on the other. Indeed, it tends to subsume the latter under the former. As a result, the poststructural account of linguistic agency forecloses any concept of human intention or of the pragmatic everyday creativity that explains how 'speech acts are not only iterations but also innovations and reinterpretations' (Benhabib 1999: 339).

NARRATIVE AND COMMUNICATIVE ETHICS

Habermas's idea of recognition as communication may well provide a more creative and pragmatic account of agency than is available within poststructural thought but it is not without its difficulties. As we saw in the previous chapter, his idea of communication is underpinned by a disembodied account of speech acts that overlooks crucial issues connected to the way in which social hierarchies are sustained through corporeal manipulation. Benhabib is mindful of these limitations and has suggested substantive revisions to overcome them. Her earlier work centred on introducing a greater sensitivity to gender differences into communicative ethics through the idea of the 'concrete other'. It is well known that Habermas borrows his idea of the moral subject and stages of moral reasoning from Thomas Kohlberg and this results in his adherence to an abstract and proceduralist concept of justice. Perhaps one of the most debated difficulties of this proceduralism is Habermas's delimitation of a proper object domain for morality from which ethical matters pertaining to virtues, emotions, life, conduct, are excluded because of their non-universalizable and non-formalizable nature. As Carole Gilligan has shown, this is particularly problematic for feminist theory because it excludes consideration of many issues associated with injustices of gender. In an exchange with Gilligan, Habermas claims that the kind of issues that she attempts to incorporate into a theory of justice such as care, affect and empathy are 'anomalies' which belong outside universalistic moral theory.

Benhabib claims that Habermas's formal conception of justice not only derives from his reliance upon an unencumbered conception of the self but also from his insistence that the universal structure of communicative competence guarantees consensus, indeed, that consensus is itself the end goal of the communicative process.[1] For Benhabib, Habermas's consequentialist formulation of universal consensus is sufficiently indeterminate with regard to the content that it cannot even yield a normatively thin prescription of 'negative duties', that is, duties not to violate the rights of humanity in oneself. In short, the abstract nature of communicative ethics serves to reinforce a conventional distinction between the impersonal sphere of justice and the more concrete issue of the ethical content of the good life; as Benhabib puts it: 'Positive moral duties cannot be deduced from the universalizability test alone but require contextual moral judgement in their concretization' (Benhabib 1992: 35–6). She seeks to overcome these difficulties by reconfiguring communicative debate as an ongoing conversation rather than being governed by the goal of reaching consensus. She also counterbalances the ethically cognitivist perspective of 'the general other' with the perspective of the 'concrete' other drawn from Gilligan's work on an ethics of care. Benhabib is critical of the 'essentialist' foundation of Gilligan's work in object relations theory and claims that its care perspective does not provide sufficient grounds for a moral theory in itself. It should, however, be integrated into an impartial justice perspective which, on its own, can have profoundly counter-intuitive implications (1992: 184). Neither justice nor care has ontogenetic primary; both are essential for the development of the autonomous, adult individual out of the dependent child: 'Modern moral philosophy, and particularly universalist moralities of justice, have emphasized our dignity and worth as moral subjects at the cost of forgetting and repressing our vulnerability and dependency as bodily selves' (1992: 189). The integration of the general with the concrete perspective is achieved through the faculty of enlarged thinking, derived from Hannah Arendt and which denotes an agonistic relation with the other where the boundaries of (self-)knowledge are constantly tested. Ethical bonds are thereby reconfigured as not just juridical in nature but as based on a postconventional *sittlichkeit* which combines demands of justice and virtue (1992: 11).

In her recent work, Benhabib continues her revision of the formal structure of communicative ethics by conceptualizing the idea of enlarged thinking through that of narrative identity. Although it is not explicitly acknowledged, her shift away from the specifically gendered idea of the concrete other to the more general idea of the narrative structure of identity might be seen partly as a response to criticisms of her earlier work (e.g. Benhabib et al. 1995; Young 1990). Jodi Dean argues, for example, that Benhabib's formulation of the distinction between the concrete and general other reinforces, rather than breaks down, a series of attendant oppositions between the public and the private, the rational and the embodied, the masculine and the feminine, and so forth. As Dean puts it: 'Benhabib links the generalized other to the public sphere and the concrete other to the private sphere. This prevents us from seeing how generalized conceptions of role identity influence our domestic and intimate interactions. In other words, Benhabib neglects the fact that norms are always generalized sets of expectations no matter where they come into play' (Dean 1996: 38). In a different vein, Iris Marion Young claims that despite her replacement of the idea of consensus with the more fluid notion of moral conversation, Benhabib still presumes untenable levels of fungibility and reflexivity between participants in debate. She underplays the ways in which structural privilege and oppression create the possibility of 'falsifying' projections: 'When members of privileged groups imaginatively try to represent to themselves the perspective of members of oppressed groups, too often those representations carry projections and fantasies through which the privileged reinforce a complementary image of themselves' (Young 1994b: 171).

The idea of narrative identity suggests a more complex conception of the interweaving of embodied and general aspects of the self than the dualist formulation of concrete and general other. It brings, in Benhabib's view, a greater sensitivity to difference into communicative ethics by invoking more particularized notions of identity and agency. Habermas does not explicitly connect communicative competence with the narrative structure of self, so instead Benhabib draws upon the work of Charles Taylor on intention and dialogically constructed narrative identity. In her subsequent work, *The Claims of Culture*, Benhabib is more critical of Taylor and claims that her source for the idea of narrative identity is in fact Arendt. Indeed, Benhabib's turn, in the first instance, to a communitarian idea of narrative is somewhat surprising because, on her own account, it shares the same relativist tendencies of poststructuralist thought. Its emphasis on the inescapable embeddedness of all knowledge within tradition forecloses the process of ideal-typical reconstruction upon which feminist critique necessarily rests. Nonetheless, Benhabib sees in the communitarian idea of narrative self-interpretation a way to modify the disembodied idea of the subject which underlies Habermas's theory of communicative ethics. To be a self, on Taylor's account, is the result of being 'thrown into' and inserting oneself into 'webs of interlocution', ranging from familial micro-narratives through to macro-narratives of gender and nation. The individual's sense of self is established through an interweaving of these multiple narrative strands which are historically and culturally specific. Narrative codes are neither freely chosen, nor, however, are they fully determining in the sense that they exhaust the capacity to 'initiate new actions and new sentences in conversation' (Benhabib 1999: 345). Benhabib differs from Taylor in rejecting his assertion that narrative identities are constructed, explicitly or implicitly, around strong evaluative commitments to certain cultural values and norms. Indeed, in Taylor's view, individuals who lack these evaluative commitments also lack the essential conditions of what he refers to as 'integral, that is, undamaged human personhood' (Taylor 1989: 27). Benhabib argues that Taylor's assertion that strong qualitative discriminations are necessarily constitutive of personhood confuses the conditions of possible human agency with a strong concept of moral integrity. Following Habermas's arguments about postconventional normativity, Benhabib asserts that the conditions of modernity are such that it is possible to live a life not within the horizons of strong evaluative commitments. The continuity of the self through time must be thought of not as attachment to a specific set of evaluative goods, but as the capacity to take and adapt attitude towards such goods, even if this entails an attitude of 'non-commitment' (Benhabib 1999: 346). On this view, selfhood is understood in terms of second-order attitudes that the self has towards making first-order commitments. It is not what the story is about that matters, but rather 'one's ability to keep telling a story about who one is that makes sense to oneself and to others' (Benhabib 1999: 347). The self is not defined by the content of the narrative but by its narratability.

It is not only Benhabib who uses the idea of narrative identity to overcome difficulties in the abstract formulation of communicative ethics. For Maria Pia Lara (1998), the excessive formalism of Habermas's notion of moral reasoning can be traced to his neglect of the expressive and creative aspects of speech. Following Wellmer's (1991) critique of Habermas, she argues that while communicative ethics accommodates a cognitive and instrumental view of rationality and its normative dimensions, it overlooks the moral and utopian thrust of aesthetic reasoning. Lara claims that the idea of narrative extends the notion of communicative praxis to include not only validity claims, but also an imaginative, performative dimension, or expressive claims. In this way, the idea of political intervention is expanded to encompass the aesthetic and utopian practices of movements such as feminism. Political movements are re-conceptualized as narrative performances within the public sphere whose collective illocutionary effects have expanded prevailing notions of justice and autonomy: 'it is evident that the "illocutionary force", derived via the transformation of gender narratives, has made a substantial impact on the values and categories which are now employed to deal with the social, political and moral dimensions of life' (Lara 1998: 80).

SELF AND CULTURE

For both Benhabib and Lara, the force of the idea of narrative identity is that it shares with poststructural theory an 'anti-essentialist' account of identity as discursively constructed and, therefore, as a culturally variable and historically specific entity. However, the idea of narrative configuration circumvents the poststructural fragmentation of the subject where self is seen as a series of unconnected episodes. By invoking notions of intention, self-expression and reflexivity, the idea of narrative yields a situated and creative concept of agency. Poststructuralism tends to view the unified subject as an exogenously imposed effect of discourse. This rests on an impoverished account of the continuity of self through time, of the different levels at which this continuity is maintained and of the relation between the coherent self and action. In contrast, the idea of narrative recognizes that a degree of coherence is an operative necessity of selfhood, but is in no sense a pre-social or inevitable characteristic. In short, the narrative view of the self seems to bypass the antinomy of essentialism versus fragmentation by suggesting that the self has unity, but it is a dynamic unity which integrates permanence in time with its contrary, namely diversity, variability, discontinuity and instability (McNay 2000: 89–94). As well as invoking a notion of dynamic coherence, narrative is also an explicitly relational category in that it draws attention to the irremediably intersubjective nature of identity. Using a phrase of Jessica Benjamin's (1998), Benhabib argues that the shadow cast by the other subject permanently prevents closure, or the achievement of an enclosed, autarkic sense of self. Even apparently solitary acts of memory and recall, for example, can only be carried out from within the temporal horizon of the present which itself is enmeshed within webs of intersubjective relations: 'narratives cannot have closure precisely because they are always aspects of the narratives of others' (Benhabib 1999: 348). In short, the idea of narrative identity emphasizes the temporal and intersubjective aspects of subjectivity and agency which are neglected in abstract, poststructural accounts.

In *The Claims of Culture*, Benhabib extends the idea of narrative to explain the formation of collective as well as individual identities and thereby to go beyond the limitations of the liberal debate over multiculturalism. The problem with liberal approaches to multiculturalism is that they rely on a reductive sociology of culture where collective identities are seen as clearly delineable and internally coherent formations. These holistic views of cultural identity result in the relativism and balkanization that is so often the problematic endpoint of debates within 'mosaic' multiculturalism. Benhabib claims that these problems can be bypassed by adopting a constructivist perspective where cultures are viewed as internally riven and contested. Any given culture is composed of multiple narrative strands which are constantly subject to processes of contestation and reinterpretation on the part of its members. There are also narratives that are shared across cultures, which means, contra claims of cultural incommensurability, that a given culture is never totally alien to another, that there will always be some basis for mutual interpretability. The narrative view of culture moves the debate about cultural difference away from arguments about maintaining the purity or distinctiveness of cultures towards one of democratic, cross-cultural dialogue. This dialogue centres not on trying to establish the merits of one entire culture versus another, because all cultures are composed of good and bad practices. Rather it is a process of mutual enlightenment with the eventual goal of justifying different narratives and practices within and across cultures according to democratic normative standards.[2] Against the idea of multiculturalism, Benhabib proposes an interactive universalism which takes the basic form of Habermas's discourse ethics but is based on the shared narrative structure of cultural life.

Benhabib justifies her view that cultures present themselves through narrative by grounding it in the ontological claim that human action has a narrative structure: 'not only are human actions and interactions constituted through narratives . . . but they are also constituted through actors' evaluative stances toward their doing . . . there are second-order narratives entailing a certain normative attitude towards accounts of first order deeds. What we call "culture" is the horizon formed by these evaluative stances' (Benhabib 2002: 7). Although the narrative view of culture is grounded in an ontological claim about human action, Benhabib maintains, nonetheless, that it is essential to maintain the distinction between individual and collective narratives. One of the weaknesses of Taylor's work on multiculturalism is that he subsumes the former under the latter, thereby problematically equating the search for authentic individual identity with the realization of collective forms of self-expression. This enables Taylor to sidestep, *inter alia*, the thorny issue of individual autonomy – most vividly exemplified in debates on women and multiculturalism. Individual autonomy is conflated with a notion of authentic identity which itself rests on conflation of the individual with the community. Against this conservative logic, Benhabib maintains that individual narratives of self-identification must not only be analytically distinguished from the ascribed narratives of the collective but they must also normatively trump them in order to preserve the autonomy of the individual: 'the goal would be to move a democratic society toward a model of public life in which narratives of self-identification would be more determinant of one's status in public life than would designators and indices imposed upon one by others' (Benhabib 2002: 80).

There is no doubt that Benhabib's reconfiguration of culture as narrative bypasses some of the conceptual and political limitations of the liberal debate on multiculturalism. The idea of narrative identity also goes further than poststructural discourse theory in generating a dynamic and creative account of agency and intersubjectivity by initiating a move from a 'negative' to a 'generative' paradigm of subject formation (McNay 2000). The attempts of Benhabib and Lara to integrate the concept into Habermas's idea of communicative ethics are problematic, however, in so far as they rely too heavily upon an over-extended and de-radicalized idea of narrative. Ultimately this is the unacknowledged effect of the latent normative demands of Habermas's model of recognition which requires an *a priori* communicative symmetry in order to be effective. I argue in the next section that both Benhabib and Lara deploy an exaggeratedly syncretic concept of narrative identity that underestimates the blocks, both psychic and social, to the formation of a coherent sense of self. This results in an over-extension of the narrative model of self, where it is used as an exhaustive account of all aspects of subjectivity. In other words, Benhabib and Lara replicate a similar ontological reduction that, as we have seen, is characteristic of the work of Benjamin, Taylor and Habermas where the idea of narrative is problematically extended to be the single constitutive feature of self and action. On this organic view, the idea of narrative comes to represent an inherently authentic expression of self-identity and is conflated with reflexive agency. This has problematic implications, in particular, for an understanding of gender identity and agency.

NARRATIVE COHERENCE AND INCOHERENCE

While it is not unreasonable to assert that aspects of self-identity have a narrative structure, it is more contentious to accord narrative an ontological status where it encompasses all aspects of experience and selfhood. Benhabib and Lara are in accord with communitarians such as Taylor and MacIntyre who reject the Sartrean and also poststructural view, that narratives are false constructs in the sense that they impose an illusion of the unity of self. For Sartre, narratives are falsifications in so far as the whole pattern of a story, the coherence of its events, is built on a false premise of retrospection, for it is only in retrospect that we can recognize events to be significant or irrelevant and contingent. The nature of living is, however, quite opposite to that of narrative fiction since, when we are acting, we never know the outcome, we are unsure of its effects and we ignore what is happening elsewhere. In so far as it attempts to conceal this temporal contradiction, narrative is regarded as a false construct. While there are certainly problems with this rather unmodulated view of narrative as a false construct, Benhabib and Lara seem to fall into a countervailing simplification by proposing a syncretic notion of narrative as an exhaustive description of the mechanisms of selfhood. Such an

over-extended and synthesizing notion of narrative ultimately forecloses an understanding of complexities and contradictions within
the construction of gender identity.

To be sure, Benhabib refers to the unfinished and 'unpredictable'
quality of narratives; stories about the self always have to be reconfigured in order to accommodate the flux of events and the narratives
of others which 'unsettle self understanding, and spoil attempts to
mastermind one's own narrative' (Benhabib 1999: 348). She also recognizes that experiences of fragmentation and the senselessness of
being are authentic and may hinder the configuration of coherent
narratives. Yet the urge to create narratives, in her view, overrides
experiences of alienation in so far as individuals will always attempt
to 'make sense of nonsense' (Benhabib 1999: 347). While narrative is
certainly a fundamental mode through which experience is rendered
meaningful, Benhabib is in danger of universalizing the idea so that
the differences between narrative structures and lived experience are
effaced. As Michael Bell puts it: 'narrative has to be a different kind
of thing from lived temporality or there is no point in drawing any
analogy between them. The meaningfulness of the comparison
depends on an implicit recognition of this difference even while it is
being denied' (Bell 1987: 174). By privileging the drive to narrative
unity, the precarious and contradictory dimensions of subjectivity
are downplayed and, so too, are the possible connections between the
unfinished quality of narratives and wider conflicts in social life. In
Lara's work, for example, the distinction, drawn from Paul Ricoeur,
between 'representational' and 'ontological' narratives is tacitly valorized by being mapped onto a dualism of ideology versus authenticity (Lara 1998: 70–1). Representational narratives are regarded as
bearers of dominating power relations, whereas ontological narratives are seen as expressions of 'authentic' experience whose illocutionary effects are held to be inherently emancipatory. By unhitching
ontological narratives from the analysis of power in this way, Lara
produces an overly syncretic and expressive account of narrative
identity. As we will see, the same problems attend the dualist distinction that Benhabib makes in *The Claims of Culture*, between narratives of self-identification and ascribed narratives.

There are many ways of examining how certain experiences elude
narration and block the formation of coherent self-understanding.
This does not mean an abandonment of the category of narrative
altogether, but it does entail a greater sensitivity to the discontinuities and fragilities of the category as it relates to an understanding
of the formation of identity at both a collective and an individual
level. In Ricoeur's view, for example, narrative is the privileged

medium through which phenomenological time is represented, but it is not the only medium of temporal experience. Binding the concept of time too closely to that of narrative implies that 'the subject would be the master of meaning, that it would hold within the narrative all the meanings that time is capable of assuming' (Ricoeur 1998: 88). Ricoeur argues that the narrative attempt to impose temporal synthesis is never fully successful and this failure results in the multiplication of temporal 'aporia'. One such aporia appears as the disjunction between different types of experience of the self; in Ricoeur's terms, *idem* and *ipseity*. These can be understood respectively as the difference between embodied identity, which works upon the principal of sameness as similitude, and selfhood where sameness is understood as continuity through time. Ricoeur (1992) emphasizes that the resolution effected by narrative between these different levels of identity, between *idem* and *ipse*, is only fleeting and fragile and, indeed, may break down altogether in the face of extreme disjunction between the two levels. For example, in the face of traumatic bodily experiences such as rape, trauma or violation, the sense of self can collapse almost entirely. An example of this disjunction between embodied identity and a more abstract sense of self can be drawn from the fifth chapter of Frantz Fanon's *Black Skin, White Masks* (1996), where he describes how being sealed into the 'crushing object-hood' of blackness by the gaze of the colonial oppressor is internalized in the form of confusion and anger. The disjunction between the 'fact of [his] blackness' and his self-understanding locks him into an 'infernal circle', an oscillation between shame and rage, which prevents him establishing an integral sense of self.

It could be countered that the kinds of experience that elude narrative synthesis are limit cases and do not represent the normal mechanisms through which selfhood is established. Indeed, Benhabib makes the strong claim that it is only when an individual is 'delusional and violent or completely rigid and fragmented' that the ability to narrate proximity and distance, intimacy and alienation is lost (Benhabib 1999: 352). Yet, writers such as Galen Strawson (1997), for example, draw attention to more mundane forms of disassociation where experience perpetually resists incorporation into a meaningful self-narrative. Strawson draws a distinction between narrative and episodic experiences, the latter being experiences that have happened to the subject but resist incorporation into a meaningful account of the self. It is such mundane disjunctions within gender identity that feminist theory has also repeatedly drawn attention to in work on the contradictory nature of dominant conceptions of femininity, on the conflict between desire and reason or on the tensions within the construction of women as political subjects (e.g. de Lauretis 1984, 1987). In the unified concepts of narrative selfhood deployed by Benhabib and Lara, there seems to be little sense of the possible gaps and discontinuities between different levels of subjective experience. Indeed, Benhabib avoids addressing such issues by setting up a misleading opposition between fragmentation and coherence of the self rather than exploring how these moments might coexist within the same self (1992: 213–8). By constructing such a false antithesis, Benhabib avoids addressing important issues, such as the nature of the boundary between the sayable and unsayable or of the passage of experience from a pre-discursive to discursive level. Benhabib is critical of poststructural thinkers who, in their focus on sexual identity, reduce subjectivity to one single aspect of embodied or *idem* identity and she rightly argues that selfhood is a more multi-dimensional entity. However, by failing to consider the often incongruous relation between embodied identity and the narrative self, she falls into a countervailing reduction of subjectivity to a free-floating *ipseity*. In this respect, she replicates a much-noted difficulty of Arendt's work on narrative identity, namely, that it is so emptied of determinate content that it is difficult to see from where it derives its meaning and substance (e.g. Honig 1992: 226).

In sum, the communicative remodelling of narrative identity forecloses a consideration of the contradictory, pre-conscious and so-called non-rational aspects of identity. The stress on narrative as a syncretic entity posits a simplistic congruence of bodily existence with consciousness of that existence. It does not rule out a consideration of the pre-rational aspects of subjectivity *per se* but, in so far as it assumes a relatively untroubled communicability of inner nature, its treatment of these issues is superficial. Only certain types of subjective experience – ones that can be linguistically expressed – are admitted into communicative formulations of narrative identity. All too often, however, this precludes non-linguistic dimensions of identity – unconscious desires, embodied norms, non-verbal forms of expression and ways of being. Ultimately this can be traced back to a 'linguistic monism' that prevails in Habermas's idea of communication, which, according to Joel Whitebook, rests on a denial of Freud's fundamental distinction between word-representations and thing-representations. By banishing the difference between images and thing-representations from a concept of subjectivity, 'the articulability of inner nature can be casually maintained because the linguisticality of inner nature is presupposed from the start' (Whitebook 1995: 89. See also Coole 1996: 239). In their work on narrative, Benhabib and Lara reproduce this linguistic abstraction in their assumption of the unproblematic transmissibility of inner nature. Indeed, this linguistic abstraction is not an incidental effect of their narrative paradigms but an intrinsic feature. It is necessary to deploy a linguistically contained notion of the agonistic aspects of subjectivity in order not to disrupt the ideas of reflexivity, reciprocity and symmetry that underpin the framework of communicative recognition within which they wish to operate. To make such a criticism is not to invoke an absolutized notion of inauthenticity in the manner of, say, Žižek's unconditional insistence on the imaginary nature of subjectivity. It is, however, to throw into question the continuous and organic relation that is posited by Habermasians between experience and different modes of narrative configuration. Although Benhabib and Lara criticize Habermas for reducing identity to a set of abstract, linguistic propositions, their idea of narrative, ultimately, does not go much further in breaking down this 'epistemocentrism' (Bourdieu 2000: 60).

NARRATIVE AND AUTHENTICITY

The one-sidedly syncretic idea of narrative deployed by Habermasian feminists not only underplays discontinuities within subjectivity but also tacitly attributes an inherently authentic status to narrative identity. This is compounded by a further conflation of narrative identity with reflexive agency, that is, that the ability to narrate a coherent account of self is taken as a guarantor of a certain level of critical self-awareness. These elisions are particularly evident in Lara's argument that, rather than understanding narratives in a representational sense as effects of power and domination, they should be construed as the self-reflexive constructions of autonomous individuals. Narrative identities are achievements, guided by a ' "cognitive role": narrative agents . . . are empowered by their own choices articulated in the agency of an enactment' (Lara 1998: 71). Similarly, for Benhabib, one of the normative conditions against which the democratic potential of different cultural practices is to be assessed is that of voluntary self-ascription. The narrative identities that a culture makes available to individuals must be freely adopted rather than imposed. The deliberative democratic theorist must have 'more faith in the capacity of ordinary political actors to renegotiate their own narratives of identity and difference through multicultural encounters in a democratic civil society' (Benhabib 2002: 104). Setting aside the normative implications of such claims, the problem with Lara and Benhabib's formulations is that individual narratives constructed from below, so to speak, are treated as inherently authentic and as somehow resistant to the ideological elements in imposed narratives of cultural domination. Everyday narratives of self are held up as intrinsically coherent, meaningful, self-aware constructions. Against this tacitly normative conception, it can be argued that there are not such bright lines between imposed narratives of domination and self-ascribed, unifying narratives of self. Narratives are not just the conveyors of structure, 'smoothing, and holding' experience as Laurence Kirmayer (1996) puts it, rather they can equally be the source of crevasses, ruptures, emptiness and deep wells of non-being. Kirmayer shows, for example, how the construction of therapeutic narratives to help individuals overcome traumatic events may promote the alienation of families, oversimplify problems with complex origins and, ultimately, disempower those it aims to help by institutionalizing the position of victim. For example, the political gains conferred by a victim identity, such as a trauma survivor, are often accessible only through expert discourses, which have their own agendas and are themselves instruments of power. By their very nature, such discourses deal in causes rather than meanings, events rather than persons, instances rather than entire lives. Re-inscribing personal into expert discourses can accentuate the gulf that exists between the narrative possibilities afforded by notions of personhood, kinship and morality, on the one hand, and the dry language of bureaucracy and biopolitics, on the other.

The presumption underlying Lara and Benhabib's idea of reflexive narratives of the self is that, left to their own devices, individuals inherently will their own freedom. As Wendy Brown puts it: 'the presumption of a subject born with a passion for freedom – self-realizing in work and self-legislating in society – is . . . unquestioned, no matter how fraught the path to gaining that freedom' (Brown 2001: 47). Such a presumption disregards the effects of symbolic violence upon individuals and the possible consequent attachment to their own subjugation. Brown uses Freud to unpick the masochistic dynamics that often underpin political identity formation. Identities that arise out of a recognition of the failings of 'the liberal promise of universal personhood' are often organized around a masochistic compulsion to repeat and relive this primal injury of exclusion. The symbolic and actual violence that gives rise to politicized gender and racial identity is constantly reiterated both through repeated acts of racism and sexism and also through the subject's own compulsion to re-experience that punishment. Beyond the erotic gratification it yields, this restaging of the original trauma is generative of psychic and political reassurances. One of these reassurances is that, in an era of declining community, it creates an imaginary bond with others who share in the suffering: 'Such restaging stabilizes an identity whose traumatic formation would render unstable its political or public face: it forges a politically coherent, continuous, and conscious identity out of conflicting unconscious desires' (Brown 2001: 55). At the same time, this psychic investment in reliving the primal injury effects a kind of political paralysis of the subject. The subject remains in thrall to a compulsive oscillation between desiring to be punished through the replaying of their injuries and aggressively desiring the punishment of others for this humiliation 'while freedom, as a wish or a practice, is nowhere to be found' (Brown 2001: 61). It is this masochistic structure that arguably underlies certain discourses of victimization that have become so central to contemporary political mobilization. For some critics, the politics of recognition is the paradigm of this masochistic presentation of the self as victim (Skeggs 2004c; Berlant 2000). From this perspective on the compulsive structure of recognition claims, the authentic status imputed to narratives of the self by Lara and Benhabib is thrown deeply into question.

In their unqualified welding of narrative to reflexivity, Benhabib and Lara sidestep the issue of how the narration of identity may involve a reification as much as a clarification of the self. As Adrienna Cavarerro points out in *Retelling Narratives*, the spontaneous experience of memory within narrative is not the same as the process of reflection taken to be a characteristic of autonomous subjects. Not all memory takes the form of an active process of remembering, it can also take the form of involuntary recall or an unreflecting knowledge of self (Cavarerro 2000: 34). The narrative reconfiguration of past experience may be strongly driven by a desire to reassert the familiar which, in fact, displaces the subject–object structure of reflexivity. This drive to maintain an 'everyday certainty of the self' may reinforce an irreflexive unity of the self – analogous to Bourdieu's notion of *habitus* – as much as contribute to a critical self-awareness (Cavarerro 2000: 43). The tendency to regard narrative identity as inherently reflexive means that Habermasian feminists are in danger of reproducing a simplified model of women's agency based in a celebration of women's experience as authentic. This kind of privileging of women's experience has long been criticized by feminists but, unless the idea of narrative is considered in the context of forms of symbolic domination, feminist Habermasians seem to come close to a form of standpoint essentialism that relies on a 'sanitized idea of embodied identity where negative and unruly aspects are defined away as "not genuine" forms of relatedness' (Flax 1993: 66).

NARRATIVES AND POWER

The fugitive and complex aspects of memory and experience that may prevent the construction of reflexive narrative identity involve not just psychological issues but also raise issues of power, ideology and exclusion. The passage from experience to narrative involves not just a transition from flux to coherence but a process whereby certain ideas or persons are silenced, constituted, displaced, controlled, modified. Such processes of marginalization and exclusion may often take place at a level removed from immediate daily experience and, therefore, from conscious awareness. As Foucault remarks: 'power relations can materially penetrate the body in depth, without depending even on the mediation of the subject's own representations. If power takes hold on the body, this isn't through its having first to be interiorized in people's consciousnesses' (Foucault 1980: 186). A powerful illustration of this abstract deformation of experience is provided by Gayatri Spivak's much-cited essay 'Can the Subaltern Speak?' on the practice of sati (the self-immolation of widows) in early-nineteenth-century Bengal. Here Spivak shows how the campaign by the British to abolish widow sacrifice is framed by the two male discourses of paternalist colonialism and a resistant, patriarchal Hinduism. Although, in a literal sense, the subaltern can speak, Spivak's point is that there is no legitimate narrative position from which the widow's experience can be expressed: 'the subaltern as female cannot be heard or read' (Spivak 1988: 308). Spivak relates the widow's silence to a 'model of social indirection' understood as the dislocation of structures of representation that occurs with the mediation of experience through the abstract, impersonal structures of globalized capital. This means that individuals are often unable to fully comprehend or speak of the nature of their oppression. The passage from 'rendering visible' abstract structures of exploitation to 'rendering vocal' the individual is far from straightforward in as much as the relation between the two levels of experience is often highly mediated and dislocated. As Spivak puts it: 'On the other side of the international division of labor, the subject cannot know and speak the text of female exploitation' (Spivak 1988: 288).

By glossing over these issues connected to the mediation of experience through abstract, global systems of power, Lara and Benhabib's idea of narrative seems to problematically assume a 'naturally articulate subject of oppression' (Spivak 1988: 288). This idea of natural articulacy informs Benhabib's distinction between ascribed and voluntary narratives and Lara's reworking of the Habermasian idea of illocutionary effects. It enables the narrative model of recognition to establish a unity between identity, action and culture and it thereby ensures the universal status of communicative ethics because no culture remains entirely opaque to another, no self wholly unrecognizable to another. Benhabib argues that the criticism that marginalized groups may be unable to articulate their oppression is a 'species of exoticism' that rests on the patronizing assumption that certain individuals are beyond the reach of reason. Such criticisms are a subset of a larger group of 'incommensurability' arguments, frequently levelled against discourses ethics, which claim that its cognitive and rationalist bias tacitly excludes many different groups from participation. Such claims, in Benhabib's view, invoke a form of essentialism wherein individuals are unable to transcend the perspective generated by their social position: 'social positionality then falls into pure essentialism in that it is premised upon the reduction of structures of individual consciousness to delineated group identities' (Benhabib 2002: 137). It is erroneous to insist upon the ineluctably situated nature of social critique because the idea that the 'view from nowhere' be replaced by the 'view from somewhere' assumes that the latter is a relatively unified, self-evident and discrete body of knowledge. This hermeneutic monism overlooks the extent to which knowledge is interwoven with complex social practices and is, therefore, fragmented, discontinuous and sometimes contradictory. Furthermore, an unqualified insistence on the situated nature of critique assumes that the constitutive norms of a given culture are sufficient to enable one to exercise criticism in the name of a desirable future. All social criticism necessarily assumes a degree of distance from everyday certitudes – even if these are to be reaffirmed at a higher level of analysis and justification. In short, then, the perspectivalism of social position brings no exemption from the responsibility of normative justification lest it lead to a 'retreat from utopia' which deprives feminism of a regulative principle of hope (Benhabib et al. 1995: 28–30).

In opposing the essentialism of social position, however, Benhabib posits a countervailing essentialism where reflexive narrative identity is attributed a crypto-normative status. To question the apodictic, emancipatory awareness that Benhabib regards as residing in narrative identity is not necessarily to fall back into an unqualified perspectivalism. Indeed, in making such an argument, Benhabib seems to fall back into the same zero-sum account of reflexivity that, as we saw in the previous chapter, characterizes Habermas's thought. Unless reflexivity conforms to certain *a priori* standards of truth, or communicative rationality, then individuals cannot be said to have genuine self-knowledge at all. Reflexivity is not, however, an absolute capacity of individuals that receives its full expression in narratively mediated structures of recognition. It is a much more incomplete and intermittent feature of social interaction. To consider reflexivity in relation to social position is, therefore, not to undermine it entirely but rather to explore, in more detail than Benhabib, how the workings of power and symbolic violence both constrain and enable the individual's ability to construct a coherent narrative. To question the inherent reflexivity of narratives of the self is not to deny that individuals are capable of distancing themselves from the certitudes of everyday life. It is, however, to assert that relations of power shape and distort embodied experience in ways that often elude the individual and therefore restrict the ability to narrate a coherent account of self. It is also to query the neat distinction between imposed and self-ascribed narratives and the series of analogous distinctions it generates between the ideological and the authentic, heteronomy and autonomy, domination and resistance. Ultimately, then, their detachment from an analysis of power relations depoliticizes narrative structures and imputes to them a questionable redemptive status. This mirrors what Bourdieu has identified as a twofold process of depoliticization in Habermas's work where political power relations are reduced to those of communication which are, in turn, neutralized by being understood as reciprocal (Bourdieu 2000: 66).

This unyoking of narratives from the analysis of power is evident in Lara's assertion that the emancipatory effects of women's narratives upon the public sphere necessarily override potential antagonisms between the differing agendas of political actors (Lara 1998: 151). The assertion of an overarching bond of solidarity that transcends the heterogeneous claims of marginalized groups can only be based on an idea of political identity formation that is separated from issues of power and struggle over resources. The abstract universal equivalence posited by Lara between different narratives of emancipation effaces the concrete particularities of specific struggles and results in a depoliticization of the political realm. The same depoliticizing effect arises from Benhabib's uncritical absolutization of the narrative model of identity. In her view, one of the central problems with Taylor's model of recognition is that its culturalist orientation ignores questions of power and struggle over resources:

'This world is without conflict and contention: self-actualization claims seem to presuppose a seamless web of interlocution through which individuals are held together' (Benhabib 2002: 57). The same criticism, however, can be levelled at Benhabib's own ontology of narrative recognition which imputes the same underlying structure to all aspects of identity and action. This both simplifies the operations of narratives within social life and reduces aspects of experience that do not fit within its universal structure to the status of the marginal or anomalous.

NARRATIVE AND THE INVISIBILITY OF GENDER

The unyoking of the idea of narrative from an analysis of power can be traced to a culturalist or 'associational' mode of thinking common amongst thinkers of recognition where gender inequalities are considered primarily as lifeworld issues of identity and not as systemically perpetuated forms of discrimination (Sayer 2000). It is obviously not the case that Habermas's work lacks a theory of power. Rather the problem lies with his dichotomous account of society as system and lifeworld where the instrumental rationality of the former has distorting effects on the communicative rationality of the latter. This dualist account of power confines an understanding of gender inequalities to the cultural realm, neglecting the systemic and material dimensions in their construction. As Nancy Fraser (1989) argues, for example, Habermas regards the family solely as an institution of the lifeworld and thereby misses its 'dual aspect', i.e., that the family perpetuates systemic relations of oppression as much as it reproduces values and cultural norms. In other words, money and power do not have only an extrinsic and incidental relation to the institutions and practices of the lifeworld but are often constitutive of its core dynamics. In an analogous fashion, Habermas understands gender only as a type of identity formation (lifeworld) and not as a structuring principle of social division (system). Furthermore, the one-sided dynamic where systems unambiguously distort the structures of the lifeworld is too simplified a model with which to analyse the uneven phenomenon of gender oppression. The extension of instrumental rationality into the lifeworld undoubtedly has corrosive effects but, at the same time, it has also created new types of autonomy for women, especially in so far as increased economic independence has liberated them from oppression within the domestic realm.

It is significant that feminists, such as Benhabib and Lara, who appropriate Habermas's thought, focus only on the normative implications of communicative ethics and ignore the adequacy of this idea for a sociological analysis of gender. Social analysis and critique cannot be separated in such a stringent fashion and, indeed, both Lara and Benhabib work within the tradition of critical theory which emphasizes the dialectical relation between the two. Yet, the normative status they impute to narrative as an ideal retroactively distorts its efficacy as a category for analysing gender identity and inequalities. Their one-sided appropriation of Habermas's thought skews the dualism of system and lifeworld, compounding a 'cultural turn' where systems are reduced to the lifeworld and gender is considered almost entirely from within the paradigm of identity issues (Ray and Sayer 1999). In the communicative paradigm, for example, the idea of narrative identity remains closely wedded to notions of community as a co-presence of subjects or as face-to-face relations and, in this stress on immediacy, it misses the ways in which gender inequalities are reproduced through impersonal and global power relations, such as the gender division of labour. It is not, of course, that the consideration of gender through the prism of identity politics doesn't inevitably raise questions of material oppression. As we will see in the next chapter, issues of material redistribution are inevitably caught up in a politics of cultural recognition. The problem is more that cultural and material inequalities not only have different dynamics but also, in many cases, they have become decoupled from each other, disrupting clear patterns of determination. As Nancy Fraser puts it, 'cultural value patterns do not strictly dictate economic allocations (*contra* the culturalist theory of society), nor do economic class inequalities simply reflect status hierarchies' (Fraser 2000: 118). It is important that these disjunctions are understood if the complexities of gender oppression are to be understood. Cultural sanctions against homosexuality, for example, do not translate in a straightforward way into forms of material oppression, indeed many gay individuals are economically privileged and relatively powerful social actors (Seideman 1993). Similarly, in the labour market, the divisions between women of different classes and generations are now often as significant as those between men and women (Walby 1997). Yet these intra-gender differences do not reflect the privileging of heterosexual masculinity over femininity that still dominates symbolic systems.

In short, in an era of increasingly formal equality, gender and other inequalities are often reproduced in discontinuous and uneven ways. Systemically maintained forms of oppression, such as segregation in the workforce, do not necessarily manifest themselves in a straight-forward way at the level of immediate daily life. As feminists like Carol Brown (1981) and Sylvia Walby (1990) have pointed out, there has been a shift in the past hundred or so years from private to public patriarchy. Echoing Spivak's idea of social indirection, they argue that gender inequalities are no longer perpetuated so much through arbitrary and direct sanctions confining women to the domestic sphere but through indirect forms of economic exploitation and state inertia. These indirect and impersonal forms of oppression render gender inequality less visible because formal equality between men and women, at the level of civil and social freedoms, appears to be upheld. The distinction between private and public patriarchy is analogous to a distinction made by Iris Marion Young (1990) between oppression and domination. Domination refers to constraints upon oppressed groups to follow rules set by others, whereas oppression refers to inequalities maintained at a structural and non-intentional level where 'an oppressed group need not have a correlate oppress-ing group' (Young 1990: 41). If this distinction is applied to the work of Benhabib and Lara, it is apparent that while the ideas of narrative and communicative rationality might be able to identify forms of gender domination as explicit patriarchal sanctions, they do not so readily capture the types of systemic and impersonal gender oppres-sion associated with public patriarchy.

The ways in which personal identity is mediated through struc-tural dynamics have been explored by Aihwa Ong in her work on female workers in Mexico and Asia. Against models of capitalist development structured around schematic core–periphery distinc-tions, she found that female workers are regulated through a specific situational amalgam of industrial and social modes of domination. Certain worker identities are created for the women by articulating culturally specific mores about women's roles through the discipli-nary techniques of factory production which are reinforced, in turn, by types of state regulation. Although these strategies of identity regulation generate a few types of resistance on the part of the women subject to them, they are, in general, overwhelmingly suc-cessful in ensuring compliance and exploitation. Their success is because they are not imposed in the form of what Burawoy has char-acterized as 'despotic regimes' of peripheral regions but precisely because they operate through the more insidious techniques of the manipulation of embodied identity: 'worker consciousness and subject constitution . . . must be investigated in contexts shaped by the intersection of state agencies, the local workings of capital, and already configured local/power culture realms' (Ong 1991: 296). In

Ong's view, this disciplinary manipulation of identity confirms Spivak's view that subaltern consciousness is shaped through the locally mediated operations of transnational capital: 'the subaltern's consciousness is situational and uneven, and the subaltern's subjectivity is locally shaped and delimited' (Ong 1991: 296).

These complex ensembles of power where systemic forms of oppression mediate embodied identity are not accessible within the concept of narrative identity as it is thematized by Habermasian feminists. On their view, narrative is understood in the context of a phenomenological analysis of social experience but this is disconnected from a sufficiently thorough analysis of power relations. It is by reconnecting these two levels of analysis that a more critical perspective can be developed on the ways in which embodied reality and the ability to turn that reality into a coherent narration are fostered and negated, over-determined and distorted by impersonal structures of power. From a conceptual perspective, Iris Marion Young's work on gender as a series spells out some of the analytical weaknesses of the theoretical commitment to the phenomenal immediacy of the notion of narrative identity. Young takes the idea of the series from Sartre's taxonomy, in *A Critique of Dialectical Reason*, of different types of collective organization in social life. The meaning of the series emerges in contrast to that of the group. The idea of the group implies high levels of internal organization, shared interests and mutual identification. This elevated level of reflexivity within the group often results in collective action: it is a 'self-consciously, mutually acknowledging collective with a self-conscious purpose' (Young 1994b: 724). The idea of the series denotes a more passive type of social collective which Sartre famously captures in the idea of the queue. The unity of the series is established by a similar orientation, amongst its members, to the material environment but this in no way implies identification with other members of the series. Unity is generated only through the rationalized conditions of social life and the accumulated force of latent social structures (*pratico-inert*). Thus, individuals waiting for a bus share a minimal collective orientation towards a material object (the bus) and all observe the social conventions of queuing. Beyond the shared goal of wanting to catch the bus, there is no mutual identification amongst members of the queue. Indeed, individuals experience each other within the series as anonymous, isolated entities (Young 1994b: 724–5). Young's central point is that the idea of the series applied to an understanding of gender can help overcome the problem of essentialism in feminist theory and politics. By conceptualizing gender as a serial collective, it is possible to understand how women are similarly situated with regard to certain materially conditioned aspects of their experience such as the gender division of labour. This shared situation does not imply anything, however, in terms of a unity of immediate experience. There is no commonality that necessarily arises from shared oppression or mutual identification. In short, the idea of the series promotes an understanding of gender as a systemically generated hierarchy and not just as a mode of embodied being created through immediate interaction. A problem with the idea of narrative recognition is that its focus on face-to-face interaction leads to a one-dimensional understanding of gender as interpersonally generated identity. This idea cannot explain how, in late-capitalist societies, gender inequalities are created as much through impersonal and structural modes of oppression as direct domination. These systemic forces may certainly manifest themselves as the felt necessities of embodied existence but the discontinuous and non-synchronous processes through which they are often mediated elude the undifferentiated phenomenalism of the idea of narrative identity. As long as it remains detached from an analysis of underlying power relations, the use of narrative as a normative category seems to be what Nancy Fraser (1995) has called 'an abstract promise' that the social order could be otherwise, which does little to explain the material and cultural forces that constitute the uneven phenomenon of gender oppression.

HAVING IT BOTH WAYS: NARRATIVE AND UNIVERSALISM

Ultimately, the difficulties with Benhabib's and Lara's formulations of narrative stem from the attempt to render the category consistent with the normative demands of communicative recognition. The idea of narrative identity is regarded as the vehicle through which an enlarged notion of subjectivity can be used to modify the rational and tacitly masculine notion of moral reasoning that underpins Habermas's thought. At the same time, however, the narratively enlarged understanding of subjectivity cannot be taken so far that it disrupts the process of the rational reconstruction of validity claims that is essential to debate in the ideal speech situation. The attempt to reconcile these two conflicting tendencies results in the reliance on normatively one-sided ideas of narrative identity as a reflexive unity. Ultimately, this reconciliation fails on more fundamental grounds, namely, on the underlying incompatibility between the particularist orientation of the idea of narrative and the universal orientation of communicative ethics.

It is significant that Habermas not only does not connect communicative competence to narrative identity but, in fact, his definition of rational discourse outlaws the narrative form from the ideal speech situation (Habermas 1998a). In order to make it possible to adjudicate between different validity claims and to render speakers equal in the ideal speech situation, language must be rendered as neutral and rational as possible. To this end, the world-disclosing function of 'poetic' uses of language must be subordinated to the bonding illocutionary force of rationally structured, communicative speech. This privileging of the illocutionary over the perlocutionary permits speakers to express themselves as sincerely as possible with regard to three types of validity claim (truth, meaningfulness, sincerity) without the playful detours of rhetoric: 'The peculiar disempowerment of speech acts, which generates fictions, consists in the fact that speech acts are robbed of their illocutionary force, retaining illocutionary meanings only as refracted by indirect reporting or quotation' (Habermas 1998a: 390). There is no doubt, as we have seen in the second chapter, that Habermas's stringent definition of rational discourse is highly problematic, but it is necessarily so in order to establish the universal grounds for open and equal debate. In the ideal speech situation, speakers must conform to the rules of rational discourse and it is only on the basis of these that they can adjudicate between different validity claims and arrive at universally legitimate conclusions. As an unstable mixture of fact and fabulation, narrative as a perlocutionary and rhetorical form of speech does not conform to Habermas's definition of rational discourse (Habermas 1998a: 391). The feminist Habermasian attempt to synthesize narrative with the communicative paradigm is problematic, therefore, in that it disrupts Habermas's distinction between poetic and communicative uses of language and, in this intermingling of the rational with the rhetorical, removes the grounds from which it is possible to adjudicate between different validity claims. In other words, in trying to modify and extend the Habermasian framework, Benhabib and Lara weaken the rational and symmetrical character of the ideal speech situation from which universal claims to truth are ultimately derived.

In her earlier work, Benhabib seems to recognize the potentially destabilizing implications that the idea of narrative may have for communicative ethics. In a response to Iris Marion Young's (1996) argument that the terms of communicative debate should be broadened to include rhetorical modes such as story telling, Benhabib accuses her of weakening the impartial status of rational debate. She argues that social justice would be limited because the rhetorical effects of narrative have an ineffable effect on individuals which is not amenable to rational reconstruction in the same way as the *post-hoc* validity claims underlying speech acts. Without some impartial standard of deliberation, the outcome of debates would be capricious and arbitrary: 'Young could not differentiate the genuine transformation of partial and situated perspectives from the mere agreements of convenience or apparent unanimity reached under conditions of duress' (Benhabib 1996: 82). Yet, in her subsequent work on narrative recognition, Benhabib seems to have abandoned these reservations altogether. It is the case that her work on narrative does not explicitly address the specific mode of debate to be undertaken within communicative ethics. Thus, it is possible that although narrative self-understanding is a crucial stage to be attained prior to communicative debate, the debate itself could assume a more rational form. It is unlikely, however, that Benhabib would make such a move, indeed it would contradict the ethos of all her revisions to communicative ethics. Given the ontological status she attributes to narrative structures in the constitution of identity, it would seem inconsistent to ban it as a legitimate form of self-expression in democratic dialogue. If narrative is as central to self-understanding as Benhabib claims, it becomes difficult to proscribe it on the grounds that it is an arbitrary rhetorical device whose capricious effects need to be excluded from rational debate. Nor does Benhabib suggest, following Habermas in his later work, that issues about identity recognition must be raised as a crucial precondition of democratic debate, but these issues cannot themselves form part of communicative debates about moral norms. Indeed, to follow Habermas in this respect would be at odds with her earlier work on the 'concrete other' where she rightly criticizes him for the arbitrary formalism of his separation of the moral from the good. Her understanding of narratives as inherently evaluative forms suggests that moral argumentation cannot be so easily detached from the structures in which it presents itself to individuals in daily life.

To point out this unaddressed conflict in the work of Benhabib and other feminist Habermasians is not to argue against narrative as a powerful political tool in democratic debate. Plenty of critics have made strong cases for narrative both as a way of rendering the process of rational deliberation and debate more inclusive and also as a key strategy for mobilization in identity politics (e.g. see Dryzek 2000: 68; Young 2000: 70–7). Nor is it to argue against the idea that democratic politics should aim to be universal in scope, at least in some sense. There are many types of political thought that attempt to ground democratic debate in a weak or qualified universalism – i.e., a universalism not derived from ontological or metaphysical arguments about human nature or rationality; the arguments, for example, of Butler, Laclau and Žižek (2000) about contingent universalism or those of Rawls, Derrida and Rorty which seek to dissociate legal universalism from any essentialist underpinnings. Benhabib rejects these delimited formulations of universalism, however, in favour of Habermas's definition of the universal in terms of the normative content of reason. It is only in the light of her commitment to the universal status of rational discourse that the idea of narrative becomes problematic because it undermines the transcendental status she wishes to claim for her reconfiguration of communicative debate. To be sure, Benhabib states that the argument about the universal rationality embedded in speech acts is only 'weakly' transcendental in the sense that it does not have any strong ontological or metaphysical entailments. But, it is not clear whether the distinction between weak and strong transcendentalism amounts to anything more than a semantic distinction. However, even if the distinction were viable, the idea of weak transcendentalism does not solve the problem for Benhabib, namely that the attempt to integrate a theory of narrative identity into communicative ethics jeopardizes the very terms in which the universal status of the latter is maintained.

CONCLUSION

In sum, feminist Habermasians cannot have it both ways. The attempt to combine a theory of narrative identity with the strong universal claims of communicative recognition results in the contradictions and limitations discussed above. Benhabib and Lara can only retain a universal basis for feminist critique by tacitly invoking a delimited and problematic concept of narrative which underplays the complexities of gender identity and, in some ways, replicates rather than overcomes the rationalist tendencies in Habermas's work. If a more complex theory of narrative identity is to be deployed then it must be at the cost of losing the communicative paradigm's claim to universal status. The tensions in Benhabib's and Lara's narrative reconfiguration of communicative ethics clarify more general difficulties confronting a feminist appropriation of the idea of recognition. Ultimately, the idea does not permit a sufficiently differentiated account of power with which to examine the reproduction of gender identity and inequality. The interpersonal conception of power inherent to their idea of narrative recognition occludes an understanding of the way in which identities are mediated through structural dynamics of inequality. Furthermore, its commitment to a concept of power as face-to-face interaction results in the deployment of normative notions of identity that have been largely purged of destructive or negative elements. Many feminists have noted the analytical difficulties that arise from a reliance on sanitized accounts of feminine identity. It seems, however, that the tendency to produce 'good girl' images of subjectivity is, nonetheless, deeply rooted in certain types of normative feminist thought and the idea of recognition only reinforces, rather than dislodges it.

4

Recognition and Redistribution

INTRODUCTION

Of all the work on recognition in the past decade, it is perhaps that of Axel Honneth and Nancy Fraser which most consistently places a discussion of identity and agency in the context of an extended analysis of power relations. Both thinkers approach the idea of recognition from the perspective of social theory and they therefore aim to ground the normative political implications of their work in a critical analysis of contemporary power relations. In their recent wide-ranging debate, a basic disagreement emerges between Fraser and Honneth about how to characterize the dynamics underlying contemporary social and political conflict. For Honneth, all such conflicts, including those over economic distribution, are variants of a fundamental struggle for recognition which itself is the key to understanding the long-term development of social interaction in capitalist societies. Against this, Fraser argues that struggles for recognition, such as identity politics, are analytically distinct from conflicts over redistribution. Both are fundamental to social justice but are irreducible to each other.

I explore this debate from the perspective of the concept of agency that each thinker deploys, in an explicit or latent way, to mobilize their political paradigms. For Honneth, social and political agency can be traced back to the moral suffering that arises from the myriad ways in which the basic human need for recognition is disregarded in unequal societies. In his view, the idea of suffering yields an account of the emotional grounds of agency that is arguably more compelling than the instrumental and interest-based conceptions that prevail in conventional sociological accounts of action. However, Honneth's social theory lacks an explanation of how this underlying affective impulse is mediated through symbolic and material power relations and he finishes with a naïve, spontaneist account of action. This lack of a theory of mediation is compounded in his subsequent thesis that, in late modernity, the subject is able to embrace difference and otherness because of an internal capacity to let down inner defensive barriers, what Honneth terms an internal 'liquefaction of the ego'. The difficulty is that Honneth derives this capacity from the argument that the internal structure of the self unproblematically mirrors the interactive structure of wider social relations. By totalizing the interactive structure of recognition in this way, however, any tension between the individual and wider social relations is dissolved. Thus he is unable to explain, in any other terms than passive conformity, how it is that individuals are able to act autonomously at all.

Nancy Fraser criticizes Honneth for the subjectivist orientation of his formulation of recognition. As an antidote to this subjectivism, she reconfigures the idea of recognition so that misrecognition is defined as a form of institutionalized status subordination rather than a psychological injury. She also supplements the idea of a cultural politics of recognition with that of a materialist politics of redistribution. While her critique of Honneth is forceful, she falls into a counter-veiling objectivism which prevents her from developing some of the central insights of her own paradigm. Her 'non-identitarian' rendering of recognition leads her to abandon an experiential or interpretative perspective that is associated with identity. Lacking this perspective she is unable to explore types of social suffering that cannot be captured in the dualism of recognition and redistribution, the emergence of agency and the ways in which the subjective and objective dimensions of oppression are related.

In developing my argument and a possible way beyond this impasse of objectivism and subjectivism, I draw on Bourdieu's notion of habitus. Expressed in this idea is the same initial insight as Honneth's work on recognition, namely that a phenomenological emphasis on experience is crucial to uncovering certain aspects of oppression and resistance. However, as a way of explaining how power relations are incorporated into the body as physical and psychological dispositions, habitus prevents the naturalization of the cluster of emotions associated with social suffering that is the consequence of Honneth's ontology of recognition. At the same time, the experiential emphasis of habitus mitigates the objectivism of

Fraser's alternative account of recognition and redistribution, showing how some of its central insights may be taken further.

HONNETH: SOCIETY AS A RECOGNITION ORDER

One of the problems with recent theories of recognition is, as we have seen, the often unacknowledged ways in which its normative sense gets entangled with its use as a heuristic tool to describe social relations. This conflation of the normative with the descriptive results in a simplification of social and political relations by positing their foundation in the interpersonal dyad of a struggle for recognition. As a result, debates on the politics of recognition often get caught up in disputes about the extent to which identities are authentic and integral. Axel Honneth's work tries to avoid some of the problems that ensue from this conflation by defining his social theory as an explicit attempt to mediate the two senses of recognition as a normative and a descriptive category. On his twofold understanding, recognition describes both the basic intersubjective structure of social relations and also refers to the overall normative direction of social development in that its most fully realized form represents the maximal conditions for positive self-realization and personal integrity. Honneth makes the further claim that, by deriving normative conclusions from empirical foundations, his critical social theory yields a formal conception of ethical life that overcomes the impasse between universal notions of morality, on the one hand, and particularist notions of ethics, on the other.

Honneth's basic argument is that the desire for recognition is so fundamental to individual self-realization that it is the motivating force behind social development. This primal need is institutionalized in distinctive ways within each of the three principal spheres of social interaction: love, law and achievement. These correspond roughly to Hegel's division of society into family, state and civil society. Of these three spheres, it is the area of love (family) which is the most fundamental because it institutionalizes social interaction based on the principles of affection and care which are essential to the emergence of stable subjectivity and self-respect (Honneth 1995: 107; Fraser and Honneth 2003: 139). Affective recognition receives its primary institutional expressions in the bourgeois 'love marriage' and the recognition of childhood as a distinct and special phase of human development. However, the growing complexity and differentiation of capitalist social relations ceaselessly multiplies and refines the demands for different types of affective recognition. For example, in late capitalist society, there is an increasing acknowledgement that the nuclear, heterosexual family is not the only 'legitimate' way to meet the needs of individuals for care and affection. Affective recognition is the fundamental bedrock from which autonomous participation in public life becomes possible and, as such, forms the 'structural core of all ethical life' (1995: 107).

From the grounds of affective recognition emerge the two further types of legal and status recognition. The emergence and growth of capitalist society is characterized by the formation of an autonomous sphere of law which institutionalizes the principle of legal equality and grants an increasing array of rights to individuals. The formal, institutional nature of legal recognition means that it cannot be said to embody an interpersonal reciprocity between subjects in the way that affective and, to some degree, status recognition clearly do. The indeterminacy inherent in notions of what constitutes a legal person and rights, however, opens up instituted forms of legal recognition to challenge from marginal and excluded social groups. There is a 'structural openness' to legal forms of recognition which means that, as they are contested, they gradually become more inclusive and precise (Honneth 1995: 110). Status recognition or social esteem is closely linked to the institutionalization of the principle of legal equality. The democratization of forms of legal recognition highlights the persistence of unjust value hierarchies and the lack of social esteem accorded to certain individuals and groups within civil society. In Marx's terms, the gap between formal and substantive rights becomes increasingly apparent. An obvious example is the discrepancy between the extension of legal rights to women and people of colour over the course of the twentieth century and the persistent denial of respect and esteem to these same groups through endemic sexism and racism (Fraser and Honneth 2003: 141). It is only through the promotion of proactive networks of social solidarity that the esteem of groups and individuals can be protected (Honneth 1995: 127–30).

The relations between these three spheres of recognition are complex and uneven and their internal levels of development are non-synchronous. These three orders share, however, a long-term trajectory towards the provision of greater opportunities for the positive expression of individuality: 'with each newly emerging sphere of mutual recognition, another aspect of human subjectivity is revealed which individuals can now positively ascribe to themselves intersubjectively' (Fraser and Honneth 2003: 143). Furthermore, underlying all three forms of mutual recognition is a discernible set of uniting normative principles that enable individuals and groups to argue that existing forms of recognition are inadequate and should be extended. Other types of social relation are not based in such normative principles and thus mutual recognition is the most fundamental type of social interaction. Indeed, Honneth makes the strong claim that modern societies are imperfect realizations of a normatively guided recognition order. The 'surplus validity' of these normative recognition orders vis-à-vis their empirically realized forms provides a moral standard and justification against which experiences of injustice and disrespect can be measured. All social and political conflict has a normative core which ultimately stems from the fundamental yearning for recognition: 'If the adjective "social" is to mean anything more than "typically found in society", social suffering and discontent possess a *normative* core . . . such feelings of discontent and suffering . . . coincide with the experience that society is doing something unjust, something unjustifiable' (Fraser and Honneth 2003: 129).

INTEREST AND ETHICS

One of the central claims that Honneth makes for his normative approach to the analysis of social recognition is that it offers a fuller account of the motivations for agency and resistance than is generally available in sociology. On Honneth's view, classical sociology either empties social change of any element of confrontation by rendering it an effect of long-term structural tendencies as, for example, in the functionalist accounts of Durkheim or Parsons. Or, it explains change in terms of individual or group struggles for power (Weber) or objective inequalities (Marx) that downplay the dimensions of moral indignation or suffering that often catalyse social conflict: 'The motives for rebellion, protest and resistance have generally been transformed into categories of "interest" and these interests are supposed to emerge from the objective inequalities in the distribution of material opportunities without ever being linked . . . to the everyday web of moral feelings' (Honneth 1995: 161). Against an interest-based conception of agency, Honneth's model highlights the emotional grounds of action, in particular the suffering that arises from disrespect and the moral insights that it generates: 'In the context of the emotional responses associated with shame, the experience of being disrespected can become the motivational impetus for a struggle for recognition' (Honneth 1995: 138). Suffering can generate moral insights which, in turn, can take the form of political resistance. While it is possible to experience shame and misrecognition in the arena of love, this most basic form of recognition cannot directly give rise to social struggle because its agonistic concerns cannot be generalized beyond the arena of primary relationships to become a matter of public concern. Claims for legal and social recognition, however, can be the basis for social conflict because they operate according to generalized criteria. In so far as individual experiences of disrespect can be interpreted as typical for an entire group, they may form the basis of struggles for recognition. Hurt feelings can become the motivational grounds for collective resistance only if individuals can articulate them within shared interpretative frameworks that are characteristic of a given group. The recognition model of struggle provides, therefore, a 'semantic bridge' between personal and impersonal goals in a way that abstract, utilitarian notion of interest cannot: 'the struggle can . . . only be determined by those *universal* ideas and appeals in which individual actors see their particular experiences of disrespect eliminated in a positive manner' (1995: 163). It has the further advantage over interest models of conflict in that it does not insist on the intentional nature of struggle; actors do not have to be aware of the latent moral motivations of their actions. It can explain, for example, movements that misidentify the moral core of their resistance by setting out their aims in terms of interest categories instead of status injury. Nonetheless, Honneth does not intend his recognition model of struggle to replace utilitarian models but rather to extend them. Indeed, the two are interlinked in that struggles for social esteem often correlate to concerns about control over certain material goods or resources.

Honneth claims a second advantage to his normative approach to recognition, namely that it generates a formal conception of ethical life that bypasses the split between universal notions of morality and particularist notions of ethics familiar from the debate between liberals and communitarians over justice and the good life. Liberals, on the one side, mobilize a neo-Kantian conception of universal morality where individuals are respected equally as ends in themselves or as autonomous persons. The Aristotelian response made by communitarians, on the other side, is that the notion of autonomy is emptied of substantive content when persons are antecedently individuated, that is, when they are detached from the ethical context of their particular lifeworld (see Mulhall and Swift 1992). In this view, the validity of moral principals is bound up with 'historically variant conceptions of the good life'; however, this inevitably seems to entail some degree of ethical relativism (Honneth 1995: 172). Honneth argues that his formulation of recognition as a structural principle governing social life bypasses this problematic relativism without resorting to the abstract procedural solutions of liberals such as Rawls. Recognition acknowledges the determinate content of individual self-realization that is manifest in a plurality of concrete instantiations. It transcends this particularism, however, in so far as it is a universal structural feature of social life and a normative precondition for individual autonomy. Recognition: 'has to do with the structural elements of ethical life, which, from the general point of view of the communicative enabling of self-realization, can be normatively extracted from the plurality of all particular forms of life' (Honneth 1995: 172). In this respect, Honneth's work on recognition resembles that of Selya Benhabib in that it attempts to revise some of the weaknesses of Habermas's discourse ethics. The idea of misrecognition as moral suffering injects a substantive, experiential dimension into the formal structure of communicative ethics whilst retaining Habermas's insight into the irremediably intersubjective structure of sociality and morality (see Honneth 1994).

Honneth claims that his formulation of the idea of recognition supplies social theory with a reconfigured notion of agency and that it overcomes the separation between the just and the good are ambitious. In what follows, I show that Honneth can only sustain them by setting up a tendentious ontology of recognition that runs counter to a social theoretical understanding of power and misrecognizes the nature of agency and oppression. He derives this ontology from object relations theory and his unqualified reliance upon it undermines an adequate understanding of the mediated nature of power relations. As a result, his construal of the suffering that catalyses struggles for recognition is naturalized to such a degree that agency is deprived of much social specificity. Furthermore, he is unable to relinquish such an ontology because then his normative claim that recognition constitutes the universal structure of ethical life would also fall.

RECOGNITION AS A UNIVERSAL STRUCTURE

What are the grounds that enable Honneth to make the strong, quasi-functionalist claim that recognition is the latent integrative principle and normative telos of the social development of modern societies? At first sight, it appears to rest on not much more than Honneth's frequent assertions that the universal scope of recognition is borne out by his empirical observations of the nature of social relations and action. Such a strategy, according to Christopher Zurn, seems to invoke an Hegelian style of argument about the immanent direction of historical progress 'as a progressive unfolding of the ideal of individual fulfilment in non-coercive social relations' (Zurn 2000: 121). It is not clear, however, that Honneth does establish empirically that the desire for recognition is a universal constant throughout history and across most or all cultures. The problem remains for Honneth to show that it is self-realization through intersubjective recognition rather than any other principle that should be the governing ideal of social organization: 'Why self-realization and not pious self-abnegation, or virtuous subservience to communal ends, or righteous obedience to the moral law, or maximization of the pleasure of others, etc?' (Zurn 2000: 121). There is also the further difficulty with this type of teleological argument that the claim of the structural inevitability of recognition comes close to rendering agency an empty category.

Even if it were possible to empirically establish that struggles for recognition were empirically universal phenomena, it would still be possible to arrive at different conclusions than the normative ones that Honneth reaches. For Foucault, for example, the pervasive desire for recognition would be a manifestation of an encroaching governmental power that controls individuals by manipulating the type of relation they have with themselves. The inculcation in individuals of a preoccupation with the self is not only compatible with an individualized consumerism, but also diffuses energies that might otherwise be directed towards more radical forms of social transformation. From a Foucauldian perspective, the quest for recognition shares the same structure as the confessional – the paradigm of disciplinary power – where individuals seek self-legitimation through being acknowledged within the normalizing discourses of authority. From this perspective, what Honneth regards as the spontaneous and innate nature of the desire for recognition is an example of how, in late modernity, disciplinary structures have been so thoroughly internalized by individuals that they have become self-policing subjects. In a similar fashion, Bourdieu understands recognition as an internalized misrecognition of the inequalities of social existence.

To sustain, therefore, the strong claim that recognition is the latent integrative principle and normative telos of modern social development, Honneth bolsters his shaky historical arguments with an ontological one. Recognition orders are accorded their universal status and normative pre-eminence over other types of social interaction on the basis that they are constitutive of human development. Honneth's primary source for his ontology of recognition is the work of object relations theorists, most notably that of Donald Winnicott and Jessica Benjamin (Honneth 1995: 96–107; 1999). As we saw in Chapter 1, both Winnicott and Benjamin use a reworked version of Hegel's master–slave dialectic to explain the primal relationship between parent and child and the establishment of the infant's ego-identity. An infant gains its primary sense of self from parental acknowledgement but her egomaniacal tendencies also drive her to want to control the process of recognition through domination and even destruction of the parent. Stable identity is established when the parent neither submits to the child's demands nor punitively withholds recognition. If the mother establishes herself as 'reliable' by neither punishing the child nor yielding to her, the child can become autonomous by developing a sense of confidence and an ability to be alone (Honneth 1995: 104). It is from this developmental account that Honneth derives the justification for the animating idea of his social theory, namely that self-realization is optimally fulfilled through recognition.

There are many problems that arise for Honneth's sociology of recognition by grounding it in such a strong ontogenetic claim. Setting aside for a moment the particular difficulties that present themselves to a social theory, there are compelling reasons, as we have already seen, to regard the object relations' conflation of the formation of subjectivity with a struggle for recognition as a tendentious view of human development. One central problem is whether it is appropriate to even characterize the primal mother–child dyad as a struggle for recognition given that the infant has not attained the level of consciousness that the model seems to require. Honneth does not appear to question this founding assumption for, if he were to do so, the primacy he accords recognition dynamics in social and ethical life would also be undermined. Even if it were possible to agree with Honneth that the desire for recognition is constitutive of the basic structure of subjectivity, it does not necessarily justify the normative status that he attributes to it. The assumption that Honneth makes is that, when it is realized in interpersonal relations, recognition forms stable and mature personalities and that this is the foundation for the generalization of the normatively desirable qualities of tolerance and the acceptance of difference to all aspects of social life. The questionable nature of these claims can be highlighted, however, by contrasting the object relations approach with other perspectives in developmental psychology. From the perspective of ego-psychologists such as Anna Freud, for example, even 'secure' and 'healthy' persons have 'complex and fragmented cognitive and affective structures' which means that they may interact defensively, aggressively and violently. As Alexander and Lara put it: '"Confident" people can be, and have been, anti-Semitic, racist and misogynist' (Alexander and Lara 1996: 131). In this regard,

Honneth's naïve psychologism reconfirms a more general critique made of object relations theory, namely that its investment in the ideal of mutual recognition necessarily downplays moments of negativity and breakdown in interaction by rendering them incidental rather than inherent to the self–other dynamic.

It is this normative version of interpersonal interaction that informs the larger, untested assumption at the heart of his work, that struggles for recognition will inevitably result in progressive social change. By positing a single underlying motor to social development, his theory of recognition posits a false unity and cohesion to social formations in a manner not unlike certain types of functionalist sociology that claim that social development is basically integrative in nature. In Honneth's case, the binding dynamic of integration is replaced by the progressive historical realization of expanded forms of recognition. This exposes Honneth's social theory to many of the criticisms levelled at functionalist explanation, *inter alia*, that social development is based on a questionable teleology and that it underestimates the negativity of social conflict and agency. The most insuperable difficulty in Honneth's recognition paradigm, however, is that power relations are always viewed as *ex posteriori* effects of a fundamental psychic dynamic. In other words, the ontology of recognition produces a psychologically reductive social theory where social relations are persistently viewed as extrapolations from the primary dyad of recognition. This both sentimentalizes social relations but also obscures their complex nature, in the sense that they are mediated through latent dynamics of money and power. This affective reductionism is evident, for example, in Honneth's account of relations within the family which are misunderstood as imperfect expressions of a principle of care. For Honneth, the family is the primary site through which the need for affective recognition is satisfied, enabling individuals to develop confidence and self-esteem. This normative view of the family is problematic on many levels. It drives a theoretical wedge between the realms of the domestic and the social, reifying the former as the emotional foundation of society. Such a view ignores the extent to which the family is no longer the exclusive locus for the reproduction of intimate relations which, according to some commentators, have become increasingly unbounded (Jamieson 1998). It also overlooks the extent to which the family and its internal dynamics are contingent historical structures shaped by the forces of money and social control (e.g. Donzelot 1979; Shapiro 2001: 58–66). From a materialist feminist perspective, Honneth's idea of affective recognition is based on a mystification of women's domestic labour (Fraser and Honneth 2003:

220; Thistle 2000). Fraser argues that 'marriage has never been regulated by the principle of care' and that such a view is underpinned by a failure to recognize that the family has always been a 'dual aspect' institution (Fraser and Honneth 2003: 219). Familial relations cannot be said to be oriented solely around a normatively secured logic; they are also traversed and determined by the steering media of money and power evident, for example, in negotiations over domestic finance, domestic violence, abuse, etc: 'families are thoroughly permeated with . . . the media of money and power. They are sites of egocentric, strategic and instrumental calculation as well as sites of usually exploitative exchanges of services, labor, cash, and sex – and, frequently, sites of coercion and violence' (Fraser 1989: 120).

The reductive consequences of interpreting social structures and relations in terms of a fundamental need for recognition are not confined to Honneth's account of the sphere of love but also limit his understanding of the legal and cultural spheres. His claim that the development of modernity is accompanied by a progressive expansion of legal forms of recognition is based on a one-sided reading of the history of the development of law. On his view, it is the generality or abstract nature of legal structures that renders them peculiarly amenable to expansion in response to the claims of different groups to autonomy and self-respect. Jeffrey Alexander and Maria Pia Lara point out, however, that the generalization of legal forms does not automatically entail the expansion of the recognition of autonomy, as is evident in the examples of the imposition of apartheid laws in South Africa during the 1940s and the more recent legal attempts to limit access to social benefits in the past twenty or so years in welfare states (Alexander and Lara 1996: 133). Furthermore, the depiction of the relation between the individual and the state as one of legal recognition rests on a naïvely reductive understanding of power relations. The idea that subjects are connected to the state through legal relations of recognition overlooks the ways in which the state uses this same idea to foreclose possibilities for radical action. It is, according to Patchen Markell, a form of 'liberal wish fulfilment' that disregards the extent to which legal recognition is formulated as an individual bourgeois property relation in order to pre-empt any possibility of collective action (Markell 2003: 187). Similarly, as numerous critics of multiculturalism have pointed out, recognition struggles within the cultural terrain might equally result in balkanization and isolationism rather than, as Honneth claims, in the expansion of more elaborate forms of social solidarity where 'subjects mutually sympathize with their various different ways of life because, among themselves, they esteem each other symmetrically' (Honneth 1995: 128).

The source of these normative psychological reductions is, according to Alexander and Lara, because Honneth fails to appreciate the 'illocutionary' dimensions of institutions and conflicts. Drawing on Habermas, they define illocutionary dimensions as the symbolic and linguistic resources available in the interactional and cultural structures of the lifeworld. It is these resources that actors draw on to frame their claims when they are engaged in social and political struggles. The idea of illocutionary force draws attention to the contingent and constructed nature of identity. Thus, for example, the success of the women's movement in the 60s and 70s was because, in part, feminists transformed gender consciousness and created new empowered subject positions for women. The idea of illocutionary effects reverses the causality that Honneth establishes, where psychological motivations precede social movements; instead, social forces are regarded as creating empowering psychological conditions: 'Women empowered themselves by the performative effectiveness of their claims to recognition, not by the psychological effectiveness of such claims' (Alexander and Lara 1996: 1320). Alexander and Lara are certainly right to draw attention to Honneth's lack of a theory of mediation; however, it is not clear that the Habermasian idea of illocutionary force that they draw upon provides sufficient conceptual resources for a more sociological account of power relations. Indeed, given that Habermas's version of recognition relies on a series of problematic linguistic reductions, it seems to raise as many difficulties in terms of an account of power as Honneth's ontology of recognition (see Chapter 2).

Honneth is not unaware of the dangers of grounding a social theory in an ontology of recognition. He claims that he does not reduce recognition struggles to effects of an overriding psychological imperative but rather proposes a model of mutual inherence and determination between psyche and society. Although the need for recognition is pre-social, it is only ever manifested in variable and socially specific forms (Fraser and Honneth 2003: 131–2). It is hard to see, however, how the claim that forms of recognition are entirely shaped by social forces is not undermined by the positing of a self-same dynamic of recognition that is the ubiquitous driving force behind social transformation. Honneth's inability to break out of this circular logic and its de-historicizing consequences can be seen most clearly if we consider his thematization of the emotional dimensions of agency as a 'phenomenology of social experiences of injustice' (Fraser and Honneth 2003: 114). One of the consequences of his ontology of recognition is that these emotions of suffering are understood as spontaneous and self-evident phenomena rather than as the effects of the operations of power upon the body. This naturalization of emotions results in a naïve and elliptical account of the movement from suffering to agency in struggles for recognition.

SUFFERING, OPPOSITIONAL CONSCIOUSNESS, ACTION

There is no doubt that Honneth's phenomenology of social suffering emphasizes a crucial realm of catalysing emotional experience that remains hidden in the rational and instrumental orientation of other sociological perspectives. The difficulty is that the unidirectional causal dynamic of his ontology of recognition, where social relations are seen as extrapolations of psychic dynamics, reifies these emotions and the realm of experience in general. The pre-political realm of social suffering is seen as a realm of unmediated experience characterized by spontaneous and authentic feelings with inherent moral status. It is not evident, however, that all suffering leads to any kind of political insight or can be accorded such moral significance in the politics of experience, and this is partly because all experience is mediated through a web of potentially distorting symbolic relations. Honneth might accept, in theory, such an idea of mediation but, in practice, his ontology of recognition prevents him from developing such an account and this results in an elliptical and spontaneist account of the relationship between suffering and agency.

The naïvety of Honneth's phenomenology of social suffering can be illustrated in comparison with the Bourdieusian idea of habitus. From this perspective, emotions are not elemental or spontaneous givens but are a type of social relation that are generated by, and mediate the interactions between, embodied subjects and social structures. Bourdieu would agree with Honneth that a phenomenological emphasis on social suffering is crucially important to bring to light hidden types of oppression and non-institutionalized forms of conflict (Bourdieu 1992, 2000). Indeed, Honneth recognizes this affinity in his debate with Fraser where he approvingly cites Bourdieu's work on social suffering (Fraser and Honneth 2003: 118–20). *Contra* Honneth, however, Bourdieu describes this recovery of an 'unformulated, repressed discourse' as part of a wider relational phenomenology that attempts to situate experience within the complex set of symbolic and material relations that explicitly and implicitly structure it (Bourdieu 1990a: 132). As Bourdieu puts it, 'the most personal is the most impersonal . . . many of the most intimate dramas, the deepest malaises, the most singular suffering that women and men can experience find their roots in the objective contradictions, constraints and double binds inscribed in the structures of the labour and housing markets, . . .' (1992: 201). This relational phenomenology does not deny the validity of suffering but it does complicate the moral status that Honneth attributes to it and the spontaneous theory of agency he derives from it. The idea of habitus as internalized misrecognition reminds us that there is no pre-political realm of suffering – no discourse that "speaks for itself" – waiting to be discovered (Bourdieu et al. 1999: 621). In a discussion of method, he warns against the 'spontaneistic illusion' of uncovering authentic experience, arguing that often the impression of authenticity arises from a 'false, collusive objectification' between sociologist and interviewee (Bourdieu et al. 1999: 216). All experience is shaped by pre-constituted discourses; in particular, hegemonic media representations which penetrate the discourse of the disadvantaged, providing them with 'ready-made terms for what they believe to be their experience' (Bourdieu et al. 1999: 620). For example, *The Weight of the World* considers the sociological issues raised when deprived individuals use racist views to express their oppression (Bourdieu et al. 1999: 80–1, 223), This is why, without wanting to devalue the experiential, Bourdieu insists that 'social agents . . . do not necessarily have access to the core principles of their discontent or malaise, and, without aiming to mislead, their most spontaneous declarations may express something quite different from what they seem to say' (Bourdieu et al. 1999: 620).

If material and symbolic violence permeates all levels of social experience by being mediated through dispositions, then there is no straightforward continuum between social suffering and its manifestation in oppositional consciousness. There is no doubt that moral suffering might reveal forms of injustice that would otherwise remain invisible from a perspective that seeks to establish a material or rational interest (e.g. Honneth 2004: 475). However, on Honneth's subjectivist model, suffering is conflated with a critical awareness of injustice which is, in turn, conflated with agency. Indeed, this presumption is so strong that, at points in his work, it appears that critical agency is the inevitable effect of withheld recognition: 'the imperative of mutual recognition . . . provides the normative pressure that *compels* individuals to remove constraints on the meaning of mutual recognition' (1995: 92, my italics). Not only does suffering not necessarily lead to the formation of oppositional consciousness but there are also many different types of oppositional consciousness, none of which occur spontaneously but are the effects of certain kinds of social and political intervention. Jane Mansbridge, for example, identifies at least six types of oppositional consciousness, none of which manifest themselves in a pure form, because they are interwoven with hegemonic types of consciousness, and none of which lead automatically to the recognition of the need for action (Mansbridge 2001: 238). There is a huge difference between recognizing injustice, identifying systemic domination and common interests, devising strategies for action and, finally, feeling able to act. Even when there is substantial misrecognition and subordination, resistance might not emerge if the symbolic resources with which to formulate agency are not present (Gal 2003: 99). Suffering might simply be negatively internalized in a habitus of resignation, frustrated rage and boredom, as Simon Charlesworth (2000) has documented in his Bourdieusian study of social deprivation in Rotherham. Critical consciousness and agency are not, therefore, the spontaneous effects of social suffering but are determined by the specific configuration of symbolic and material relations – the space of possibles and structure of positions – in a given field of action.

The notion of habitus reinforces the view that suffering is no guarantee of injustice and genuine political grievance. Its socio-centric treatment of emotions calls into the question the legitimacy that is attributed to a rhetoric of suffering in identity politics where 'trauma stands as truth' (Berlant 2000: 41). According to Lauren Berlant, there is a certain manufactured discourse of suffering which has become prevalent in contemporary social and political life and which is a symptom of a wider neo-liberal de-politicization of citizenship. From the Reagan period onwards, US citizenship has been reconfigured in the language of privatized individualism in order to diffuse the critical energies that emerge from politicized movements in civil society. A key strategy in this privatization has been the manipulation of a rhetoric of intimacy and, in particular, of personal suffering. A 'vicious yet sentimental' discourse of individual suffering has become the *sine qua non* of making any kind of political claim and one of the effects of its pervasiveness is to deflect attention away from the suffering that arises from genuine oppression: 'the public rhetoric of citizen trauma has become so pervasive and competitive in the United States that it obscures basic differences among modes of identity, hierarchy, and violence. Mass national pain threatens to turn into banality' (Berlant 1997: 2). Such an analysis of the discourse of suffering as a political construct is foregone in Honneth's subjectivist account where it is taken as the almost automatic guarantee of injustice and oppositional consciousness. The naturalization of emotions prevents a consideration of, for example, some of the more negative political implications of individuals and groups becoming attached to identities that are fetishistically constructed around the idea of suffering. In her work on wounded attachments, for example, Wendy Brown argues that adherence to a politics of injury and pain prevents the exploration of more positive and emancipatory forms of agency and being: 'politicized identity thus enunciates itself . . . only by entrenching . . . and inscribing its pain in politics; it can hold out no future that triumphs over this pain' (Brown 1995: 74). The treatment of emotions as irreducible givens also forecloses an analysis of how their supposed authenticity can be deployed to regulate oppressed groups by those who bestow recognition. It is precisely these normalizing effects that Elizabeth Povinelli (2002) explores in her work on how the granting of recognition rights to aboriginal groups exacerbated their oppression by compelling them to enact a colonial conception of 'authentic' aboriginal culture.

In sum, Bourdieu's idea of emotions engendered through the complex of embodied tendencies, intentional relations with the world and social structures highlights the ellipses in Honneth's account where agency is assumed to be a spontaneous effect of primal social suffering. Habitus does not deny that feelings of pain and suffering are indicative of oppression, but they cannot be taken as reliable or automatic indicators of that fact. In linking emotions to social structure, habitus treats suffering as a socially specific entity rather than as a universal *a priori* or what Berlant calls a 'prelapsarian knowledge' (Berlant 2000: 43). It is the exteriorization of the seemingly ineffable realm of affect in relation to objective structures that enables crucial forms of political discrimination to be made between competing claims to recognition (see Williams 1998: 176–202).

LIQUEFACTION OF THE EGO

In his work subsequent to *The Struggle for Recognition*, Honneth sets out renewed grounds for the relevance of object relations theory for his social theory of recognition. Postmodern claims about the multiple nature of identity in late capitalist society seemingly render orthodox psychoanalytical explanations of individuality obsolescent. In psychoanalysis, individuality is formed around the strength of the ego which is supposed to strike a balance between the unconscious demands of the drives and social norms. This rational control model of the ego seems to be at odds with the socio-cultural tendencies of late modern society where individuality is posited not so much around self-mastery but around an inner fluidity and porosity of the self. The force of object relations theory is that it posits subject formation as an agonistic process of internalizing interactive relations and this produces an ideal of mature identity as the capacity to bear conflict and tension – in a fashion similar to Benjamin's notion of splitting – rather than as rational ego strength. This capacity, which Honneth describes as a 'communicative liquefaction of the identity of the ego', offers a more substantive account of how individuals cope with the heterogeneous demands arising from social complexity than the essentially defensive logic of egological accounts (1999: 22). In developing this communicative account of subject formation, Honneth seems to correct the psychological determinism of his earlier work on recognition. The implication is that autonomous subjectivity is an effect of the internalization of patterns of social interaction rather than the projection outwards of the need for recognition: 'the individual subject becomes independent by internalizing external patterns of interaction, by means of which a kind of space of communication can develop within the psyche' (1999: 235). The idea of the interactive structure of subjectivity is also used as the basis for a reworked theory of the drives. The drives are no longer conceived as disruptive and destructive forces, in the manner of the Freudian Id. Rather, their energy is what propels the process of individuation after the early stage of symbiosis with the mother. The drives provide the imperative to internalize the various schemata of interaction that arise from multifarious social encounters. This process of internalization is continual and produces the ceaseless refinement of the psychic resources and abilities – what Honneth calls the 'functionally efficient organizational units in the inner world' – with which the individual learns to deal with varied modes of interaction (1999: 237).

In setting out this interactive account of subject formation, Honneth seems to be trying to produce a socialized account of the formation of the psyche in the manner of other thinkers such as Butler (1997b) and Castoriadis (1987). The relation between psyche and society is one of inherence and mutual determination rather than a uni-directional causality. A central difference, however, between the work of these thinkers and of Honneth is that, in the latter's account, the interactional structure of recognition is so exhaustively generalized to all aspects of social existence that any distinction between the individual and wider social relations seems to also disappear. This totalization of the structure of recognition forecloses any explanation of why individuals should be motivated to act in anything other than a conformist manner. Castoriadis, for example, shares with Honneth the general aim of formulating a socialized account of the psyche; however, in his idea of the radical imagination, he posits a psychic energy that perpetually resists incorporation into the symbolic and social structures of the world. The disruptive force of the radical imagination – conceived of as a ceaseless flux of primal images – is intended to explain the source of the creative aspects of action. By this Castoriadis means the capacity of individuals to act in ways that are unpredictable and innovative and that cannot be foreseen from their social conditions of existence because they emerge *ex nihilo*. Honneth also wishes to explain the creativity of action; how it is that individuals have the capacity to respond to the multiple demands of complex societies in a manner that is neither defensive nor, as in the postmodern account, involves a fragmentation of the self. Yet this creativity is a strangely domesticated capacity that is derived from a putative complementarity between the internal structure of the self and external social relations. It is one thing to assert that the self is formed and shaped through interaction; it is another, however, to render it virtually indistinguishable from internalized patterns of recognition. If there is no essential dissonance between the subject and social relations then it becomes hard to explain how individuals can act in any other than a conformist fashion.

The idea that, in response to the heterogeneity of social life, individuals develop an ever-refined capacity for the liquefaction of the self is a questionably normative account of action. In emphasizing the individual's accommodative capacities, it underplays the likelihood of negative and aggressive responses to difference. Arguably, phenomena such as fundamentalism, terrorism and ethnic cleansing are as characteristic responses to increasing social complexity as tolerance and the embrace of difference. Castoriadis, for example, was emphatic that the creativity of action should not be interpreted, in a superficial fashion, as an individual's capacity to create goodness or positive values: 'Auschwitz and the Gulag are creations just as much as the Parthenon and the *Principia Mathematica*' (Castoriadis 1991: 3–4).

The normative, redemptive force that Honneth invests in the idea of recognition skews its analytical adequacy as a depiction of the relation between the human psyche and social relations. This normative skewing is in fact crucial for Honneth to be able to sustain his claims that recognition represents the universal ethical structure of social life. Its transcendental status can only be assured by underplaying the negative effects of power upon subjectivity, by construing them as secondary distortions extrinsic to a primal dynamic of mutuality. In this respect, Honneth's claim that his idea of recognition modifies the rationalist orientation of Habermas's communicative ethics is open to question. On his account, the idea of recognition adds to discourse ethics 'richer conceptions of positive liberty, of moral motivation and its link to social struggle, and of the ethically particular concerns bound up with the forms of recognition enabling both self-confidence and self esteem' (Zurn 2000: 120). In fact, far from injecting determinate content into the communicative paradigm, Honneth replicates the same normative sanitization of subjectivity as Habermas (see Chapter 2). He follows his teacher in that subjectivity is emptied of any non-identitical elements and is, hence, domesticated by being imputed a communicative structure understood as an 'intrapsychic capacity for dialogue'. It is these covert elisions that ensure the sociological and normative pre-eminence of the idea of recognition.

ORGANIZED SELF-REALIZATION

If Honneth's work on recognition is characterized by a spontaneist and normative account of agency, his more recent work seems to deny the possibility of political agency altogether. This apparent reversal of position is underpinned, however, by a similarly inadequate account of the mediating effects of power upon social forms that limits his previous work. In two recent articles, Honneth appears to backtrack on one of his central normative claims, namely that through the expansion of relations of recognition, modern societies offer ever-increasing opportunities for self-realization (Honneth 2004; Hartmann and Honneth 2006). He argues instead that, as a consequence of the intensification of capitalist modernization over the past few decades, the expansion of recognition norms is no longer emancipating but has turned into a normalizing type of self-realization. One of the features of flexible, 'network' capitalism is that individuals are no longer treated as workers, who are compelled to participate in capitalist production, but as self-determining entrepreneurs or 'entreployees', who are required to display a 'readiness to self-responsibly bring one's own abilities and emotional resources to bear in the service of . . . individualized projects' (Hartmann and Honneth 2006: 45). In a manner not dissimilar to Foucault's idea of the government of individualization, Honneth claims that any apparent increase in individual autonomy in fact represents an intensification of a disciplinary power that operates by blurring the boundaries between the public and private realms. This erosion takes the form, on the one hand, of an 'informalization of the economy' where interpersonal communicative and emotional skills are increasingly required in utility-based work processes. This ultimately renders distinctions between instrumental and non-instrumental types of intersubjective relation unclear and this has a deleterious impact upon the individual because 'the "true" intentions with which others encounter us can scarcely be discerned' (Hartmann and Honneth 2006: 50). On the other hand, there is a process of the 'economization of the informal' where civil and private areas of social life are increasingly permeated by principles of individual achievement and exchange, breaking down communal affective bonds: 'the changed demands require one to remain so open with regard to choice of location, use of time, and type of activity that friendships, love relationships, and even families are exposed to a high degree of pressure' (Honneth 2004: 49). The overall effect of these erosions is to instil in the individual a seemingly paradoxical compulsion to self-responsibility. The normative and emancipatory force that originally inhered in the idea of personal responsibility is eroded as individuals are forced to assume responsibility for states of affairs for which they are not responsible. The wider consequences of this are a fragmentation of social values and a process of 'social desolidarization' which manifests itself in elevated levels of depression and mental illness and the emptying out of any meaning to the achievement principle other than maximization of profit. This ubiquitous and insidious compulsion to responsibility ultimately destroys the individual's normative bearings: 'in network capitalism . . . citizens tend to perceive their efforts . . . as individualized, so that a reference to the greater whole scarcely seems possible any longer' (Hartmann and Honneth 2006: 52).

Although it reaches the opposite conclusion to the work on recognition, the unmitigated pessimism of the thesis of organized self-realization is underpinned by a similarly undeveloped account of power relations. One aspect of this is a simplified understanding of the relation between the economic and cultural realms. Honneth seems to assume that, in previous phases of capitalist accumulation, economic and cultural forces have been separate and it is their increasing interpenetration in the past few decades that has had such pernicious effects on social values and norms. Without wanting to underestimate the commodifying scope of global capitalism, it is an error to assume that the economy and culture have ever operated as autonomous systems with an exclusively external relation to each other. As Ray and Sayer point out, although the spheres have their own respective logics, economy and culture have always historically been caught up in each other (Ray and Sayer 1999: 1–24). This imbrication is denoted in Geoffrey Hodson's principle of impurity, which asserts that no single type of economic or organizational system can exist entirely on its own. Instrumental relations can only function to some degree with the support of communicative relations and vice versa. Not only is it simplistic to assume that instrumental economic relations are extrinsic to normative, interactive ones but it is also misleading to assume, as Honneth does, that their impact is solely negative. As Ray and Sayer put it: 'The relationship between culture and economy should therefore not be coded: culture (good), economy (bad)' (1999: 6). Women's increasing autonomy has been, for example, the result in part of an intrusion of economic forces into the cultural sphere which has freed them from conventional domestic expectations and has given them the material resources with which to exit from traditional family situations. Although he does not address the situation of women explicitly, the conservative implications of Honneth's position are evident from the overstated claims he makes about the deleterious effects of economic forces on intimate relations. Stable, intimate relations are being eroded by instrumental considerations: 'what rather seems to be emerging as a new model of behaviour is the tendency to calculate the long-term chances of such love relationships according to their compatibility with the future mobility demands of a career path that can only be planned in the short term' (Hartmann and Honneth 2006: 56). In this respect, Honneth reproduces the same one-sided arguments as Habermas's problematic thesis of the colonization of the lifeworld where the effects of systemic intrusion in the social realm are conceptualized as uni-directional and unequivocally negative. Habermas's claim that bourgeois institutions such as the family are being non-renewably dismantled by the steering media of money and power gives rise to a deeply conservative analysis of changing gender relations. Like Habermas, Honneth's thesis of organized self-realization disregards these complex relations, mobilizing a dualist account of power which institutes a false separation between intimate and instrumental relations and assumes the unmitigated negative effects of the former upon the latter. He cannot explain, for example, how individualizing tendencies, which are undoubtedly corrosive in some respects, have contributed to the emergence of gay identities (D'Emilio 1984).

In effacing these complexities in the nature of freedom, Honneth's work on self-realization is underpinned, ultimately, by the same subjectivist adherence to a notion of authentic identity as the work on recognition. The difference being that, in the latter, this authentic core to the self comes to be expressed in social life with relatively little difficulty whilst in the former, its expression is endlessly thwarted. Power relations do indeed organize everyday existence in insidious and compelling ways and it is undoubtedly the case that individual identity is increasingly the focus for strategies of commodification and social control. However, *contra* the thesis of organized self-realization, individuals engage with the world in a variety of ways; they are not just the passive subjects of a disciplinary manipulation. Agency is a complex phenomenon which is not just motivated by a desire for recognition or thwarted by an insidious compulsion to self-realization. Rather it is realized unevenly in the complex interplay between embodied being and social position. This idea of liberty in constraint or what Bourdieu calls 'regulated liberties' will be taken up in more detail in the final chapter.

FRASER: RECOGNITION AND REDISTRIBUTION

In a series of essays over the past few years Nancy Fraser has produced one of the most cogent and sustained critiques of the idea of the politics of recognition. Fraser's main claim is that the predominant formulation of the idea of recognition results in an understanding of politics as primarily about symbolic and cultural struggles over identity. This skewed understanding of social conflict as a struggle for recognition carries with it the risks of *displacing* economic inequalities from view and *reifying* oppression as an injury to the self's eternal need for affirmation (Fraser 2000: 112–13). With regard to the problem of displacement, Fraser argues that there are many kinds of conflict that are redistributive in nature, that is, they deal with oppression arising from unequal distribution of economic resources and cannot, therefore, be encompassed under the idea of cultural struggles for identity recognition. There are also many types of distributive injustice that are not accompanied by any sense of personal injury or shame at all and would therefore not be identifiable within a recognition paradigm (Fraser and Honneth 2003: 34–5). With regard to the problem of reification, she claims that, by simplifying the process of identity formation, the recognition model ends up as a 'vehicle of misrecognition' that all too easily reinforces 'repressive forms of communitarianism, which promote conformism, intolerance, and patriarchalism' (Fraser 2003: 26). Along these lines, Fraser's central criticism of Honneth is that his depiction of all social and political conflict as expressions of a fundamental struggle for recognition is sociologically inaccurate, ahistorical and psychologically reductionist. Although Honneth does not ignore distributive injustices, his claim that they can be remedied through a politics of recognition is erroneous.

Against Honneth's normative monism, Fraser proposes a 'perspectival dualism' of recognition and redistribution where oppression is understood as both institutional subordination and as maldistribution or denial of economic resources. The dualism is perspectival because it does not denote two distinct societal domains of economy and culture, rather it is a heuristic tool to identify power relations that, in reality, are ineluctably entwined. Fraser is emphatic that this dualism of recognition and redistribution is not analogous to the base–superstructure or material–cultural hierarchies of Marxist analysis. Neither type of injustice is an indirect effect of the other, both are 'primary and co-original' (Fraser and Honneth 2003: 19). Capitalism is now so complex that identity depreciation does not translate directly into economic injustice or vice versa: 'markets follow a logic of their own, neither wholly constrained by culture nor subordinated to it: as a result they generate economic inequalities that are not mere expressions of identity hierarchies' (Fraser 2000: 111–12). The complex ways in which economic and cultural forces create oppressions is exemplified in gender hierarchies which are generated by injustices of both redistribution and recognition. Gender has a 'dilemmatic structure' in so far as the remedies for these two types of injustice are potentially contradictory (Fraser and Honneth 2003: 19–22). The elimination of women's economic exploitation revolves around transformative strategies which would create distributive equality. The problem of misrecognition is combated, however, through affirmative strategies that revalue practices and ways of being associated with women that have conventionally been accorded an inferior status. In other words, the dissolution of gender difference that is the result of transformative strategies potentially conflicts with the assertion of gender difference that results from affirmative strategies. Gender is, then, a paradigm of the multifaceted nature of oppression where the interpenetration of economic and cultural forces may, in certain instances, conflict with each other and, in certain instances, reinforce each other.

In addition to insisting on the irreducibility of issues of redistribution to those of recognition, Fraser also produces a revised notion of recognition as status subordination. Although it may provide insights into the emotional effects of phenomena such as racism and sexism, recognition is better conceived, not as a psychological dynamic, but as institutionalized cultural value patterns that have discriminatory effects on the equal standing of social actors. Status subordination takes the concrete forms of juridical discrimination, government policy, professional practice or sedimented moral and ideological codes. It judges them from the perspective of whether they promote reciprocal recognition and status equality: 'when . . . institutionalized patterns of cultural value constitute some actors as inferior . . . as less than full partners in social interaction, then we can speak of *misrecognition* and *status subordination*' (2003: 27).

An advantage of formulating misrecognition as status subordination is that it overcomes the vagueness of the psychological model which relies too heavily on what Fraser terms 'free floating' notions of personal harm and ungrounded ideas of injurious cultural representation. By adding institutional specificity to the idea of misrecognition, it becomes easier to adjudicate between genuine and opportunistic claims to recognition. A central problem, for example, with Honneth's work on social suffering is that it is construed in such loose psychological terms that it does not provide criteria against which the racist's claims for recognition can be distinguished from others. On Fraser's model, the norm of participatory parity provides the standard in relation to which individuals and groups must justify their claims about misrecognition. Such claims cannot derive their authority by reference only to personal experience; rather they must demonstrate how the intersubjective conditions necessary for participatory parity are being violated by institutionalized patterns of cultural value (Fraser and Honneth 2003: 38). In other words, by rendering the category more objective, or in Fraser's words 'non-identitarian', some of the problems associated with an uncritical phenomenology of social suffering, such as false consciousness, are avoided. As Christopher Zurn puts it: 'The status model gains its strength here by simply avoiding reference to the psychological states of victims of subordination, and so avoids traditional problems associated with theoretical reliance on potentially distorted or manipulated ideas held by social actors' (Zurn 2003: 533).

Fraser also claims that her objectivist rendering of the category of recognition permits the implementation of concrete remedies aimed at removing subordination. This contrasts with the free-floating recognition model which adduces strategies for valorizing reviled identities and, in so doing, risks reifying identity further. The status model is not *a priori* committed to any particular remedy; rather it seeks specific remedies to overcome the institutional barriers that prevent a given group from equal participation in social life. Ensuring parity may involve deploying strategies of transformation or affirmation or it may involve distributive strategies in so far as democratic participation can be impeded as much by unequal distribution of economic resources as it is by discriminatory patterns of value. Unlike the identity model of recognition, therefore, the status model of subordination does not displace distributive issues but rather highlights the intertwined but mutually irreducible nature of economic and cultural barriers to participatory parity. Economic issues often have a recognition subtext, for example, the devaluation of women's work in the labour market. Conversely, recognition issues have distributive subtexts, for example the 'underclass' often lack sufficient political representation.

FROM IDENTITY TO STATUS SUBORDINATION

Fraser's formulation of the politics of redistribution and recognition offers a compelling critique of the limitations of the identity model of recognition. She rightly criticizes Honneth for the dehistoricizing effects of grounding his theory in a moral psychology where all social struggle is viewed as a version of an eternally recurrent need for recognition. She is also right to insist on the complex and often indirect ways in which oppressions are created. Yet Fraser's critique of the subjectivism inherent in the idea of recognition is so emphatic that it leads to an objectivist style of analysis that forecloses most understanding of the subjective dimensions of identity. The non-identitarian rendering of misrecognition is oriented to an objective analysis of status subordination to such a degree that it neglects to consider how many types of ideological and institutional discrimination are rooted in extra-institutional modes of being. In other words, identity injustices are considered primarily as externally imposed injuries rather than as lived identities. It is as if Fraser accepts on face value that the concept of identity is irremediably subjectivist and, therefore, cannot be reconfigured in a praxeological manner that connects the analysis of lived experience to a theory of power. Rather than reformulate the notion of identity so that it is compatible with a critical social theory, she objectivizes the category and this creates gaps in the analytical purchase of her model.

The foreclosure of any experiential or subjective dimension in her understanding of identity has its roots in Fraser's rather overstated critique of the recognition paradigm. In order to justify the objectivist reframing of recognition as status subordination, Fraser unnecessarily simplifies the complexity of the work that she deems to be representative of the 'free-floating' paradigm of recognition. She underplays, for example, the differences between thinkers such as Butler, Honneth and Taylor, who are all, at various points in her work, labelled as recognition thinkers. Her blanket criticism that the recognition paradigm reifies identity is based on a failure to acknowledge that many of these explicitly seek to formulate non-essentialist understandings of identity even if, ultimately, they may not be entirely successful (Yar 2001: 296–7; Zurn 2003). Furthermore, there is a sense in which Fraser herself does not in fact entirely succeed in detaching the idea of recognition from 'subjectivist' formulations of identity. The latter are rather displaced as the unthought pre-conditions of her idea of status subordination. The definition of recognition as 'status injury', for example, ranges from specific institutional discriminations to 'sedimented ideological codes'. Whilst institutional discrimination might be relatively easy to identify, it is less easy to examine the entrenched operations of ideology without some notion of how it effects the formation of subjectivity. The force of the notion of habitus in this regard is that it moves away from a crude notion of ideological mystification to show how structures of symbolic violence are reproduced through corporeal dispositions. Because, however, habitus is an active not passive concept in that it is generative of practice, this process of reproduction is never automatic, internally monolithic or unchangeable. Without some such subjective category to show how ideological codes are anchored in daily life, it is unclear how Fraser's idea of status subordination differs fundamentally from the idea of 'free floating cultural harm' of which she is so critical in psychological models of recognition. In this respect, her model could also be said to be free floating in that she takes institutional discriminations as already given without exploring their origins in, and connection to, a substrate of experiences and beliefs that sustain misrecognition. As Patchen Markell puts it, Fraser focuses on the 'symptoms of injustice' and treats misrecognition as an 'unfortunate fact' rather than engaging with 'the deeper question of the *sources* of misrecognition' (Markell 2003: 21).

In important respects, then, the one-sided objective and institutional focus of the idea of status subordination limits the analytical depth of Fraser's understanding of misrecognition. Her non-identitarian version of recognition may circumvent ungrounded cultural notions of identity and subjectivity and attendant problems of subjectivism but it does have significant blind-spots. One of these is that Fraser's paradigm is deprived of a perspective upon the submerged experiences of everyday life which precede any politics of recognition. The move away from a focus on subjective experience means that she cannot adequately address pre-political and hidden forms of social suffering and this leads to a narrow focus in her work on already established movements for recognition. It is precisely this point that Honneth makes when he claims that Fraser's failure to establish a phenomenology of social experiences of injustice results in an element of uncritical empiricism in her work (Fraser and Honneth 2003: 114). The starting point of Fraser's theory is established social movements that have already achieved a certain level of political mobilization within the bourgeois public sphere. Types of social suffering that have not already crossed a certain perceptual threshold of public attention are disregarded. Indeed, as commentators have noted, there is a further skewing in her depiction of recognition struggles in that they are identified only with progressive and not regressive socio-political movements (e.g. Blum 1998: 63). This 'filtering effect', where a relatively few types of conflict are deemed representative struggles, leaves unaddressed marginal forms of social suffering that do not conform to the paradigm of post-socialist conflict (Fraser and Honneth 2003: 120). In this respect, Honneth's claim that his notion of social suffering gives him improved insight into the hidden sources of resistance and discontent seems to be justified. This extra-institutional realm has to be approached through some kind of phenomenal or hermeneutic understanding of identity as lived experience if certain potential types of invisible oppression and incipient political struggle are to be identified. However, as the idea of habitus demonstrates, it is not necessary to impute to this submerged level of experience an authenticity or ontological priority vis-à-vis already established recognition struggles.

There is another type of social experience related to the disciplinary manipulation of identity that also potentially falls beneath the radar of Fraser's objectivist rendering of the idea of recognition. Without a category of subjectivity or identity, Fraser is unable to address the ways in which identities have increasingly becoming the focus for strategies of social control in the manner raised by Foucault's idea of the government of individualization or Honneth's work on organized self-realization. Although, Honneth overstates the extent to which insidious strategies of normalization have taken hold upon individuals, there is no doubt that late-modernity has been characterized by the spread of an intensified consumerist individualism. Some aspects of this phenomenon, such as the increasing commodification of social life, have become important areas of struggle, for example movements against globalization and consumerism. The sources of these movements lie in the submerged experiences of everyday life and it is this pre-political ground of struggle that Fraser's institutional and objectivist category of recognition disregards. A reason why this terrain of experience remains unexplored is that issues connected with the normalization and commodification of identity do not fall neatly into one category or the other of the binary recognition and redistribution. Although normalization strategies target identity, they do so in an often diffuse and generalized manner (for example, through methods of population control or information monitoring) that does not express itself in the form of the direct subordination of a specific group and, therefore, does not give rise to focused oppositional struggles.

Furthermore, some of these strategies of normalization, such as the commodification of social life, are driven by obvious profit motives and are, therefore, as relevant to struggles over redistribution as they are to identity politics. At the same time, issues of normalization are not strictly redistributive in nature either, because their effects are often displaced onto issues of identity instead of involving struggle over the allocation of resources. A further reason why Fraser is unable to address certain issues pertaining to the government of individualization is that, in so far as they can be construed as cultural problems, her materialist paradigm disregards them. The institutional bias of her idea of recognition as status subordination seems to render culture an analytically insubstantial category. Cultural struggles for recognition acquire authenticity only from how strongly they can be related to materialist struggles. As Anne Phillips puts it: 'It seems that the separation between the economic and the cultural . . . has emptied the cultural of much of its meaning. Despite Fraser's declared objective, redistribution emerges as the central site of a political struggle, with a rather cursory nod in the direction of recognition' (Phillips 1997: 152).

Struggles against the government of individualization are not the only issues that do not fit neatly into one side or the other of her dualism of recognition and redistribution. There are many different sorts of political issue connected with the embodied aspects of existence, such as rape, domestic violence or child abuse, that escape categorization in this way. There is a blind-spot, then, in Fraser's perspectival dualism which 'cannot accommodate forms of injustice which are in principle non-economic and non-communicative in character' (Yar 2001: 300). In response to this analytical gap, Majid Yar proposes that Fraser's dualism be replaced by a single multi-axial category that acknowledges that there are different orders and different types of recognition claim, each of which corresponds to a different dimension of human need. In this respect she follows Honneth's strategy of normative monism by arguing that recognition is a moral meta-category or 'first-order logical reconstruction of the basis upon which all appeals to social justice are constituted' (Yar 2001: 293). While it is certainly the case that there are significant types of social conflict that cannot be captured in the distinction of recognition and redistribution, it is not clear that a single multi-axial theory of recognition can solve the problem. From the perspective of social theory, a single theory of recognition too easily leads to a type of functionalist analysis that has a reductive account of power relations emptying political movements of their specific logic. The problem with Fraser's approach is that its objectivist orientation disregards the sociological relevance of concepts of self-identity and thereby weakens the scope of her dualism of redistribution and recognition. A consequence of the dismissal of the category of identity as a psychological and cultural abstraction is that Fraser loses the theoretical grounds upon which to base a notion of agency. Without a concept of agency, however, she cannot develop very far one of the central insights of her own paradigm, namely, how it is that the cultural and economic forces interact with each other in order to create social injustices.

OVERCOMING DUALISM

Perhaps one of the most significant consequences of the objectivist turn that under-emphasizes the social relevance of concepts of self-identity is that Fraser is unable to provide a robust account of social agency. If Honneth's subjectivist phenomenology leads him to make the move too easily from suffering to political agency, then Fraser's objectivism leads her to disregard a host of issues such as political mobilization and the formation of oppositional consciousness that pertain to agency. Her objectivism means that these are taken as the always-already achieved background to established movements of recognition and redistribution. It is this lack of attention to a notion of agency that leads to Fraser's arguably overstated critique of the politics of recognition. By considering it only as an abstract paradigm, she fails to view it from the practical perspective of political mobilization. Anne Phillips points out that many recognition struggles do not involve the simple assertion of collective identities but rather are about self-organization and the struggle by certain groups to be recognized as political actors in their own right. This construal of recognition struggles as a form of mobilization to achieve political voice renders the problem of reification less significant. As Phillips puts it: 'the insistence on difference can be contingent rather than a claim about the group's distinctive qualities or concerns' (Phillips 2003: 266). By failing to consider the idea of recognition in relation to political and social agency, Fraser's own critique inadvertently compounds the problem of the reification of identity rather than deconstructing it. Her objectivist approach is unable to explain how an individual's understanding of their own identity and place in the world can motivate them to action.

A focus on agency not only undercuts Fraser's claim that the idea of recognition reifies identity, but would also animate one of the central insights of her paradigm and thereby move it away from dualism. One of Fraser's repeatedly emphasized claims is that the economic and cultural dimensions of oppression have a complex and indirect relation with each other: 'perspectival dualism allows us to theorize the complex connections between two orders of subordination, grasping at once their conceptual irreducibility, empirical divergence, and practical entwinement' (Fraser and Honneth 2003: 64). However, because she construes the categories of recognition and redistribution in objectivist terms, she can only posit their imbrication from an abstract perspective. A construal of agency from the perspective of a relational phenomenology that connects identities to deeper social structures is one way of exploring the interpenetrations of cultural and economic forces. The forces that create injustices of recognition and redistribution often only reveal themselves in the lived reality of social relations. Ellen Meiksins Wood makes precisely this point when she uses E. P. Thompson's notion of experience against Althusserian definitions of class as an abstract structural location: 'since people are never actually "assembled in classes", the determining pressure exerted by a mode of production in the formation of classes cannot be easily expressed without reference to something like a common experience, – a lived experience of . . . the conflicts and struggles inherent in relations of exploitation' (Wood 1995: 96). Rosemary Hennessey also draws on Thompson's concept of 'experience' to provide an interpretative perspective on the imbrication of economic and cultural forces in daily life. She is particularly concerned to explain how capitalist economic structures have a primacy in determining social existence but not in an absolute or mechanical sense. One of the weaknesses of Fraser's work in this regard is that it construes class as an abstract distributive mechanism and thereby fails to understand how it deeply penetrates the formation of cultural identities. As Hennessey puts it: 'under capitalism there are and historically have always been uneven, complex material connections between the unequal relations of production (another way of understanding class) and the production of identities, knowledge and culture' (Hennessey 2000: 221). In order to explore these subjective effects, Hennessey uses Thompson's idea of experience to develop a notion of class, not as an objective position, but as a 'structured process' that is always present, in an explicit or latent form, in the antagonisms and conflicts of daily experience. Class relations remain the 'kernel of human relationships' in so far as they structure emotions and legitimate or 'outlaw' need, but in ways that are indirect rather than causal. The concept of experience allows a systematic examination of the ambivalent forms of identification and affective force that characterize social relations by making visible the fundamental social structures from which they emerge.

Hennessey's remarks on how it is possible to connect even the most intimate experiences of daily life to global structures of capital are suggestive but they are also rather elliptical. Furthermore, her assertion of the centrality of class would not only be problematic for many feminists but also it raises, rather than resolves, well-known difficulties with class analysis, notably the problem of determination in the last instance. Part of the problem is that although it provides the necessary subjective emphasis that is lacking in Fraser's objectivist framework, the category of experience may be too undifferentiated to be effective as a transitional category that mediates between the levels of phenomenal experience and social structure. Perhaps because it is ultimately a relatively passive category, the idea of experience seems to be intrinsically unifying in that it construes social existence as a self-evident state. Thus, although she claims that class doesn't determine experience in a straightforward sense, Hennessey's analysis lacks intermediate concepts with which to analyse the indirect flows of power. This results, therefore, in a residual class determinism evident, for example, in her dismissal of certain types of identity formation as 'dead identities'. Whilst it might be the case, for example, that some work on identity fails to interrogate the class implications underlying its fetishization of certain 'ambivalent' subject positions, it is, nonetheless, a form of class reductionism to deny them any experiential validity by describing them as 'dead identities'. In this respect, the action-theoretic concept of habitus escapes the essentializing tendencies of the idea of experience through the alternative idea of practice. Practice denotes an interpretative perspective on the active realization of embodied social relations in context. This idea will be discussed at greater length in the final chapter; here, however, it suffices to note that this idea of practical agency provides interpretative depth to Fraser's objectivist formulation of the interpenetration of economic and cultural dimensions of power. In so far as it involves the practical negotiation of power relations, a praxeological idea of agency can illuminate how cultural and economic forces play themselves out in daily life as constraints and resources for action. The unequal distribution of economic resources is lived as the 'shame' of the class habitus or the 'superior taste' of the middle classes. Conversely, until the civil partnerships bill, homophobic cultural norms were lived as the reality of economic discrimination. Habitus shows us, in short, how economic imperatives are lived through cultural identities and that cultural norms can be lived as economic realities. The debate over recognition–redistribution is, after all, partly about the type of constraints that operate upon social action and how it may be possible to overcome these constraints. It is important, therefore, to move beyond objectivism, because agency cannot be deduced from abstract social structures. Even if it were possible, for example, to tell whether it is economic deprivation or lack of social recognition that is the principal motivation behind social action, this would tell us little about why individuals act in some circumstances rather than others, and why it is that only some individuals rather than all will act faced with the same circumstances. It follows that the subjective dimensions of oppression, the perceptions and evaluations that individuals have of the social world and that might impel them to act also need to be taken into account.

Fraser's failure to provide categories through which to examine the impact of economic and cultural forces on daily life means that her theory has a tendency towards dualism. Several commentators have criticized her for dualism, arguing that she is simply reinstating a version of a Marxist base–superstructure distinction with all its attendant problems (Butler 1998; Markell 2003; Oliver 2001; Yar 2001). Iris Marion Young (1997) is one of Fraser's most trenchant critics in this regard; she claims that, far from breaking down the opposition between economy and culture, the categories of redistribution and recognition reinforce it by being unjustified and 'brazenly dichotomous'. The dualism of recognition and redistribution creates a false separation between the cultural and material aspects of identity claims. For example, Fraser categorizes the gay and lesbian struggle against heterosexism as an 'ideal type' of the politics of recognition. Yet, echoing a point made by Judith Butler (1998), Young argues that even if the causes of homophobia can be classified as cultural, its oppressive effects are material and require remedies of redistribution as much as recognition: 'those on the wrong side of the heterosexual matrix experience systematic limits to their freedom, constant risk of abuse, violence and death, and unjustly limited access to resources and opportunities' (Young 1997: 157). If social life is indeed permeated by multifarious power relations then it would make sense to deploy a plural categorization of oppression rather than a simplifying dualism. Young argues that Fraser's discernment of a dilemmatic structure within, say, gender oppression and politics is purely the result of her bipolar analysis rather than being an actual contradiction. Fraser 'finds contradiction where none exists' (Young 1997: 158). Overcoming gender oppression involves complex strategies that, at times, may aim to eliminate gender difference and, at other times, affirm it; however, there is no reason not to suppose that these strategies indirectly reinforce each other rather than conflict. Young suggests an alternative typology of oppression based on the five axes of exploitation, marginalization, powerlessness, cultural imperialism and violence. This five-fold distinction avoids reductionism and accommodates a political and legal aspect to social struggles which, in her view, is occluded by Fraser's bifocal analysis (Young 1997: 151).[1]

Young's critique is cogent but, like Fraser, she seems to accept on face value that the notion of identity is irretrievably subjectivist. She likewise fails to develop any praxeological categories to show how her abstract typology of power is played out in social life. She argues in *Inclusion and Democracy*, for example, that social difference should be unyoked from the idea of identity in order to overcome the essentializing logic that understands social groups as having substantively unified identities. Class, gender, race, ethnicity, etc., should not be understood as group attributes but rather as structural relations of power and the individual's relation to these is one of position, not one of identity. The position of an individual within social structures conditions their identity but does not determine it in a straightforward way. This loosening of the link between social difference and identity gives Young a critical perspective on the politics of recognition. In her view, it is misguided to characterize movements attempting to overcome hierarchical social differences as a politics of recognition. Such movements may occasionally involve claims of recognition but more often they are tied to 'questions of control over resources, exclusions from benefits of political influence or economic participation, strategic power or segregation from opportunities. A politics of recognition . . . usually is part of or a means to claims for political and social inclusion or an end to structural inequalities that disadvantage them' (2000: 105). Young's decoupling of social difference from the idea of identity is not without merit but, like Fraser, her shift to an objectivist mode of analysis leaves her without a basis from which to develop a substantive account of agency. Her only discussion of agency amounts to a few general remarks upon Giddens' theory of structuration, which posits that individuals fashion their identities as active agents from an array of options that they do not determine but from amongst which they can choose.[2] This assertion that social position conditions, but does not determine, individual identity is undoubtedly correct but it is formulated in such an abstract manner that it leaves unexplained many aspects of how these choices are realized in daily life. Individuals may very well actively fashion their identities but, as Foucault has observed, some practices of the self are imposed upon individuals in the form of cultural imperatives and others are merely suggested. If Bourdieu is right to claim that self-recognition is always bound up with processes of misrecognition, then the idea that the individual autonomously constitutes their own identity needs considerable elaboration vis-à-vis the internalization of symbolic norms. There are types of identity, racial identity, for example, that may, in certain circumstances, be felt by individuals to be totally defining of their social existence, and other types, national identity, for example, that are not experienced in such a compelling manner. There are other types of identity, gender most obviously, whose phenomenal significance may fluctuate for the individual even though it may, at a latent level, be determining of an individual's ability to intervene in the world. To analyse these types of identity only as relations of power and not in terms of the subjective meaning they have for individuals or in terms of the investments, conscious or unconscious, that individuals make in them leaves many aspects to the question of agency unanswered.

The objectivism of Young's position prevents her from correctly identifying the cause of the dualist tendencies in Fraser's thought. The latter's dualism is not because she covertly adheres to a residual economic determinism where the base–superstructure distinction is transposed onto that of redistribution and recognition. Indeed, Fraser goes to some lengths to avoid economic reductionism, including her materialist redefinition of status subordination. The problem is that her objectivist formulation of the categories of recognition and redistribution leave her without any way of 'teasing out the complex imbrications of status with economic class' (Fraser 2003: 31). Thus a complex phenomenal reality remains an abstract dualism. Given Young's similarly objectivist tendencies, it ultimately seems rather tangential whether she replaces Fraser's dichotomy with a five-fold or a nine-fold typology of power; arguably it remains just as schematic and unjustified. Like Fraser, Young also states that symbolic and material power relations are intertwined yet irreducible to each other but, by remaining at the level of macro-structural analysis, neither develops mediatory categories such as embodied agency through which it is possible to map these imbrications.

IDENTITY AND NORMS

The normative elements of Fraser's work are more firmly grounded than Honneth's in a socio-theoretic sensitivity to the complex and ineluctable workings of power on social relations. Fraser's recognition paradigm is not destabilized in the same way by Bourdieu's critique of power; indeed, there is a fundamental affinity between the two in so far as habitus potentially provides interpretative depth to her analytical dualism. The phenomenological orientation of habitus emphasizes, however, that there is a normative as well as an analytical cost to

Fraser's rejection of the concept of identity and consequent move to objectivism. It is not clear, as we have seen, that all forms of misrecognition can be adequately captured by eschewing any hermeneutic orientation to embodied identity and agency and focusing only on institutionally anchored types of injury. Thus, a significant normative gap in Fraser's framework is that it overlooks types of suffering that fall below the perceptual threshold of the recognition and redistribution distinction. Another normative oversight is that it is not clear that Fraser's deontological treatment of status subordination provides much help in adjudicating between and remedying concrete instances of misrecognition (Markell 2003: 30; Zurn 2003: 534). For Bourdieu, there is a double naturalization of the social world that operates through both 'objective systems of positions' and 'subjective bundles of dispositions' (Wacquant 2005: 3). By focusing only on the objective dimension, perhaps the most significant normative gap in Fraser's model is that it cannot explore how misrecognition can arise even within formally egalitarian structures. Without any orientation to the subjective dimensions of identity, Fraser has no category through which to address the unforeseen exclusions and psychic harms that inevitably accompany the institution of any democratic system. As Christopher Zurn puts it: 'there is a serious risk of foreclosing from theoretical view precisely what theories of recognition were designed to bring into view in the first place: the way in which, even . . . where relevant rules and norms have been structured to overcome unjust subordination, there are still harms felt by individuals and carried by denigrating cultural-symbolic patterns of evaluation' (Zurn 2003: 534). The reintroduction of a concept of identity into an analysis of social suffering need not involve the restoration of subjectivist notions of psychological interiority. As a relational concept, habitus connects the subjective to the objective dimensions of oppression in a way that furthers Fraser's general insight into the interconnected, but mutually irreducible nature of cultural and economic harms.

The final question for Fraser is if, on Bourdieu's account, the idea of recognition is a form of epistemic universalism that simplifies the social realm and obscures the complex logic of subordination, whether her analysis requires the distinction between recognition and redistribution at all. The social theoretical aim of Fraser's thought is to develop a multidimensional account of power relations and the variable ways in which they overlap in the creation of social hierarchies. In the light of this aim, it would be possible for her to analyse the imbrications of cultural and economic inequalities, and indeed to pay more attention to the role played by the neglected dimensions of politics and law, without mapping them onto the perspectival dualism of recognition and redistribution. In other words, there is an unresolved tension in her thought between the analysis of power that draws attention to the specificity of the dynamics of social oppression and the adherence to a categorical dualism that stymies that analysis by attributing too unified a logic to social formations and practices.

CONCLUSION

The trouble with the idea of recognition is, then, twofold. First, it effaces the diversity of political conflicts by falsely unifying them as manifestations of a basic ontological struggle. This dehistoricization of agency is the difficulty with Honneth's subjectivist formulation of recognition struggles springing from an authentic form of suffering. Second, it institutes an analytical break between culture and economy which disconnects identities from their material conditions of emergence. This is the difficulty with Fraser's objectivist formulation of recognition and redistribution which empties the analysis of counter-hegemonic political movements of any active agents. The concept of habitus potentially helps to push the debate between Honneth and Fraser onto new ground by mediating the dualism of objectivism and subjectivism through its agent-centred or praxeological orientation. Beyond the specific insights into how latent structures of power exert their effects in daily life, there is a more general implication of this agent-centred perspective. Social theory should dispense with the idea of recognition and seek to untangle, in their singularity, the indirect routes of power that connect specific identity formations to the invisible structures underlying them.

5

Beyond Recognition: Identity and Agency

INTRODUCTION

One of the problems of the limited conception of power that is
deployed by thinkers in their work on recognition is that the idea of
agency is often yoked too closely to unified ideas of identity. On this
view, social action is impelled by the individual's primordial desire
for recognition. This simplifies the diverse logic of action, by imput-
ing to it a single cause and a relatively unmediated relation to
embodied existence. In short, this ontology of recognition natural-
izes agency. Recent feminist theory has, in many respects, a far more
developed understanding of the impact of power upon subjectivity
and, therefore, does not construe agency as directly governed by a
need to express authentic identity. Despite this, feminist theory also
finishes by binding agency too tightly to a problematic conception of
identity. The performative accounts of agency that prevail in cultural
feminism are based on a discursively objectivist understanding of
subject formation, a consequence of which is the elevation of one
aspect of women's identity over all others, namely sexuality. It is not
so much the focus on sexuality itself that is a problem as the failure
to integrate it with an account of other aspects of embodied identity,
notably class. This leads to a narrowly sexualized view of agency
and women's social existence in general. The objectivism of theories
of performativity also means that crucial political dimensions of
agency, connected to the embodied context of action, are foreclosed.

If women are to be understood as social and not just sexual subjects then the connections between embodied identity and agency

need to be understood through a more differentiated and flexible model of power other than discourse. In so far as the idea of habitus expresses a socio-centric understanding of embodied existence, it suggests some useful insights into the conceptualization of agency in relation to gender. The idea of practice that is central to the concept of habitus counters the objectivism of cultural feminist accounts of embodiment, suggesting that agency is not only a discursively generated capacity but also a lived relation. However, by positing an intrinsic connection between the body and power, the idea of practice avoids some of the essentialist tendencies that hamper some phenomenological treatments of embodiment through the idea of experience. In this regard, feminist standpoint theory has revised many of its more generalized assertions about the nature of women's practices and perspectives yet, nonetheless, it still invokes an over-unified conception of experience through which to examine them. By exteriorizing aspects of embodied identity – emotions, for example – in relation to different dimensions of power, habitus offers a way of exploring how the formation of sexual identity is intertwined with other aspects of identity, notably class. This socio-centric orientation towards embodiment does not undermine an account of agency by asserting an indivisible complicity between dispositions and social structures, it rather construes it in terms of 'regulated liberties'. This idea goes beyond dualisms of domination and resistance and also militates against the uncritical phenomenalism that often informs certain feminist ideas of embodied resistance. Against these conceptions, agency is construed as a specific engagement with the world whose meaning can only be derived from its location in the social order. Ultimately, this gives a better understanding of the power relations that divide women than accounts of agency in terms of resistance or in terms of the universalized ideas of performativity or recognition.

CONNECTING IDENTITY AND AGENCY

There is no doubt that the emphasis placed by thinkers of recognition on the dialogical aspects of subject formation initiates an important shift in conceptualizing identity and agency. The formulation of these concepts through ideas of embodiment, interaction and practice represents a significant move in overcoming some of the limitations of the disembodied and instrumental concepts that prevail in social and political theory. In this respect, there is a particularly productive affinity between theories of recognition and feminists working on ideas of gender and agency who seek to go beyond not just the abstract and monological conceptions of 'patriarchal' thought but also neo-Nietzschean ideas of agency as self-fashioning that predominate in poststructural theory. The normative force of the idea of recognition for feminists resides in part, then, in the extent to which it overcomes the poststructural hypostatization of difference. By highlighting the interactive and shared features of existence, it sketches out potential grounds for mutual understanding and common action. The potential of these dialogical and embodied accounts of identity and agency are stymied, however, by the inadequate theory of power deployed by thinkers of recognition. Their tendency to understand social relations as extrapolations from a foundational dyad of recognition results in a reductive account of subject formation in relation to inequalities of power. One of the most problematic of these reductions is that the concept of recognition tends to bind an account of social action too tightly to the idea of identity. Agency is understood as impelled, in the final instance, by the desire for recognition in whatever form it may take: self-expression (Taylor and Honneth), mutual understanding (Habermas and Benhabib) or emotional autonomy (Benjamin). The ontology of recognition thus has the problematic consequence of naturalizing agency.

There are many interrelated reasons why this short-circuited connection between identity and agency needs to be unpicked. It presumes a univocal model of subject formation which underplays the problems of multiple and contingent identifications. It presumes that agency derives its shape from identity rather than action itself being constitutive of identity. It thus fails to differentiate adequately between different types of social and political agency or between available discursive resources, framing strategies and opportunity structures (Hobson 2003: 5). In overlooking these distinctions, it simplifies the relation between individual and collective identities, most especially by blurring the differences between types of identity that are chosen and types that are imposed. As a consequence, its own limitations as a comprehensive model for the politics of identity are not interrogated. In the case of ascribed identities, such as those associated with race, individuals may simply not seek any kind of recognition vis-à-vis an unwanted identity (see Appiah 1996). It may be that individuals have the same experiences of social exclusion and discrimination but this need not have any implications for a common identity. In this case, individuals share a 'formal commonality' where they are linked in the shared reality of 'permanent, structural misrecognition and discrimination' but they do not share 'any authentic core of convictions and values'. They are defined not by 'what they are' but 'what was done to them' (Emcke 2000: 492). The recognition theorist might respond that such individuals are nonetheless motivated by the desire to have an as yet unformulated, chosen identity recognized. This is, however, to fall back into an invocation of a problematic ontology that construes agency in psychological rather than social terms. It represents what Carolin Emcke calls a 're-essentializing' gesture that tries to pull all dimensions of social action back to the core logic of identity. In short, the desire to eliminate social injustice need not necessarily be accompanied by the parallel aim of asserting group identity. The organization of gender hierarchies in industrialized societies provides a paradigm of this discontinuous relation between identity and action. Women may occupy a similar social position with regard to the types of systemic and institutional discrimination that structure social life but, arguably, this has few implications for a shared, substantive identity. They may struggle, for example, for equal pay in the workplace without wanting to make any claims about a common feminine identity. To claim, as, say, Honneth does, that ultimately such struggles over resources can be characterized as variants of a fundamental struggle for recognition, is illustrative of yet another danger with the concept, namely that it is often generalized so far that it loses any determinate content. There are many reasons for action – routinization, impulse, strategic interests, belief in social justice – that cannot be incorporated easily into a logic of identity recognition. In setting it up as an explanatory meta-category, thinkers of recognition empty the category of action of any diversity in terms of its internal logic.

This is not of course to argue that an individual's identity has no bearing on how they act in the world. It is to assert, however, that identity does not govern agency in the direct sense proposed by the idea of recognition. By tying the idea of agency too closely to that of identity the idea of recognition comes close to replicating the very same individualist and voluntarist concepts of subjectivity and action that it originally seeks to dislodge. Action and interaction are understood as governed by 'arriving at a clear understanding of who you are and of the nature of the larger groups and communities to which you belong, and of securing the respectful recognition of these same facts by others' (Markell 2003). If action is driven by a logic of identity, which itself is understood as a *fait accompli*, then the fragilities and indeterminacies of the relation between self and others are obscured. In criticizing the false unity that the idea of identity imposes on that of action, it is important, however, to avoid falling into an equally as problematic assertion of the indeterminate or open-ended nature of action. The logic of action is one of neither pure determinacy nor indeterminacy. The uncertainties of social existence are always mediated through determinate social relations which themselves are at least partially expressed in the entrenched dispositions and tendencies of embodied subjects. Thus action is both routinized and creative; it is freedom-in-constraint, or what Bourdieu calls a regulated liberty. It is not sufficient, therefore, to decouple identity from agency through a simple assertion of their inherent indeterminacy. The discontinuous relation between embodied identity and agency can be better understood instead through developing a differentiated account of the impact of power relations upon subject formation.

In important respects, feminist theory has been at the forefront of developing an account of the way in which power mediates the relation between identity and agency. Simone de Beauvoir's famous statement that 'one is not born, but rather becomes, a woman' can be interpreted as meaning that, although embodied identity inescapably situates women in the world, it does not fully determine their social existence. Through their daily actions and practices, women routinely transcend the sexualized notions of feminine identity that they are partially compelled to inhabit (e.g. Moi 1999: 177–202). The desire not to construe women's actions as directly governed by embodied identity has, of course, become more important in the wake of the debate over essentialism. Feminist thinkers have been forced to shed many of their early assumptions about how the dynamics of patriarchal oppression create a shared identity and common cause for action amongst women. As a result, feminist theorists have developed notions of identity and agency that are highly attuned to the complex operations of power around the embodied subject. However, as I will show in the next section, although, on one level, feminist theorists question any direct relation between identity and action, on another level, they reaffirm it by focusing on only one aspect of embodied identity, namely sexuality, and basing a theory of agency around it. It is not that such theories of sexual agency are not necessary, but they tend to be one-dimensional in that they are not sufficiently integrated into a wider understanding of other relations of power such as class. As I will argue in relation to the work of Judith Butler, these libidinalized accounts of agency are partly the result of the abstract model of power as discourse that is deployed. The idea of discourse construes agency in an objectivist manner as primarily a property of language rather than of subjects engaged in the world. This objectivism not only produces a narrowly sexualized account of agency but it also forecloses exploration of subjective dimensions to action, such as intention and understanding, which are crucial, *inter alia*, to assessing its political implications.

PERFORMATIVE AGENCY

Cultural feminism has been in the forefront of formulating sophisticated accounts of gender identity and agency using primarily Foucauldian ideas of the discursive realization of embodied identity. The work of Judith Butler on the performative construction of identity is a paradigm of this kind of cultural feminism. On her account, gender is materialized through the ceaseless and repeated ways in which cultures inscribe sexual norms upon the body. The cultural compulsion to reiterate these norms is indicative of the deeply entrenched and inescapable nature of gender identity. At the same time, however, the anxiety around issues of gender and sexuality points to the extent to which these identities are not innate or assured but are arbitrary cultural constructions. Dominant heteronormativity can be challenged, therefore, by prizing open these anxieties and instabilities surrounding the enactment of gender in order to create space for subversive gender practices. Agency, then, is conceived in the primarily discursive terms of resignification or the displacement of hegemonic meaning.

Butler's idea of performative agency has been justifiably influential, yet, despite this, it is limited, in certain crucial senses, by the abstract and rarified notion of discourse which she deploys (e.g. Sedgwick 2003: 6). The linking of linguistic agency to the reiterative structure of language is a deliberate move by Butler to circumvent crudely voluntarist interpretations of performativity as the freely willed performance of gender identity. There are many senses in which gender is an imposed, compulsory identity not a chosen one. Nonetheless, by conceiving of language as an abstract system of signification rather than as a type of pragmatic interaction, she falls into a 'negative paradigm' of subject formation where the individual is conceived as the passive effect of discourse. On this view, the idea of performativity is not an account of practical agency but an account of some of the discursive pre-conditions that must prevail for certain types of linguistic innovation to be possible (McNay 2000: 44–5). In short, agency is conceived primarily as a property of linguistic structures rather than of individuals engaged in the world. One of the theoretical consequences of this linguistic abstraction is that it forecloses an examination of certain subjective features of agency, such as intention and reflexivity, which emerge in the embodied context of action. These subjective or voluntarist aspects of action cannot be easily bypassed because they are crucial when it comes to a political assessment of the subversive impact of any given act of resignification. There is nothing inherently subversive to an act of cross-dressing, as many commentators have pointed out, rather it acquires contestatory significance only in relation to its context, the intention of the performer and the interpretation of the audience (e.g. Osborne and Segal 1994; Lloyd 1999). To understand agency as a political act, therefore, it is necessary to have some interpretative insight into the embodied context of action, which includes the intentions, motives and responses of the individuals involved. Such terms as intention, motivation and interpretation associated with the subjective aspects of action are, however, inaccessible to Butler because of the structural bias of her theory which rules them out as *per se* voluntarist.

In her subsequent work on melancholia, Butler appears to modify the hyper-structuralism of her account of performative agency by arguing that the displacement of hegemonic power formations is never an inevitable or 'mechanical' effect of the inherent instability of language. Agency is not automatic because it involves 'the willed effect of the subject' (Butler 1997b: 14). This may be a more equivocal approach to the subjective aspects of agency but it is no less problematic. This is because it is not clear how Butler's idea of 'willed effect' differs from a more conventional notion of will which, at its most minimal, must entail the capacity for reflexivity and conscience if it is to be anything more than a linguistic abstraction. The introduction of such concepts makes no sense, according to David Weberman, unless there is a tacit adherence by Butler to some kind of humanist notion of individual autonomy:

> What is the nature of the 'willed effect' if not a conscious choice . . . underneath Butler's rejection of humanist illusions about the subject's autonomy is the belief that to be a subject or a self is to possess certain rational capacities for deliberation and will formation without which subjects would not be subjects and could not be said to be free agents able to resist and transform existing power relations (Weberman 2000: 267).

It is not necessary to concur with Weberman's conclusion that Butler tacitly restores a humanist account of the rational subject in order to accept that there are problems with her conceptualization of agency. Indeed, to reclaim her to rationalism in the way that Weberman attempts could be said to show a disregard for the central problem motivating Butler's thought, namely, how it is that, as a compulsory and imposed form of identity, gender is nonetheless amenable to displacement and change. The invocation of an unmodified rationalist discourse of the reflexive, autonomous subject does not get very far in unpicking this conundrum. It is not so much, therefore, that Butler restores a rational subject to the centre of her thought. Rather, the structural orientation of her discursive paradigm does not provide the conceptual resources to elaborate certain crucial aspects of agency pertaining to its embodied context, which inevitably include ideas of will and intention and which are necessary for explaining the political implications of action.

A significant difference that an interpretative focus on embodied context makes to an understanding of agency is that it brings to the fore conflicts inherent to the reproduction of normative forms of gender identity that are otherwise obscured in Butler's discursive model. Although Butler certainly stresses the complexities inherent in all identities, these are conceived, by and large, in the abstract terms of the effects of the relational nature of language. A consequence of regarding gender largely as a question of position within language and not as embodied social relations is that dominant identities are left under-problematized. The reproduction of normative types of gender identity is construed in terms of an exogenous imposition of symbolic norms, rather than as a process that involves some degree of negotiation on the part of subjects. It is an error, however, to assume that hegemonic heterosexuality passively exists as a form of dominance, rather it 'has continually to be renewed, recreated, defended, and . . . also continually resisted, limited, altered, challenged by pressures not at all its own' (Williams 1977: 112). On this view, the reproduction of normative identities cannot be understood simply as a question of positioning within language but as a lived social relation that necessarily involves the negotiation of conflict and tension. Such conflicts and tension can be illustrated by Beverly Skeggs' (1997) study of the ways in which working-class women position themselves and are positioned by dominant conceptions of femininity. Skeggs argues that, as a consequence of their locations of class and sexuality, the women occupied a series of contradictory subject positions. On the one hand, working-class women have an uneasy relation to dominant norms of femininity because these have evolved historically from idealized notions of bourgeois womanhood. Traditionally, working-class women have been positioned as the 'Other' of such norms. Against bourgeois ideals of elegance, refinement and controlled eroticism, they have been defined as common, bawdy and sexually promiscuous. This uneasy relation to the middle-class norm of femininity is negotiated, in part, through the idea of 'respectability' that provides an interpretative trope for them to construct their own version of femininity distinct from stereotypes of the working-class slattern. The idea of 'glamour' is another trope that also provides a particularly effective tool in enabling them to hold together femininity and sexuality in a 'respectable' performance. Skeggs' point is that the idea of respectability is used by these women as a means to accrue some symbolic value to their devalued and vulnerable class position. To become respectable or to 'pass' as middle class, working-class women make strong investments in bodies, clothes, consumption practices, leisure pursuits, homes, etc. And yet, at the same time, they remain wary of many middle-class dispositions and values, retaining a strong sense of the injustice of their social and economic positioning. In short, the women both identified and dis-identified with their class position and lived these ambivalences as the 'hidden injuries' of shame, awkwardness and the sense of being judged by others (see Sennett and Cobb 1977).

This perspective on embodied agency in context not only powerfully illustrates the uncertainties and negotiations that accompany the reproduction of normative gender identity but it also brings into view other dimensions of power apart from the symbolic medium of language, most notably, class. Butler certainly problematizes the idea that there can be any stable identity, dominant or otherwise, but it is done from the perspective of the relational nature of meaning and, in her later work on melancholia, in terms of a perpetual dislocation between unconscious attachments and fixed subject positions. It is also the case that she frequently argues that her theory is socio-centric in that the performative construction of the subject takes place through other systems of power apart from language. Ultimately, however, her adherence to a linguistically abstract account of subjectivity prevents her from integrating an account of sexuality with other types of identity and it therefore lacks any kind of social or historical specificity. For Skeggs, in contrast, femininity is a difficult place for certain women to occupy, not because of an invariant logic of semantic or psychic instability, but because of class dynamics. To put it bluntly, for many working-class women, it is because their prospects of achieving respect through educational achievement, occupational success or any other conventional indices of social prestige are so minimal that they invest so heavily in themselves. In the absence of economic and social capital, the only capital in which they have to invest is their own body and appearance. Yet, despite this heavy investment, many of these women feel like interlopers in their enactment of femininity because it is associated with an unattainable middle-class elegance and 'savoir faire'. Furthermore, they cannot take themselves too seriously in case they are 'seen' as taking themselves too seriously and, by implication, as betraying their class origins. It is their class position that also generates a refusal of feminism which is regarded as the discourse of privileged women and irrelevant to their lives. Indeed, from their perspective, feminist critiques of conventional femininity undermine one of the few ways open to them to achieve any kind of social recognition, as fleeting and unstable as it might be. These experiential dilemmas of class and gender are occluded in Butler's discursive model of agency which theorizes the complexity of identity in the objectivist register of linguistically generated sexual difference. The effect of this is to collapse agency back into sexual identity or to produce an over-sexualized model of agency. While sexuality is a significant part of identity, a perspective on embodied being in context reveals that it is of fluctuating importance in the flow of existence where individuals are situated as citizens, workers, mothers, consumers, etc. As Moi puts it: 'The sex of the body is always there, but it is not always the most important fact about the body. The dying body or the body in pain is not necessarily grasped primarily in terms of sexual difference' (Moi 1999: 201). Rosemary Hennessey also criticizes this sexualization of agency, arguing that it is an effect of the reification of identity that abstracts an account of sexuality from the historical and social relations that produce and sustain them. Attacking Butler amongst others, she claims that the cultural feminist preoccupation with a certain notion of ambivalent lesbian desire rests on an unexamined perspective of middle-class privilege. The celebration of the lesbian 'as a figure of unfettered lust' fails to examine the social conditions which allow it to arise at the same time as 'welfare reform debates in which the sexuality and needs of unmarried poor women and their children have become the punitive targets of state mandated "personal responsibility"' (Hennessey 2000: 197). Ultimately, this fetishization of 'dead identities' freezes experience, blocks the establishment of connections with other types of 'outlawed need' and narrows the field of possible action and collective agency (Hennessey 2000: 228–9). Furthermore, such libidinalized notions of agency are congruent with an increasing commodification of the lifeworld: 'These more open, fluid, ambivalent sexual identities . . . are quite compatible with the mobility, adaptability, and ambivalence required of service workers today and with the new more fluid forms of the commodity. While they may disrupt norms and challenge state practices that are indeed oppressive, they do not necessarily challenge neoliberalism or disrupt capitalism' (Hennessey 2000: 108–9).

Ultimately, then, both cultural feminists such as Butler and thinkers of recognition produce reductive concepts of agency by binding them too closely to identity. The latter reduce the diverse logic of action by seeing it as governed by desire for self-expression, whereas the former reduce the logic of action by extrapolating one aspect of identity – sexuality – and defining women's agency around it. This replicates a reductive tendency in other types of feminist work, such as the ethics of care, where women's agency is defined around the maternal function. Unlike work on maternal ethics, however, the one-dimensional theorization of agency around sexuality is by no means an intentional effect of the work of Judith Butler and others, it is rather an indirect consequence of the inherent objectivism of their linguistic paradigms. Materialist feminists have produced powerful critiques of the cultural feminist preoccupation with ideas of identity and sexuality and of their more general symbolic 'reduction upwards' (Hall 1997: 33). An upshot of these critiques has been, however, that materialist feminists have retreated from the concepts of identity, subjectivity and agency altogether, explaining issues of change in terms of impersonal processes of structural transformation. Echoing the objectivist critiques of the idea of recognition made by Fraser and Young, there has been little attempt to reformulate these concepts in more materialist terms. Rather there has been a tendency to regard the cluster of concepts associated with identity as inherently subjectivist and, therefore, to abandon them. Thus, materialist feminists have reproduced, albeit in a reconfigured form, a similar move towards an objectivist mode of analysis made by cultural feminists. This move and its problematic consequences for an understanding of agency will be discussed in the next section.

MATERIALIST OBJECTIVISM

Materialist feminists have argued that, by absorbing society into language, cultural feminists privilege issues of identity, sexuality and agency over other aspects of gender inequality. They also underestimate the intractability of systemic forms of oppression and overestimate changes that can be brought about by an individualist identity politics. Nicola Field, for example, criticizes certain types of gay politics whose visibility rests on a disregard of class inequalities: 'gay lifestyle is visible as a specialized form of middle-class lifestyle and therefore is second nature to some, completely unattainable and meaningless to many' (Field 1997: 260). Against the cultural feminist stress on language and the mutability of identity, materialist feminists often proffer more cautious accounts of change. If gender relations can be said to be changing at all, then it is in a gradual and complex fashion where the emergence of new forms of autonomy coincides with the creation of new types of dependency and subordination. The cultural feminist emphasis on discursive instabilities within symbolic norms of gender is countered by a stress on the regular and predictable features of gender relations: 'while gender relations could potentially take an infinite number of forms, in actuality there are some widely repeated features' (Walby 1990: 16). This stress on entrenched regularities within the reproduction of gender relations involves drawing attention to economic and other material conditions which form the condition of possibility of identity politics. Sources of change are not located in individual action so much as in friction between social structures. For instance, transformations in the gender division of labour and the access it gives to material resources are regarded as more crucial determinant of levels of emancipation or subordination than shifts within gender ideologies and norms. If agency is considered, it is in its collective forms around so-called redistributive issues and not so much in its individualized manifestations around a politics of identity and sexuality. Indeed, Janet Saltzman Chafetz asserts that, although issues pertaining to sexual orientation are not irrelevant to gender system maintenance, compulsive and exclusive heterosexuality is not a fundamental bulwark of systemic reproduction. In contrast to the prevailing focus in cultural feminism on sexuality, lesbianism, in her view, is only harshly sanctioned when it is tied to social rebellion. Societal repression is most strongly directed, therefore, against rebellion and not sexual preference *per se* (Saltzman Chafetz 1990: 90).

The materialist feminist argument about the deep-rooted nature of gender inequalities and the gradual and uneven nature of any process of transformation is undoubtedly very powerful. However, their critique often seems to invoke a materialist objectivism that reproduces some of the difficulties with the symbolic objectivism that is so problematic in certain types of cultural feminism. Thus, materialist feminists assert a countervailing objectivism where the determining priority of economic structures is unambiguously asserted over other types of social and cultural experience. What often gets lost in the assertion of determining priority is the attempt to think through ideas of identity and agency in a materialist framework. Some of the difficulties that this move to a materialist objectivism presents for an understanding of agency can be illustrated in a consideration of Iris Marion Young's essay on gender as a serial structure. As we saw in Chapter 3, Young's claim is that if women are conceptualized as a social collective positioned by practico-inert structures, then certain of the difficulties associated with essentialism may be overcome. It becomes possible to understand how women are similarly situated with regard to certain materially conditioned aspects of their experience, such as the gender division of labour, without attributing fixed attributes or a common identity to them. This disconnection of gender from notions of identity allows the possibility of conceiving of political action based on shared interests rather than on the essentializing idea of recognition claims (Young 1994b: 722). Young's arguments are important in many respects but it is not so clear that the idea of gender can be so unambiguously disconnected from notions of identity without some theoretical losses. One significant loss is that it becomes difficult to explain aspects of social action without a concept of identity. Young argues, for example, that the claim that a common identity amongst women can be based on one or more of any number of shared characteristics seems to make feminist politics arbitrary. The idea of the series overcomes this arbitrariness in that it establishes a commonality amongst women on the basis of a shared position vis-à-vis certain relations of exploitation rather than on the questionable assertion of shared psychological characteristics. The problem for Young, however, is that it is not clear how she moves from the idea of gender as a series to the idea of women as political agents without some notion of mobilization. The idea of shared interests that she deploys as the basis for explaining political mobilization is, in many ways, no less arbitrary than the idea of common characteristics. There are as many difficulties in defining a so-called objective set of interests – not least amongst which is the problem of conflicting interests – as there are in delineating a set of shared subjective dispositions. Furthermore, the subjective grounds for mobilization, such as shared values or characteristics, are often theoretically more effective in explaining how individuals are galvanized into political action. Even if the idea of a common identity may be arbitrary or 'imagined', it brings into play certain affective and subjective dimensions to action which are crucial in understanding the mobilization of individuals and which remain obscure in the idea objective interests. It is not possible, then, to entirely disconnect an account of gender politics from notions of identity and subjectivity without losing certain insights into the nature of agency.

The materialist emphasis on objective structures forecloses important agentic dimensions to social change such as the extent to which attitudinal shifts contribute to social transformation. It may be difficult to plot a direct causal link between attitudinal shifts and structural transformation; nonetheless, the former may equally contribute to a gradual alteration in shared social practices which, in turn, may have a transforming impact on systemic tendencies in the manner of the so-called new social movements. In this respect, change is not the result of 'the vague tendency of the system, nor the undefined drive of change-oriented collectivities . . . but [of] the everyday conduct of common people, often quite far removed from any reformist intentions that are found to shape and reshape human societies' (Sztompka 1994: 39). An act that may seem conformist, from a structural perspective, may in fact entail either a non-propositional content or, conversely, high levels of self-consciousness, both of which may be indicative of slow but far-reaching cultural shifts. An often semi-articulated disjunction between expectations and actuality illustrates how the non-propositional or pre-rational content of agency may contribute to a transformation in social relations in the manner suggested by Raymond Williams' 'structures of feeling'. This denotes a type of lived experience – social experience 'in solution' – that transcends the merely personal or idiosyncratic, although, in its nascent stages, it may be experienced as private and isolating. It refers to certain affectual or emotional dimensions of social life which manifest themselves as the uncertain and often confused present of lived experience understood as 'elements of impulse, restraint, and tone; specifically affective elements of consciousness and relationships: not feelings against thought, but thought as felt and feeling as thought: practical consciousness of a present kind, in a living and interrelating continuity' (Williams 1977: 132). It is a form or quality of social experience that is indicative of the emergence of new practices and norms that may be in an embryonic phase but will become recognizable at a later historical stage. In this sense, although they may not be explicitly articulated, structures of feeling are not simply flux but should be conceived as structured formations that can 'exert palpable pressures and set effective limits on experience and on action' (Williams 1977: 132). Identity tends to be the category through which these psychological and affectual dimensions to action are thought and therefore to entirely disconnect gender from identity would be to weaken feminist thought on agency.

An underlying assumption of the materialist feminist move towards objectivism is that ideas of identity, agency and so forth are irremediably subjectivist and that this inevitably pulls feminist analysis back into either an individualistic or essentialist stance. This assumption is exemplified in Young's definition of identity as denoting either 'who persons are in a deep psychological sense' or as 'self ascription, as belonging to a group with others who similarly identify themselves' (Young 1994b: 734). Instead of viewing it as a deep psychological interiority, Young fails to consider how it might be possible to externalize the notion of identity with regard to a differentiated account of power relations. Although it takes divergent forms, the objectivism of both material and cultural feminism means ultimately that they are both unable to address certain subjective dimensions of agency that are important to an understanding of change in gender relations. It is with regard to overcoming some of these theoretical limitations that many feminists have seen in the phenomenological tradition of thought an alternative way of conceptualizing subjectivity and agency as a 'lived' relation rather than only as an objective position within social structures. The move towards a phenomenological perspective on embodied practice is undoubtedly important for understanding agency; however, theoretical difficulties arise because of the centrality of a certain troubling category of experience to these analyses. Feminists have long been aware of the essentializing implications of the idea of experience and have revised the category accordingly. However, despite these revisions, it still seems to exert a problematic unifying effect upon an understanding of women's social existence. As we will see in relation to feminist standpoint theory, there remains a residual investment in attributing an epistemological privilege to women's experience and this undercuts the attempt to situate a phenomenological perspective on embodied agency more securely within a mediated account of power relations.

THE PROBLEM OF EXPERIENCE

The category of experience has been central to the interpretative feminist attempt to explore neglected aspects of women's social existence, as Judith Stacey says: 'most feminist scholars advocate an integrative trans-disciplinary approach to knowledge which grounds theory contextually in the concrete realm of women's everyday lives' (Stacey 1988: 23). Yet, although the uncovering and revaluation of women's experience is central to the feminist project, the theoretical category of experience has been notoriously problematic on several counts. Ideas of experience have been crucial levers for criticizing the apparent objectivity of the natural and social sciences, yet, the ways in which they have been deployed often reinforce, rather than undo, the impacted dichotomies associated with the objectivity–subjectivity distinction. Against the objectivism of scientific knowledge, early feminist standpoint theory, for example, asserted a countervailing primacy of the subjective realm which privileged experience as the grounds of genuine, emancipatory knowledge. In this respect, experience is often associated with emotion and affect and imputed an authenticity that is counter-posed to abstract male reason (Scott 1992: 31). Experience, in this sense, is generally taken as a given, self-explanatory concept that each feminist specifies in her own way. Thus it is used to refer alternately to 'feelings, emotions, the personal, personality' (Lazreg 1994: 50). The granting of an epistemological privilege to experience in this way is a contentious strategy because it pushes feminism dangerously close to an unexamined empiricism which does not scrutinize the conditions that determine how experience relates to knowledge: 'To claim that women's experience is a source of true knowledge as well as the substance of the world to be known . . . constitutes the same "epistemic fallacy" as the one encountered by classical empiricists' (see Lazreg 1994: 52). The debate over essentialism highlighted how the idea of experience was often used to establish a tendentious unity between women. The absence of a clear definition for the category allows it to 'create a sense of consensus by attributing to it an assumed, stable and shared meaning' (Scott 1992: 32).

In its move to make women's experience the basis of a radical feminist critique, standpoint theory has, in particular, been widely criticized for its essentialism (e.g. Calhoun 1995: 162–92). In response to such criticisms, however, standpoint thinkers such as Sandra Harding and Dorothy Smith have modified their positions considerably, arguing that, while the experience of oppressed groups must be the starting point for the construction of more inclusive types of knowledge about the world, they must not be falsely unified or granted an absolute epistemological privilege. There is, for example, no pure realm of women's experience; it is always mediated through other power relations such as class. This means that although experience is the starting point of the project to construct alternative epistemologies, it cannot be its finishing point. It remains, however, important to reconstruct the experiential standpoint of marginalized groups because domination, of all different types, operates through the organization and objectification of the phenomenal world. One of the effects of this objectification is to undermine the validity of the individual's knowledge of her everyday world and thus to deny her agency. The attempt to reconstruct women's experience in a non-objectified manner constitutes a challenge to domination, although such counter-hegemonic attempts always run the risk of themselves becoming new modes of objectification. An experiential standpoint is not a guarantee of authentic, non-objectified knowledge, since all experience is constituted by power relations. It is possible, however, to revise relations of knowing by constructing knowledge ensembles based not on a single transcendent viewpoint but on the multiple perspectives of subjects in everyday life.

Although feminist standpoint thinkers have revised the status of experience vis-à-vis the construction of a counter-hegemonic sociology, they do not entirely avoid the problem of essentialism and this is partly, as is evident in the work of Dorothy Smith, because of the model of power as textual relations that is deployed. An understanding of power as text does not provide a sufficiently differentiated model of the logic of social relations and, as a consequence, results in an overstated account of domination and resistance. Smith's idea of text is certainly intended to be broad in that it denotes the centrality of technologies of print in disseminating a certain neutral objectified discourse through which the world is viewed. The textual formation of a dominant social consciousness does not operate through crude strategies of manipulation or domination but through the coordination of social practices and the objectification of certain perspectives upon the world: 'a complex of text-mediated relations evolves constituting a division of the labour of consciousness that objectifies in its hyper-realities the formerly individual attributes of knowledge, judgement and will as a field of *action* and domination' (Smith 1999: 91). Ruling relations do not operate outside everyday experience but permeate it: individuals participate in the world through forms of agency and subjectivity that ruling relations provide (Smith 1999: 77). The difficulty is that it is unclear how Smith moves from the assertion that ruling relations are inescapable in that they structure everyday practices and organize consciousness to the claim that the immediacy and multifarious nature of everyday social practice renders them resistant to incorporation into hegemonic discourses. Smith seems to invoke an aporetic conception of domination as all-pervasive, on the one hand, and as somehow external to everyday activities, on the other. This aporia is connected to the resurfacing of problematic 'essentialist' claims in her work about the inherently subversive nature of the standpoint of experience. Smith claims, for example, that standpoint theory must work 'from that site of knowing that is prior to the differentiation of subjective and objective' (1999: 49). This seems to impute an authenticity or cognitive privilege to everyday experience that, on the face of it, should be prohibited by her other claim that everyday life is always already organized by objectified relations of knowing. No less problematic is the assertion that the aim of stand-point theory is to construct an insider's sociology based on experi-ence where there is 'no contrast between thought and practice' (Smith 1999: 49). This replays a dilemma central to certain types of interpretative sociology, namely that by attributing an epistemolog-ical privilege to experience, any kind of sociological abstraction comes to be regarded as inherently alienating. Taken to its conclu-sion, this logic implies that sociology should limit itself to a faithful description of experience rather than any kind of objectifying analy-sis. Thus, despite her acknowledgement that there can be no unified women's perspective because it is always traversed by the other per-spectives of class, race, ethnicity, etc., Smith nonetheless finishes by asserting that there is indeed a standpoint that is 'distinctive to women and in important ways has marked us off from men and still continues to do so' (1999: 45). The problem, in the final analysis, is that Smith's textual model of power is not sufficiently differentiated to formulate the relation between social control and individual prac-tices in anything other than simplified and, at points, contradictory ideas of domination and resistance. Her insights about how objecti-fying perspectives can be modified through reference to experience are important but they are theoretically undeveloped because of the lack of a theory of mediation.

In her well-known article on experience, Joan Scott (1992) points out that some of the problems with the concept stem from metaphors of visibility and invisibility that often govern the exploration of mar-ginal experiences in historical analysis. While the project of making experience visible may bring to light the impact of repression upon the lives of marginalized groups, it often hinders a critical examina-tion of the way in which categories through which experience is rep-resented are themselves historically constituted. The metaphor of visibility exposes the mechanics of repression along a vertical analy-sis of the explicit and the latent, the dominant and the marginal, but it does not have a horizontal analysis of the way in which these cat-egories of representation are relationally constructed: 'Making visible the experience of a different group exposes the existence of repressive mechanisms, but not their inner workings or logics; we know that difference exists, but we don't understand it as consti-tuted relationally. For that we need to attend to the historical processes that, through discourse, position subjects and produce their experiences' (Scott 1992: 25). To overthrow the metaphor of vis-ibility is to consider experience itself as discursively constructed rather than to impute to it an incontestable authority. This process of historicization involves treating the emergence of concepts and identities not as unproblematic givens but as social and discursive events, in the manner of, say, Foucault's (1978) analysis of the construction of a notion of 'perversion' in nineteenth-century discourses of medicine and psychiatry. To analyse the construction of experience in this way is not, in Scott's view, to retreat to a form of linguistic determinism or to deny historical agency. As Scott puts it: 'Experience is a subject's history. Language is the site of history's enactment. Historical explanation cannot, therefore, separate the two' (Scott 1992: 34). It does, however, involve a consideration of how the idea of experience is linked, as a legitimating principle, to the construction of truth and knowledge effects in any given era.

Scott claims that her historicist, rather than foundational, approach to experience does not dissolve agency because conflicts between discursive systems enable individuals to make 'choices'. Her depiction of agency in such voluntarist terms is surprising and because she does not theoretically develop the idea, it operates in the same way as Butler's idea of 'willed effect', namely, as a kind of conceptual 'black box' which raises more questions than it answers. The idea of agency as choice seems to imply some pre-existing meta-subject who is able to move between and evaluate different discursive systems. As Sonia Kruks notes: 'what is tacitly posited here is a notion of a freedom that escapes and transcends discourse and of a subject that, although discursively positioned, still remains capable of rational reflection upon discourse from the perspective of its own freely chosen values or ends' (Kruks 2001: 143). In Kruks' view, Scott's critique of experience relies on a series of false antitheses, including that of foundationalism versus historicism and of an essentialist constituent self versus a discursively constituted subject. Her critique elevates the second terms over the first without any *a priori* reason for doing so, rather than showing how the idea of experience as lived process is not necessarily opposed to the idea of discursive construction. In the final instance, and despite her claims to the contrary, Scott falls back into a narrowly discursive model of power relations and a problematic linguistic abstraction which hamper her ability to think through certain subjective aspects of identity and agency.

EMBODIED PRACTICE AND HOPE

The difficulties with the idea of experience turn, ultimately, around integrating it within a sufficiently differentiated theory of power which finds a way between fetishizing it as a realm of epistemological authenticity and negating its lived validity in the emphasis on underlying structuring forces. In this regard, Bourdieu's idea of habitus provides some valuable insights into embodied agency because it provides a more mediated account of the way in which experience is connected to wider social structures.

Throughout his work, Bourdieu argues that an analysis of experience, defined as the subject's direct understanding of her conditions of existence, is crucial to an account of agency and to the more general project of reflexive sociology. The study of experience must not remain at the level of phenomenal immediacy, however, but must be integrated into a relational analysis of power relations. This analysis of power, which he calls a phenomenology of social space, is developed as part of his more general opposition to the objectivist and subjectivist approaches that he regards as dominating in the human sciences. The problem with objectivism is that its concern with social structures disregards the issue of agency and questions of recognition and misrecognition. Subjectivism, on the other hand, suffers from a 'substantialist illusion' and reduces the social world to nothing but the representations of actors, recognizing no other reality other than that which is available to direct intuition. If social action is to be properly understood, then, it is important to analyse the representations that actors have of the world and the way these inform action and interaction. Such representations cannot be deduced from social structures. Nor, however, do they encompass social reality in that they are determined by structures that are at one remove from immediate experience: 'the visible, that which is immediately given, hides the invisible which determines it. One thus forgets that the truth of any interaction is never entirely to be found within the interaction as it avails itself for observation' (Bourdieu 1990a: 126–7).

Thus although Bourdieu places the idea of experience at the centre of an understanding of agency, he understands it as a relative rather than absolute category. The recuperation of an experiential perspective is not an end in itself but is an heuristic tool that yields certain insights into embodied subjectivity and agency. The relativization of the category of experience is achieved through the concept of habitus and the idea of practice around which it turns. The idea of practice implies, on the one hand, that oppression is deeply rooted in psychological and physical dispositions. Practice is the result of the habitus that is itself the incorporation of temporal structures or the regularities and tendencies of the world into the body. The living-through of these embodied tendencies serves to endlessly sediment naturalized social hierarchies. Given this intrinsic connection between embodied identity and power, it is never possible to retrieve some authentic, experiential perspective that, in itself, could be the basis for counter-hegemonic knowledge. On the other hand, however, the idea of practice is also generative of a notion of agency in that it necessarily has a future-oriented or anticipatory dimension. In so far as the living through of embodied tendencies involves encounters with unanticipated or unknown social factors, then they are also the source of potential creativity and innovation in daily life. Identity emerges through practice, and practice is both the product of power relations that have been internalized into the body and also of an active engagement with social structures, as we 'intentionally shape ourselves in relation to them' (Kruks 2001: 123).

The idea of agency generated from embodied practice shares the emphasis of standpoint theory on the practical and intuitive dimensions of action but these are not understood as relatively spontaneous effects but as somatized power relations. The intrinsic connection between bodily experience and power is further contextualized by the idea of the 'field' that situates embodied agents within a given set of relations that comprise distinct spheres of social action. Each field has its own logic which arises in part from the struggles over its specific resources and relations of power. These are conceived as different types of 'capital', ranging from relations of meaning through to access to economic resources. Fields of action are interrelated but mutually irreducible and individuals move between fields of action. One of the advantages of the concept of the field, for an analysis of gender division, is that it provides a way of conceptualizing differentiated power relations which escape the dualisms of the public and the private. Given phenomena such as the changing nature of intimacy, the increased entry of women into work and other areas of public life and the demassification of gender divisions along class, racial and generational lines, feminist analysis requires a more differentiated model of power relations than is available in these dualisms. It is such a dualist account of power which, in a latent way, informs the standpoint theory assertion that, despite the complexities of social identities, it is nonetheless possible to recover a woman's perspective on the world. The multidimensional account of power relations inherent in the ideas of habitus and field forecloses such a possibility. A perspective on experience is the starting point for an understanding of social action but there can be no epistemological privilege attributed to such a perspective. The singularity of experience cannot be derived from 'a naively personalist view of the uniqueness of social persons' (Bourdieu et al. 1999: 618).

Rather, the complexity of embodied experience must be analysed simultaneously on several levels: in terms of the relation between individual habitus and field; the specific interactions between individuals within a field; the relations between different fields of action; and the way that general systemic tendencies (inequalities of race, gender and class, for example) are mediated through specific fields.

By positing an intrinsic relation between embodied existence and power, habitus moves away from the essentialism of certain phenomenological perspectives. It does not, however, abandon the ideas of subjectivity and agency as inherently subjectivist, as other materialist approaches often do. Even though the ideas of subjectivity, identity and agency partially denote some kind of psychological interiority, it is not enough to understand them only in this way. Habitus represents a materialist attempt to reconfigure these concepts as exteriorized relations to the social world. They are the product of the subject's exteriorized relation with social structures which is both intentional and non-intentional. It is non-intentional in that it expresses the latent tendencies of the world that have been absorbed into the body as a set of physical and psychological dispositions. However, it is also an intentional engagement with other individuals and social structures and, in this sense, identity is actively created through action. The idea of embodied identity as an active creation is also central to theories of performativity but whilst these propose a universal linguistic structure to agency, the idea of practice points towards its specificity. On this socio-centric account, the meaning of agency can only be derived from its position within the social order. The differences between the performative and socio-centric approaches to embodiment can be illustrated in a comparison of Butler's and Bourdieu's treatment of the anticipatory structure of action.

Both Bourdieu and Butler share the idea that agency arises from the future-oriented dimensions of practice. The open-ended nature of temporality, that we never know what is going to happen next, means that action is never simply reproduction, it potentially involves innovation and creation as part of the response to an uncertain future. Butler conceives of this temporal open-endedness in terms of a Derridean notion of *différence* which, because of the abstract level on which it is postulated, cannot address certain social dimensions of agency. It cannot explain, for example, why it is that, given that the uncertainty of the future is a universal condition, individuals act in such different ways faced with similar circumstances. In contrast, Bourdieu ties his discussion of temporal uncertainty to a discussion of the emotion of hope which itself is connected to social location. Hope is an emotional expression of protension defined as a practical sense of the forthcoming: 'the imminent forth-coming is present, immediately visible, as a present property of things' (Bourdieu 2000: 207). It is this idea of the practical anticipation of the immanent tendencies of the field which generates agency. Although protension is a general feature of agency, an individual's capacity to experience hope is conditioned by the ways in which power relations shape the agent's expectations and orientation towards the future: 'the practical relation to the forth-coming, in which the experience of time is generated, depends on power and the objective chances it opens' (2000: 231). The phenomenological experience of time is altered by relations of power which operate through an alignment of the subjective structure of hopes and expectations with the objective structure of probabilities. To put it schematically, class inequalities partially express themselves in the empty time of the dispossessed which contrasts with the full time of the busy person. There is a tendency for hope to increase proportionally with social power which enables an agent to manipulate the potentialities of the present in order to realize some future project. Or conversely, levels of resignation are often inversely proportional to class position (2000: 228). The most oppressed groups in society oscillate between fantasy and surrender which reflects how, below a certain threshold of objective chances, the strategic and anticipatory disposition diminishes. Instead, a generalized and lasting disorganization of behaviour and thought prevails which is linked to the disappearance of any coherent vision of the future: 'The real ambition to control the future . . . varies with the real power to control that future, which means first of all having a grasp on the present itself' (2000: 221).[1] Loss of hope and uncertainty are by no means only linked to class inequalities. Systemic tendencies towards social complexity and uncertainty such as increasing occupational insecurity, social mobility and the expansion of higher education lead increasingly to mismatches between expectations and objective chances: 'the lack of a future, previously reserved for the "wretched of the earth" is an increasingly widespread, even modal experience' (2000: 234).

The difficulty with Butler's account of the anticipatory structure of action is that it is detached from any kind of phenomenal or social context; it is an abstract logic without any emotional content or social logic. A consequence of this abstraction from social location is, as Eve Sedgwick has observed, that the 'internally complex field of drag performance suffers a seemingly unavoidable simplification and reification' (Sedgwick 2003: 9). Against this, Bourdieu's model restores a specific subject to action whose capacity to act arises from the interplay between emotional dispositions (habitus), social context (field) and class relations (structure and capital). It is precisely this tying of emotions to social location which renders Bourdieu's work vulnerable to charges of determinism, where agency is understood as the acting out of somatized power relations pertaining to an individual's position within the social structure. Such a view is based on a misunderstanding of the nature of habitus and its relational dynamics with the field and general social structures. This relation is an active, not a passive one, whose outcome is practice. Emotions emerge through practice and practice is both the product of power relations that have been internalized into the body and also of an active engagement with social structures. In so far as they are the product of intentional engagement with other individuals and social structures, there is never one way in which an individual may act in response to a situation but a range of possible responses which gives social life its spontaneous and complex character. It creates what Bourdieu calls a 'margin of freedom', the space of creative agency (2000: 235). A field of action is constituted as a complex imbrication of material and symbolic relations of power, expressed as the intertwinement of the structure of 'positions' within the 'space of possibles'. The space of possibles means that interactions within a field can be generative of 'cognitive and motivating structures' that can override the entrenched dispositions of actors, pushing them to unexpected or nonconformist types of actions. For example, individuals may break the 'feeling rules' of a particular situation because of spontaneous emotions experienced in their relationship to a situation or another person (Burkitt 1997: 49). Nonetheless, because of the way in which power relations become sedimented in the body, this contingency of action is patterned and not entirely random: 'the opacity of historical processes derives from the fact that human actions are the non-random and yet never radically mastered product of countless self-obscure encounters between habitus . . . and social universes' (Bourdieu 2000: 116).

EMOTIONS AND ACTION

The implications of this socio-centric perspective on the embodied, affectual dimensions of agency for a feminist understanding of gender can be illustrated if we return to the central question of this chapter, namely the relation between identity and action. In so far as embodied practice is determined by a complex of interiorized and exterior relations of power, habitus suggests a variable relation between identity and action. In other words, action is not directly governed by identity in the way that theorists of recognition and certain types of feminism suggest. It is particularly important for feminists to theorize the often indirect connections between embodied identity and action, if the reductive implications of connecting women's agency to only one aspect of their social existence are to be avoided. In this regard, the difficulties with maternal theories of agency have been much discussed, not least their tendency to sentimentalize motherhood by highlighting its features of altruism and care and downplaying its negative features. This reinforces a more general trend in feminism to 'assign women only positive characteristics, thus revaluing traditional femininity' (Gardiner 1995: 3). Likewise, it is easy for feminist work on emotions to replicate a tendency in the work of recognition theorists like Taylor and Honneth, in that by treating the affectual dimensions of existence in a straightforwardly expressive manner, a naturalized social or moral consensus can be tacitly constructed. In other words, unified notions of women's experience can be sustained through a latent reliance upon an uncritical phenomenology of emotions. In so far as it is indicative of a self-present subject, this spontaneist understanding of emotions has been thrown into question by the Foucauldian focus on an analytics of desire (see Terada 2001).[2] By detaching an analysis of 'passionate attachments' from other structures of power, a consequence of this discursive constructionism is that it individualizes an understanding of emotions in so far as they are related to only intrapsychic dynamics of desire. Although it may be unintended, these individualistic tendencies are compounded by the elevation of one aspect of identity – sexuality – over others in the conception of agency. Butler's focus on resistance as libidinal activity or a 'style of the flesh' (Butler 1990: 139) remains caught within a privatized and individualist conception of activity whose radical political status is open to question in so far as it is complicit with, rather than disruptive of, capitalism (Hennessey 2000: 108–9).

From the perspective of habitus, emotions are neither purely 'natural' nor discursive effects; they are generated in and mediate the interactions between embodied subjects and social structures. There are, of course, many socio-centric approaches to the emotional dimensions of action available within sociological literature. The burgeoning sociology of emotions has emerged as part of the displacement of the heroic, rational accounts of agency characteristic of Weberian theory and of the narrow interest-based theory of action in rational choice theory (see Williams and Bendelow 1998: 131–54). Although they are diverse, these sociological approaches share a relational account of emotions; they do not inhere within individuals but are types of social interaction. This 'deep sociality' of emotions resides in the way they are held to mediate not only intersubjective relations but also the relationship between individuals and social structures and processes. One of the weaknesses of the sociology of emotions is, however, that its constructionist emphasis often overemphasizes emotions as managed, as a part of social role playing (see Burkitt 1997). Bourdieu's idea of habitus moves away from this intentional and subject-centred approach, suggesting instead that emotions are multidimensional complexes generated through the interplay of bodily dispositions, the intersubjective relations of the field and social structures. The interplay of an individual's latent emotional dispositions and tendencies with emotions generated through specific interaction suggests a more varied and discontinuous way of understanding how emotions are played out in action. For example, many socially effectual emotions – in the sense of mobilizing agency – are likely to be experienced below the threshold of awareness. Unlike psychoanalysis, however, this pre-reflexive emotional substratum is not explained through the idea of intra-psychic dilemmas but is related to the complexities of social position. Habitus is generative of emotional dispositions but these do not necessarily manifest themselves in action in any simple way; there is a difference between emotions as dispositions and emotions as direct motivations for action. As Burkitt puts it: 'dispositions are not mechanical responses to a given situation, but are more like conditions which may or may not become manifested in certain contexts' (Burkitt 1997: 43). On this socio-centric view, the latent intentionality of embodied emotional dispositions might be at odds with the explicit intentionality of emotions as motivations for action.[3] Thus, for example, Bottero and Irwin have shown how the idea of choice is an inadequate way of explaining increasing childlessness amongst women (Bottero and Irwin 2003: 478–9). Sociological studies have shown that women do not perceive themselves as having made a deliberate choice to remain childless but rather see it as an outcome of a variety of circumstances. The conflicting expectations of their personal and professional identities engender complex emotional responses which are effaced by using the voluntarist language of choice or by theorizing emotions only around one dimension of embodied identity.

One consequence of viewing multilayered emotions as responses to the complexities of social location is that the intertwinement of sexuality with other structures of power comes into view. Thus using the idea of habitus, Walkerdine, Lucey and Melody show how, despite increased opportunities, class remains a fundamental determinant of young girls' life trajectories, not so much in terms of objective access to resources but as a set of class-specific emotional dispositions. On this view, the reproduction of sexual identity is inseparable from the reproduction of structures of feeling pertaining to class. The production of bourgeois feminine identity, for example, is bound up with anxieties about performance that derive from a middle-class orientation towards educational success. Intellectual achievement is acquired often at the price of sustaining emotional well-being, which was manifested in the middle-class girls' ambivalent and punitive attitudes towards their sexuality. For the working-class girls, their sexuality was not seen as a threat to educational attainment and, on one level, they displayed a greater acceptance of their sexualized identities, in particular, their reproductive capacities. However, this apparent straightforwardness was also a psychic defence against the destabilizing possibilities of class mobility that academic achievement presented. This ambivalence towards achievement, that it is something to be desired but also feared, was mediated through the working-class girls' seemingly carefree attitude to the possibility of becoming pregnant: 'it was the fecund body that asserted itself as the rock in her pathway, the very thing that might thwart her ambition and place her in that much more familiar and safe territory of young motherhood'. In short, understanding emotions in relation to social location rather than intra-psychic dynamics serves to situate sexuality within a broader sociological account of power and also construes class, not just as an abstract social location, but as a set of persistent emotional dispositions. As Dianne Reay puts it: 'despite a pervasive denial of class status, there are emotional intimacies of class which continue to shape individuals' everyday understandings, attitudes and actions' (Reay 1998: 267). In a similar fashion, Skeggs draws attention to the consequences of a set of latent emotional dispositions of class upon a politics of recognition. In her view, a politics of recognition relies on a manipulation of a rhetoric of suffering which is more easily managed by privileged social groups and which gives their claims a certain moral authorization. This rhetoric of suffering and distress is, however, ultimately an unreliable indicator of injustice because it has a 'long route through the development of the bourgeois individual' (Skeggs 2004c: 58). According to Skeggs, the discourse of recognition is the most recent manifestation of a conception of the body and self as property that has always been characteristic of the bourgeois classes. Thus, the discourse of suffering and vulnerability is often paradoxically underpinned by an unacknowledged confidence derived from a privileged class habitus. According to Skeggs, less privileged groups are unable or dispositionally disinclined to reconfigure their experiences in such a manner: 'Only some groups can articulate their identities through wound or pain and only some groups would want to. Only some groups can produce their subjectivity in this way and focus on themselves and their experience as the basis for knowledge (Skeggs 2004c: 58).

It is the idea of emotions engendered through the complex of embodied tendencies, intentional relations with the world and social structures that disrupts the tendency to explain agency through a fixed set of emotional dispositions or a single dimension of embodied identity. It is important to develop such socio-centric ways of understanding embodied existence to avoid the reproduction of a concept of agency that 'locks women up in their particularized female subjectivity' (Moi 1999: 204). Women's self-awareness of themselves as sexualized subjects has intermittent significance according to the particular situation they find themselves in.[4] Denise Riley's much-quoted example of the jolt experienced by women when they are the recipients of wolf whistles is a mundane example of the way in which awareness of sexual identity waxes and wanes in the course of everyday practices. Toril Moi explains these variations in gender self-awareness in terms of Beauvoir's phenomenological idea of the body as background:

> To say that the body is the inevitable background for all our acts, is at once to claim that it is always a potential source of meaning, and to deny that it always holds the key to the meaning of a woman's acts . . . the sex of a body is always there, but it is not always the most important fact about that body (Moi 1999: 201).

Habitus captures certain dimensions of the social complexity of women's embodied existence. Although the gendered habitus is the most profound and ensures the inscription of certain affectual and psychological dispositions in women, these dispositions do not manifest themselves in action in any simple way. As women move across different social fields, they will engage in varying types of practice, some of which reinforce latent bodily predispositions, some of which are only tangentially related or are even disruptive of these dispositions. This leads to an understanding of the emotional dimensions of agency where women are understood as social beings rather than as unvaryingly sexual or maternal ones. From this perspective, agency is not a generalized capacity – e.g. the performative – but an unevenly realized and specific mode of embodied intervention in the world which is determined by a certain configuration of power relations.

AGENCY AND RESISTANCE

Many feminists would be unconvinced by the socio-centric account of embodied emotions yielded by the idea of habitus and, to an extent, their doubts are not unfounded. In Bourdieu's account of masculine domination, habitus is used to theorize, in a rather crude fashion, the idea that women are actively complicit in their own subordination (Bourdieu 1990b: 26).[5] This idea of complicity forecloses many of the tensions and complexities that characterize the way in which men and women assume gender identities. Beverley Skeggs, for example, is critical of the idea of complicity because, on the basis of her study of working-class women, she found that the process whereby they construct meaningful identities for themselves, beyond the parameters of middle-class norms, is not one of passive accommodation. Far from being complicit, these women had high levels of self-awareness and a critical understanding of the nature of their oppression: 'their experience was not an unconscious pre-reflexive gendered experience based on misrecognition, but a specifically class-gendered experienced, one of which they were highly critical and highly attuned' (Skeggs 2004a: 25). Likewise, Angela McRobbie (2002) argues, in *The Weight of the World*, that the idea of habitus is used to generate a one-sidedly negative account of working-class experience where all signs of cultural and social vitality – what Gilroy has called the 'syncretic dynamism of contemporary metropolitan life' – has been removed (Gilroy 2000: 245). So too, Elspeth Probyn argues that although the idea of habitus gestures towards a promising account of the affectual dimensions of embodied existence, its potential is never realized because of its instrumental bias. On Bourdieu's account, emotions always reinforce rather than disrupt the 'finality of the habitus', thus ensuring the correspondence between an individual's dispositions and the objective field of power relations (Probyn 2004: 232). Emotion is little more than a 'cognitive adjustment mechanism' which disregards the body's 'physiological and emotional unruliness' (Probyn 2004: 232, 236). In this regard, Bourdieu's work reflects a wider tendency in the sociology of emotions, namely the emptying of the body of any innate dynamism and 'of any interest except as a screen for the social' (2004: 238).

It is the case that the habitus does not emphasize emotion as a form of corporeal unruliness, rather emotion is conceived in a more mundane sense, as a constant aspect of our milieu. In highlighting this emotional subtext, Bourdieu's aim is primarily to show the deep entrenchment of arbitrary social hierarchies upon the body, but its praxis orientation does not necessarily rule out ideas of agency and change. What is at stake, then, is not so much that the idea of habitus forecloses a dynamic account of agency, but rather how agency and change are conceptualized. Underlying Probyn's and Skeggs' critiques of Bourdieu is a problematic formulation of agency as resistance where the unruly and nonconformist moments of existence, *qua* emotions, are invested with an inherently subversive status. On an explicit level, writers such as Probyn and Skeggs are well aware of the limitations of the idea of resistance which revolve largely around its invocation of romantic and heroized ideas of working-class practice (Rose 1999: 65). It is often not clear what it is precisely that is being resisted and, as Pamela Fox has pointed out, theorists of resistance are often very selective in focusing only on certain progressive practices and in underestimating the costs of exclusion from controlling culture. As a consequence of such criticisms, explicitly celebratory ideas of resistance have been abandoned. However, they often resurface in work on identity where resistance is based on ideas of unruly emotion, disruptive desires and other indeterminate features of social existence. These moments of non-identity are thereby invested with a problematic contestatory status. This is not to deny that certain ineffable and indeterminate aspects of existence are harbingers of change in the manner suggested by Williams' idea of structures of feeling. It is certainly the case that everyday life is frequently marked by emotional and corporeal experiences whose meaning is opaque but which are profoundly felt and disrupt the closure of routinized existence. But to attribute to these inchoate and ineffable emotions a resistant status is to implicitly invoke an uncritical phenomenology which fails to connect emotions and bodily affects to underlying power structures.

Some of the problematic political implications of such ideas of resistance as indeterminate emotion can be seen in Skeggs' work on working-class affect. The problem with the idea of habitus, in her view, is that it depicts many of the negative emotions of working-class life as expressions of resignation or adjustment. This reading denudes working-class experience of its dynamic emotions and energy: 'We need to know about the cramped spaces of politics where libidinal energies break through the processes of inscription that attempt to contain and govern' (Skeggs 2004: 89). Such explosive expressions of emotion should be interpreted, then, as displaced outrage at the injustices of the class system. These 'periperformative' utterances fall outside a dominant symbolic logic in that the volatile emotions they express cannot be contained or appropriated. They have no value other than the immediate use value of expressing a disengagement from the social order. They can, however, be viewed as a continuation of the class struggle in an affectual mode. It is this last claim that is troubling because it reveals how emotions have been invested with an apodictically resistant status. Bourdieu would not deny that expressions of rage have an immediate emotional use value to the excluded, or that they are underpinned by an acute sense of the injustices of class inequality. Dominant values are inescapable and their symbolic violence shapes all areas of social experience, often being expressed as psychological and corporeal negativity. Outbursts of rage may express simultaneously a psychological form of non-accommodation and, at the same time, a feeling of powerlessness in the face of economic deprivation and exclusion. Similarly, shame can be interpreted as both a recognition of the inadequacy of a society that thwarts the self-expression of certain groups of individuals and, simultaneously, as self-hatred based on the internalization of those very same dominant values (Fox 1994). However, Bourdieu would refrain from attributing to these negative emotions any subversive or resistant force because, beyond the immediate phenomenal level, their impact is limited and fleeting. They therefore cannot really be heralded as an indirect form of class struggle or resistance which, to be meaningful, in his view, has to have a deeper impact upon entrenched social structures and therefore broader social and political implications.

In order to address the contradictory effects of relations of power upon agency, it is important, therefore, to deploy a more flexible set of concepts than what Fox calls the 'circuit model of resistance'. It is also important to avoid an all too easy conflation of the idea of agency with resistance. In so far as any action is never one of simple mechanical reproduction, nonconformity is a widespread characteristic of social agency, but this cannot be taken as an automatic guarantor of its resistant status. Indeed, in the light of the diverse nature of an intensified consumerism and of changes in methods of social control, what appears to be a nonconformist or resistant act at one level might, at another level, be its opposite. It is these complex imbrications of freedoms with constraints that Nicholas Rose has in mind when he argues that, in an era where the regulation of identity is a central mode of social control, it is necessary to break away from the simplifying couplet of domination and resistance. Generalizing Foucault's idea of governmentality as the 'conduct of conduct', Rose argues that individuals are controlled, not through explicit forms of domination, but through rationalized techniques and devices which orient action to certain socially useful ends. The shaping of identity is a key strategy of these techniques of government. Through a wide range of practical, procedural and technical interventions we are encouraged to relate to ourselves as self-responsible and self-mastering individuals. These new forms of government force us to rethink identity beyond the formula that regimes of power necessarily falsify or distort human subjectivity. Rather these styles of government produce new modes of subjectification, ways of being and acting that 'make up subjects as free persons' in a manner that is neither authentic nor inauthentic (Rose 1999: 95). This mode of government of the self ultimately leads away from ideas of freedom as resistance towards the idea of freedom as a form of power, as a capacity for liberty that is drawn out of individuals through the government of social practices. Freedom is not the obverse of domination or order or control, rather it is 'the name we give to a kind of power one brings to bear upon oneself and a mode of bringing power to bear on others' (Rose 1999: 95–6).

It is a similar idea of freedom in constraint that is expressed in Bourdieu's idea of 'regulated liberties' which are manifest in embodied practice. Bourdieu objects to ideas of resistance because they are based in absolutized ideas of indeterminacy which fail to take account of the deep-rooted hold that power has over bodies: 'even the most subversive symbolic actions, if they are not to condemn themselves to failure, must reckon with dispositions, and with the limitations these impose on innovative imagination and action' (2000: 234–5). Against unqualified ideas of indeterminacy, Bourdieu understands change as generated by the interplay of necessity and contingency. Habitus is in a state of permanent revision, but this revision is rarely radical because the new and unexpected is always incorporated upon the basis of previously established, embodied dispositions. Bourdieu does not deny the importance of acts of iconoclasm and subversion which challenge social boundaries by enacting the previously unthinkable. However, for these acts of subversion to have lasting force, they must have some impact on social structures, revealing them to be 'in a state of uncertainty and crisis' or awakening a 'critical consciousness of their arbitrariness and fragility'. This does not amount to a denial of the creative agency or vibrancy on the part of oppressed groups and individuals. There is always a margin of freedom in the workings of symbolic power and this is created in the same instant as individuals are aligned to the status quo: 'symbolic power, which can manipulate hopes and expectations . . . can introduce a degree of play into the correspondence between expectations and changes and open up a space of freedom' (2000: 235). It is, however, to recognize the importance of putting the creative dimensions of action in the context of immediate and latent relations of power that operate in any situation. The idea of regulated liberties yields a more gradual and uneven concept of change than the idea of resistance where it is construed as a phenomenal immediacy. The sources of change are varied and their manifestations are discontinuous and non-synchronous in so far as they are mediated through different fields of action. Change may occur within gender relations, for example, because of the interplay between cultural norms and embodied dispositions. The 'hysteresis' effect refers to the generational dislocation that can arise between norms and dispositions, where cultural values have historically outstripped the expectations that individuals have largely inherited from their parents. Such a dislocation is arguably generative of new freedoms and insecurities in contemporary gender relations where the expectation of long-term monogamous intimacy is increasingly belied by emergent contemporary practices and norms. Or, conversely, expectations of equality in relationships are undermined by entrenched gender asymmetries in the behaviours of men and women (e.g. Lewis 2001). The emotional implications of such dissonances are neither wholly positive or negative, neither straightforwardly emancipating or constraining, resistant or conformist. Furthermore, the full significance of such emotional shifts vis-à-vis change within gender relations can only be considered in relation to the extent they interact with other transformations in the structural organization of gender (e.g. Bottero and Irwin 2003: 478). Habitus illuminates only one incarnate dimension of such processes of gender restructuring but, in so far as it exteriorizes embodied practice in relation to social structures, it gestures towards a more mediated and nuanced understanding of change than the ideas of emotional indeterminacy that underlie ideas of resistance. It also highlights the necessity of distinguishing more clearly between two senses of agency that are often conflated in the idea of resistance. Agency denotes both the sense in which individuals are not just passive bearers of social roles and a more politicized sense, where individuals are understood to actively challenge their conditions of existence. Given that under conditions of global capital so many areas of individual activity are subject to commodifying forces, many practices that are hailed as resistant in fact have little political bite. This is neither to fall back into unmitigated cynicism nor to resuscitate infeasible ideas of revolutionary change. It is rather to emphasize that in thinking about change, it is important to go beyond dualisms of domination and resistance in order to situate identity and agency more securely within a social theoretical account of power relations.

CONCLUSION

One of the central problems of the way in which the idea of recognition has often been developed is that it finishes by binding agency too tightly to particular concepts of identity. It tends to frame agency as an unmediated expression of an individual's desire for recognition. This inadequate understanding of the way in which power constitutes subjectivity and identity finishes by naturalizing the idea of agency. Feminist theory is more attuned to the operations of power around subjectivity but the objectivist way this has been conceptualized, through an abstract notion of discourse, leaves crucial aspects of identity and agency unexplained. In particular, it cannot explain certain subjective dimensions of agency such as will, self-understanding and intention which are crucial to explaining some of the political implications of action. Moreover, the objectivist tendencies of feminist theory lead to a preoccupation with construing subjectivity in terms of the construction of desire in language and this results in accounts of agency formulated primarily around one aspect of identity – sexuality. Thus, albeit in a different manner, feminist theory often finishes by yoking an account of agency too tightly to a certain narrow conception of identity. Against these general construals of agency as recognition or as performativity, I have suggested that the idea of habitus yields a more specific notion of agency as embodied practice that is realized in different ways through particular configurations of power. The idea of practice exteriorizes dimensions of embodied existence – for example, emotions – in respect to social relations and thereby avoids the simplification and naturalization of agency. It is important to think about women's agency in these terms if their social existence is not to be reduced to a single aspect of embodied existence, such as sexuality. It is also important to think in these socio-centric terms if the differences between women as social rather than sexual subjects are to be understood.

More generally, I have argued against the idea of recognition in so far as it is used to naturalize particular accounts of subject formation and is consequently deployed as a universal model of social interaction and agency. The way in which certain thinkers tend to analytically over-extend the idea of recognition is an example of what Bourdieu calls a 'scholastic epistemocentrism' where the specificity of social practice is neutralized by being assimilated to an intellectual construct (2000: 52). I have argued, furthermore, that these tendencies to naturalization and universalization are integral rather than extrinsic to recent elaborations of the idea of recognition in so far as they are the necessary consequence of the redemptive force with which it is invested. In order to sustain the ideas of communicative or expressive mutuality that, for the thinkers considered here, constitutes the normative heart of the idea of recognition, it is necessary to underplay the pervasive and often insidious ways in which social inequalities are reproduced through embodied identity.

It follows from the logic of my argument that the idea of recognition need not necessarily be so problematic if its analytical and normative scope is more delimited. It may have a certain descriptive value, for example, as an ideal type with which to characterize a small subsection of cultural struggles that make claims about justice through the assertion of a particular group identity. Beyond such constrained uses, however, it seems to me that the idea of recognition cannot be usefully generalized as a model for non-distributive types of social conflict without certain foreclosures in terms of an understanding of the ways in which social inequalities are reproduced through subject formation. Above all, it appears that the idea of recognition is a particularly inappropriate theoretical lens through which to examine a range of issues pertaining to sexual division, such as the restructuring of gender relations and the nature of embodied agency. At the most basic descriptive level, it is difficult, if not impossible, to classify women (and men) as a coherent class or group with a common identity or a shared set of interests. This is not to say that women do not act as coherent groups but such types of collective action are not the result of an intrinsic, shared identity but rather of a determinate set of social relations. At a conceptual level, the idea of recognition is constraining for an analysis of gender because it remains committed to a face-to-face model of power that obscures the systemic ways in which sexual and other inequalities are produced. While the master–slave dialectic of recognition struggles can identify interpersonally generated modes of domination, it tends to disconnect embodied existence from impersonal forms of social regulation. Against the one-dimensionality of the idea of recognition, therefore, the analysis of issues of gender requires a multidimensional model of social relations that allows an account of how it is organized around different social axes, such as race, class and generation, and also that connects the phenomenal realm of embodied sociality to underlying structures of power. The normative force of the idea of recognition does not seem sufficient, moreover, to offset these analytical limitations in its account of power. As a regulative ideal, recognition seems to invoke almost

inevitably a sanitized idea of embodied identity that returns feminist thought to problematically normative accounts of women's
social existence. Furthermore, the argument that, in order to prevent
the slide into a relativist politics of difference, feminist thought necessarily requires the universal ethical foundations and intersubjective binding force of the idea of recognition is overstated. To say that
the concern with the construction of social differences necessarily
undermines any common ground for political critique is to set up a
false polarity. On the contrary, it could be argued that feminist
thought develops and renews itself only by constantly refining its
understanding of the multifarious ways in which hierarchies of
power divide and unite men and women. There are many other
ways of formulating a universal framework for emancipatory critique that do not require the type of problematic ontological claim
that latently informs the work of so many recent thinkers of recognition. Thus, the final sense in which I am against recognition is that,
even if it can be constructively used to examine certain specific types
of cultural struggle, it has little sustained analytical and normative
relevance for an analysis of gender.

Notes

INTRODUCTION

1 Social reproduction becomes a quasi-automatic process because the idea of habitus filters out indeterminacy and struggle from an understanding of individual action. According to Dreyfus and Rabinow, the idea of misrecognition that is central to habitus conflicts with Bourdieu's notion of embodied agency because each generates an antithetical ontology of practice (Dreyfus and Rabinow 1993: 43). On the one hand, habitus emphasizes that practice is thoroughly social, that its meaning can only be derived from its position within the social order. This specificity is undercut, on the other hand, by Bourdieu's claim that practices across diverse fields have the same concealed or misrecognized underlying motive, namely competition for material and symbolic advantage: 'the field as a structure of the objective relations between positions of force undergirds and guides the strategies whereby the occupants of these positions seek, individually or collectively, to safeguard or improve their position and to impose the principle of hierarchization most favourable to their own products' (Bourdieu 1992: 101). This second, instrumental rendering of action gives rise to criticisms that Bourdieu's concept of agency is, ultimately, not that dissimilar to rational choice accounts where action is always motivated by the maximization of interests. From a Habermasian perspective, such an instrumental formulation of agency forecloses alternative accounts of the interpretative and cognitive capacities displayed by social actors. Likewise, James Bohman (1999) argues

that any account of agency must not only consider ways in which actors are caught within structures of power and domination, authorization and marginalization but must also include an account of their capacity for practical reflection: 'to give convincing reasons, to back up claims made in speech when challenged by other speakers' (Bohman 1999: 140). Ultimately, the account of agency as the realization of symbolic profits says little about the causes of action because symbolic advantage has necessarily to be construed so widely to establish it as a universal motive that it is emptied of content and: 'To say that whatever people do they do for social profit does not tell us anything if profit is defined as whatever people pursue in a given society' (Dreyfus and Rabinow 1993: 42).

Bourdieu defends himself against these criticisms by claiming that they are based on a narrowly economic interpretation of his idea that actors always have strategic interests. Interest need not necessarily mean the maximization of utility but rather can be interpreted in the more general sense of an investment or sense that something is worthwhile: 'To be interested is to accord a given social game that what happens in it matters, that its stakes are important . . . and worth pursuing' (Bourdieu 1992: 116). This is certainly the way in which it has been used by thinkers such as Wendy Holloway to explain the often unconscious motivations that lead women to adopt subject positions that are widely regarded as subordinate (Holloway 1984). Despite construing interest in a more general sense, arguably it is still a narrow depiction of the diverse causes for action. Motivations such as altruism, loyalty, faith or fear, for example, fit uneasily into the idea of interest. The account of action as motivated by symbolic profit produces, in Andrew Sayer's words, a 'universal deflation of actors' normative claims' (Sayer 1999: 61). The idea that individuals might be impelled to act because of their beliefs in what is right, good or just is undermined by being presented as a rationalization of a prior struggle for power. From a feminist perspective, there are many areas of gendered agency, mothering being the prime example, that cannot be construed in such terms.

2 In this respect, I follow thinkers such as Sonia Kruks (2001) and Toril Moi (1999) who argue that the conceptual legacy of phenomenology has been relatively neglected in feminist thinking on gender identity with the ascendancy of poststructural theory. The tradition of existential phenomenology provides important intellectual resources for feminists because of its shared orientation towards understanding the centrality of embodied being in social existence.

3 I have discussed the internal complexity of the field at greater length elsewhere. See McNay 2001.

CHAPTER 1

1 Butler suggests the idea of 'cultural translation' as a way of grasping the perpetual failure of the universal ever to fully cover its concrete contents not as a formal or empty (in the sense of the transcendental) relation but as a socially variable one (Butler 2000b: 136–81).

2 There are different ways in which the unconscious might be reconceptualized. Cornelius Castoriadis (1987), for example, conceives of the unconscious not as an original lack but as a radical imaginary, that is, a primal representative flux or capacity to create representations *ex nihilo*. An implication of this attribution of a positivity to prelinguistic being is that subjectivity is regarded not just as an imaginary suturing of a primal lack but as having a substantive motivational basis. The originary capacity for figuration explains why it is that individuals are motivated to act in creative or unanticipated ways.

3 The historian Laura Downs has argued, for example, that Benjamin's work provides a 'structural and historically specific ground' for analysing how inequalities are woven into psychic and social structures. Downs claims that: 'By exploring the genesis (in time) of this polarity at the interwoven levels of culture and the individual psyche, Benjamin is able to offer a historical account of how equality and difference have been lined up as the asymmetrical antinomy on which . . . liberal conceptions of social and political equality rest' (Downs 1993: 426). See also, Joan Scott's (1993) critical response to Downs.

4 For some thinkers, the divergences between Benjamin and Butler are superficial and can be attributed to the different registers at which each theorist operates – one at the level of the operations of meaning, the other at the level of the analytical encounter – then their projects can be seen to be complementary rather than conflicting. In this view, Benjamin's idea of over-inclusiveness might be seen as a concrete illustration of the performative ambivalences that Butler only considers from the abstract perspective of the symbolic construction of desire. This is the view of Stephen Frosh, for example, who argues that 'Benjamin's careful description of the way subjects can take up positions integrating the different identi-

fications available to them is a useful counterpoint to the possible pessimistic outcome of performativity theory' (Frosh 1999: 238).

5 In a striking passage, Steedman shows what this might mean when she discusses a form of shared identification between mothers and daughters in the nineteenth century based on the maintenance of social standing:

> Ambivalence has been characterized as a mental structure unique to the bourgeois family, the route by which a child purchases a parent's love in exchange for finding its own body disgusting . . . the drama of ambivalence resulted in a child's being able to internalize a rule-system which was represented by its authority/love relationship with its parents. But there is another drama of ambivalence . . . which is the child's recognition that whilst she is wanted, she is also resented: that it is economic and social circumstances that make a burden out of her, that make her a difficult item of expenditure (Steedman 1986: 90).

6 Although gender inequalities may be generated at an anonymous, abstract level, their consequences are nonetheless experienced in immediate interaction as felt necessities. It is, therefore, not just a question of asserting that the reproduction of gender hierarchies takes place at a systemic as well as an interpersonal level. It is also a question of showing how these systemic relations are manifest in immediate interaction as felt necessities. For example, Susan Thistle (2000) shows how the increased entry of women into the labour force in the middle of the twentieth century was generative of dissatisfaction amongst men who increasingly experience 'traditional' marriage relations as restrictive (see also Fraser 1997: 230). Tracing the connections between a cultural politics of identity and materialist issues is not simple because these connections can be indirect and abstract in the sense that they are not always visible from the perspective of everyday life.

CHAPTER 2

1 This runs counter to the claim of Anglo-American political philosophers that ideal thought should not be concerned with a critique of social relations and is necessarily free-standing; e.g. Miller and Dagger (2003).

2 Alexander Garcia Duttman (2000) argues, for example, that the assumption that recognition involves the expression of a stable

identity obscures its status as an 'event', as an open-ended process where identities are constituted, shaped and dissolved. Thinkers such as Habermas and Honneth conceal the essential instabilities in the performative construction of identity by imposing a unifying construction of recognition. This reification of identity ultimately serves to normalize the unstable process of politics by admitting only those highly delimited differences that do not disrupt the overall structure of a struggle for recognition.

3 This is evident in Markell's discussion of the spatialization of time where he argues that, by attributing a false temporal unity to identity and action, the idea of recognition cannot capture many types of subordination which operate through the conversion of temporal open-endedness into problems of spatial organization (Markell 2003: 10). Markell's dualist opposition of an emancipatory temporal openness to a limited economy of spatial fixity obscures the much more complex ways in which space and time are interwoven and which have been documented in the work of, for example, Fabian (2002) and Lefebvre (1991).

4 In Habermas's conception of a communicatively guided democracy, there is an intrinsic connection between all levels of society, the political, legal and social. When the principle of individual autonomy is properly implemented in all realms of the democratic state, it renders the liberal opposition between individual and collective rights redundant. All levels of society should be characterized by open structures of communication which promote discussions oriented to self-understanding and the protection of intersubjectively shared experiences and life contexts. Individual autonomy can then be protected in the context of a critical discussion about the value of cultural traditions and norms. Given that the identity of the individual is interwoven with cultural identities, it is not necessary, as Taylor claims, to protect cultures through specific collective rights based on cultural survival. Cultural identities can be protected through the actualization of individual autonomy and equality which presupposes the value of specific life contexts, in the context of open democratic debate: 'Cultures survive only if they draw the strength to transform themselves from criticism and secession. Legal guarantees can be based only on the fact that within his or her own cultural milieu, each person retains the possibility of regenerating this strength. And this in turn develops not only by setting oneself apart but at least as much through exchanges with strangers and things alien' (Habermas 1994: 223).

5 For Habermas, the work of social reproduction in modern societies takes place on two levels, namely the reproduction of material

needs and the reproduction of symbolic norms. The reproduction of material needs occurs principally in the specialized realms, or subsystems of the economy and the state which are dominated by an instrumental rationality expressed in the 'egocentric calculations' of the steering media of money and power. The generation and maintenance of symbolic norms and values takes place within the 'lifeworld' which comprises the private sphere, the modern restricted nuclear family and the 'public sphere' or 'space of political participation, debate and opinion formation'. In opposition to the systemic integration of the economy and state, both these spheres are socially integrated, that is to say, guided by normative orientation and conventional prereflective reasoning. When this reasoning is rendered more conscious, it may form the basis of communicatively oriented rationality, that is, 'actions coordinated on the basis of explicit, reflectively achieved consensus (Habermas 1987: 153–97). This consensus is reached by unconstrained discussion under conditions of freedom, equality and fairness. The two spheres of system and lifeworld are connected by interchange relations which crystallize around the roles of employee and consumer (connecting the private sphere to the economy) and client and citizen (connecting public sphere to the state) (1987: 319–20). The differentiation of society is attached to a teleological view of societal development associated with the 'colonization of the lifeworld' thesis where the system imperatives of monetarization and bureaucratization 'work back upon contexts of communicative action and set their own imperatives against the marginalized lifeworld' (1987: 318). Continuous societal rationalization has the effect of *uncoupling* system from lifeworld which initially emphasizes the differentiation of two types of action coordination, one coming about through the consensus of those involved, the other through functional interconnections of action (1987: 186). However, for reasons that are not entirely clear, but are related to systemic crisis, forms of system integration begin to intervene within forms of social integration, tending to the communicatively structured lifeworld. This form of *structural violence* has the effect of distorting modes of communication through the imposition of systematic restrictions such as access to resources and power (1987: 187). Eventually this *mediatization* of the lifeworld turns into its *colonization* (1987: 318), calling forth the pathological effects of loss of meaning, alienation and fragmentation (1987: 326–7): 'The lifeworld is assimilated to juridified, formally organized domains of action and simultaneously cut off from the influx of an intact cultural tradition. In the deformations of everyday practice,

symptoms of rigidification combine with symptoms of desolation'
(1987: 327).

6 According to Habermas's theory of universal pragmatics, anyone
engaging in communication, in performing a speech act, necessarily raises validity claims and presupposes that they can be vindi-
cated or justified when challenged. The assumption of a claim to
validity and its justification form the conditions of possibility for all
speech acts or communication. On the basis of this assumption,
Habermas derives the idea of an ideal speech situation, characterized as 'pure intersubjectivity', i.e. by the absence of any barrier
which would hinder communication (see Thompson and Held
1982: 123–4). The ideal speech situation is a 'metanorm' in that it
delineates aspects of an argumentation process – around the validity claims raised by speech – which would lead to a rationally motivated agreement, as opposed to a false or apparent consensus. In
respect to this notion of rational consensus, the ideal speech situation rests on four conditions: first, each participant must have an
equal chance to initiate and continue communication; second, each
must have a chance to make assertions, recommendations and
explanations, and to challenge justifications; third, all must have
equal chances to express their wishes, feelings and intentions;
finally, the speaker must act as if in contexts of action there is an
equal distribution of chances to order and to resist orders, to be
accountable for one's conduct and to demand accountability
from others (see Benhabib 1986: 285; Thompson and Held 1982:
124). Although actual speech situations rarely correspond to this
ideal, nevertheless, such an ideal is always presupposed in all
communication. It is on this notion of an ideal speech situation that
Habermas rests his definition of truth. Truth is defined essentially
in terms of rational consensus: 'The condition for the truth of
statements is the potential consent for all others . . . Truth means the
promise to attain a rational consensus' (Habermas quoted in
Thompson and Held 1982: 124). Furthermore, Habermas links
emancipatory critique to this notion of rational consensus.
Emancipatory critique is governed by the idea that a rational consensus could be achieved not only with regard to problematic truth
claims, but also with regard to problematic norms.

7 Judith Butler argues that Bourdieu's materialist understanding of
speech acts underplays the autonomy of language and the way it
can be subverted for resistant ends. Speech acts are too closely tied
to their institutional context and miss the processes of temporal
deferral and dissemination that are constitutive of the indeterminacy of the performative. It is this indeterminacy that is essential

to understanding how it is that dominant norms may be appropriated and subverted by marginal groups. Bourdieu perpetuates a materialist reductionism in the separation of the social from the linguistic in his insistence that the 'magical efficacity' of a performative act derives not from the linguistic utterance itself but from the surrounding social and institutional context (Butler 1999: 109–10). The consequent claim that heterogeneity is not a property of language itself but rather that 'social heterogeneity is inherent in language' raises the issue of the precise status of the heterogeneous. The stringent separation made between the realms of the linguistic and the social leads to the paradox of whether the social heterogeneity that is internal to language is 'self-identically social' or whether it is a specific dimension of the linguistic itself. The distinction between the social and the linguistic leads to Bourdieu's reliance upon a simplified mimetic relation between language and society where the former reflects the latter. It also suggests an exterior and instrumental relation between the utterance and its subject who pre-exists in the social. For Bourdieu, the subject who utters the performative is 'positioned on a map of social power in a fairly fixed way. The performative will or will not be effective depending on whether the subject who performs the utterance is already authorized to make it work by the position of social power it occupies' (Butler 1999: 122).

For Butler, the domains of the social and the linguistic cannot be separated in such a distinct way because 'the discursive constitution of the subject [is] inextricable from the social constitution of the subject (Butler 1999: 120). The repeated effects of racial slurs, for example, live and thrive in the flesh of the addressee. The performative interpellation of the subject in terms of race or gender is not dependent on a specific 'authorized' subject but is the effect of a generalized process of subjectification. The diffuse nature of the process of interpellation renders the effects of the performative potentially indeterminate and open to subversion. The performative utterance cannot exclude the possibility of going awry, of being appropriated by marginal groups in, for example, the resignification of terms of degradation such as queer or nigger: 'it is precisely the expropriability of the dominant, "authorized" discourse that constitutes one potential site of its subversive resignification' (Butler 1999: 123). It is this re-appropriation of the authorized position within language which serves to expose prevailing forms of authority. Bourdieu cannot explain the troubling effects of such indeterminacy because of the causal priority accorded to the social over the linguistic and the fixity of the subject over the utterance and, in the final analysis, this undercuts claims about the generative nature of the habitus.

8 Habermas quoted in Culler 1985: 141: 'The ideal speech situation . . . is neither an empirical phenomenon nor a mere construct but rather an unavoidable supposition reciprocally made in discourse'.

CHAPTER 3

1 Habermas revises this stipulation in his later work.

2 The three normative conditions against which the narrative strands of different cultures should be evaluated are: 1. egalitarian reciprocity; 2. voluntary self-ascription; 3. freedom of exit and association (Benhabib 2002: 19–20).

CHAPTER 4

1 Fraser's response to these criticisms is that Young deploys a notion of the social group that is defined around a narrow and excessively unified idea of cultural identity. The unexamined cultural bias of the model leads Young to defend a 'wholesale, undifferentiated and uncritical version of the politics of difference' (Fraser 1997: 190). It might be the case that 'political economy is cultural and culture is economic' but it is still necessary to have a specific analysis of the way these forces manifest themselves in social life, which, for Fraser, means a more differentiated understanding of group formation and a greater attunement to the conflicts between systems of power relations. As Anne Philips puts it: 'even if we describe political economy as cultural, and culture as economic, we will still want to be able to talk of economic resources that sustain cultural identity or the cultural resources that enable people to press their economic claims' (Phillips 1997: 149).

2 Young argues that social structures should not be thought of as existing independently of social actors. Drawing on Anthony Giddens' theory of structuration, she argues that social structures should be conceptualized more along the lines of 'rules and resources', in that they constrain social agents but also facilitate agency and indeed are themselves the sedimented effects of agents' interventions in the world. She draws out the implications that this idea of the duality of structure has for the relation

between social groups and personal identity. For Young, social groups may position individuals in a certain way, but they do not constitute an individual's identity in any comprehensive sense. It is individuals themselves who actively fashion their own identities, within the particular constellation of material and symbolic resources in which they are situated. 'Social processes and interactions position individual subjects in prior relations and structures, and this positioning conditions who they are. But position neither determines nor defines individual identity. Individuals are agents: we constitute our own identities, and each person's identity is unique' (2000: 101). A consequence of this is that difference is understood as a political resource rather than a fixed attribute of individuals or groups.

CHAPTER 5

1 The discussion of hope also runs counter to the narrowly strategic view of agency that operates elsewhere in Bourdieu's work. On this account, agency has little to do with calculation of interests but has more to do with a socially realized capacity for hope. Unlike other emotions, hope does not have a discrete other as its object, rather its object is the expression of a degree of confidence vis-à-vis the future. Given that the future is unknowable, then action can only proceed on a certain level of confidence about one's ability to realize a possible future in the present. It is crucial underpinning of action in a state of emotional anticipation that is unacknowledged in strategic models of action. As Jacques Barbalet puts it: 'as the future is in principle unknowable, it is not possible for actors to operate in terms of calculations based on information . . . calculative reason necessarily gives way to emotion as the basis of action' (Barbalet 1998: 87). Levels of social recognition, experienced as assurance about one's past behaviour, confirm in the actor confidence about their prospective behaviour or ability to make a difference in the future.

2 The claim that poststructuralism disregards feelings is not wholly without foundation, as Frederic Jameson's remarks illustrate: 'As for expressions and feelings or emotions, the liberation, in contemporary society, from the older anomie of the centred subject may also mean not merely a liberation from anxiety but a liberation from every other kind of feeling as well, since there is no longer a self present to do the feeling' (quoted in Terada 2001: 1–2).

3 The phenomenological tradition in which Bourdieu works has a notion of an embodied relation to the world which is 'pre-objective', pre-reflective, pre-intellectual yet purposive and intentional' (Williams 2001: 57).

4 The varying significance that sexuality has for a sense of self is illustrated in Catherine Lutz's (1990) study of emotional control in men and women. In interview, women were found to express a far greater concern about appearing emotionally self-controlled than men. This concern can be seen as a straightforward internalization of hegemonic associations of women with the realm of affect and feeling. It expresses the idea that women are supposed to be better at handling feelings and also brings into play the opposite view of women as the victims of uncontrollable and irrational emotions However, on the level of a detailed syntactic analysis of transcribed interviews, there was minimal gender difference in the use of personalizing or non-distancing discursive strategies. This runs against the expectation, set up by the cultural model of women as more emotionally expressive, that they would use more personalizing syntactic forms than men. Lutz relates this absence of gender differences to 'gaps and fissures in the construction of a hegemonic discourse' (1990: 83). It also speaks to the fact that although gender differences profoundly inform embodied existence, they do not influence women's self-understanding or action in an unvarying way.

5 These problems in Bourdieu's account of the formation of gender identity as misrecognition are compounded by limitations in his wider understanding of the gendered nature of social structures. His claim that the same principles of masculinity and femininity that structure social space in primitive societies are operative in industrial societies results in a simplistic and dualist sociological account of gender divisions (McNay 2000: 55–7). Furthermore, there is some confusion, for instance, about whether Bourdieu understands gender as a field, a form of capital or type of symbolic violence (Adkins 2004: 6), although on this point I think that Bourdieu is quite clear. Gender is a primary form of symbolic violence which is realized in different ways across all social fields. Gender does not constitute a discrete field of action because the opposition between masculinity and femininity is an explicit or latent organizing principle in all social fields. Nor is it a form of capital, although the distribution of capital in a given field can be strongly determined, even dictated, by the symbolic organization of gender within that field.

Bibliography

Aboulafia, Mitchell (1999) 'A (neo)American in Paris: Bourdieu, Mead and Pragmatism' in Richard Schusterman (ed.) *Bourdieu: A Critical Reader* (pp. 153–74). Oxford: Blackwell.

Adkins, Lisa (2004) 'Introduction: Feminism, Bourdieu and After' in Lisa Adkins and Beverley Skeggs (eds) *Feminism After Bourdieu* (pp. 3–18). Oxford: Blackwell.

Adkins, Lisa (1995) *Gendered Work: Sexuality, Family and the Labour Market*. Buckingham: Open University Press.

Alexander, Jeffrey and Lara, Maria Pia (1996) 'Honneth's New Critical Theory of Recognition', *New Left Review*, 220: 126–36.

Amit, Vered and Rapport, Nigel (2002) *The Trouble with Community: Anthropological Reflections on Movement, Identity and Collectivity*. London: Pluto Press.

Appiah, Anthony (1996) 'Race, Culture, Identity: Misunderstood Connections' in Anthony Appiah and Amy Guttman (eds) *Color Conscious* (pp. 30–105). Princeton, NJ: Princeton University Press.

Appiah, Anthony (1994) 'Identity, Authenticity, Survival: Multicultural Societies and Social Reproduction' in Amy Gutmann (ed.) *Multiculturalism: Examining the Politics of Recognition* (pp. 149–63). Princeton, NJ: Princeton University Press/Oxford University Press.

Barbalet, Jack (1998) *Emotion, Social Theory, and Social Structure: A Macrosociological Approach*. Cambridge: Cambridge University Press.

Bell, Michael (1987) 'How Primordial is Narrative?' in C. Nash (ed.) *Narrative and Morality* (pp. 172–98). University Park, PA: Pennsylvania State University Press.

Benhabib, Selya (2002) *The Claims of Culture: Equality and Diversity in the Global Era*. Princeton, NJ: Princeton University Press.

Benhabib, Selya (1999) 'Sexual Difference and Collective Identities: The New Global Constellation', *Signs: Journal of Women in Culture and Society*, 24: 335–61.

Benhabib, Selya (1996) 'Toward a Deliberative Model of Democratic Legitimacy' in Selya Benhabib (ed.) *Democracy and Difference: Contesting the Boundaries of the Political* (pp. 67–94). Princeton, NJ: Princeton University Press.

Benhabib, Selya (1992) *Situating the Self: Gender, Community and Postmodernism in Contemporary Ethics*. Cambridge: Polity Press.

Benhabib, Selya (1986) *Critique, Norm and Utopia: A Study of the Foundations of Critical Theory*. New York: Columbia University Press.

Benhabib, Selya et al. (1995) *Feminist Contentions: A Philosophical Exchange*. London: Routledge.

Benjamin, Jessica (1998) *Shadow of the Other: Intersubjectivity and Gender in Psychoanalysis*. London: Routledge.

Benjamin, Jessica (1995) *Like Subjects, Love Objects: Essays on Recognition and Sexual Difference*. London: Yale University Press.

Benjamin, Jessica (1988) *The Bonds of Love: Psychoanalysis, Feminism, and the Problem of Domination*. New York: Pantheon.

Berlant, Lauren (2000) 'The subject of true feeling' in Sara Ahmed, Jane Kilby, Celia Lury, Maureen McNeil and Beverley Skeggs (eds) *Transformations: Thinking Through Feminism* (pp. 32–47). London: Routledge.

Berlant, Lauren (1997) *The Queen of America Goes to Washington City: Essays on Sex and Citizenship*. Durham, NC: Duke University Press.

Blum, Lawrence (1998) 'Recognition, Value and Equality: A Critique of Charles Taylor's and Nancy Fraser's Accounts of Multiculturalism', *Constellations*, 5, 1: 51–68.

Bohman, James (1999) 'Practical Reason and Cultural Constraint' in Richard Schusterman (ed.) *Bourdieu: A Critical Reader* (pp. 129–52). Oxford: Blackwell.

Bottero, Wendy and Irwin, Sarah (2003) 'Locating Difference: Class, "Race" and Gender, and the Shaping of Social Inequalities', *Sociological Review*, 51, 4: 463–83.

Bourdieu, Pierre (2001) *Masculine Domination*. Cambridge: Polity Press.

Bourdieu, Pierre (2000) *Pascalian Meditations*. Cambridge: Polity Press.

Bourdieu, Pierre (1998) *Practical Reason: On the Theory of Action*. Cambridge: Polity Press.

Bourdieu, Pierre (1993) *Sociology in Question*. London: Sage.

Bourdieu, Pierre (1992) *An Invitation to Reflexive Sociology*. Cambridge: Polity Press.

Bourdieu, Pierre (1991) *Language and Symbolic Power*. Cambridge: Polity Press.

Bourdieu, Pierre (1990a) *In Other Words: Essays Towards Reflexive Sociology*. Cambridge: Polity Press.

Bourdieu, Pierre (1990b) 'la domination masculine', *Actes de la Recherche en Sciences Sociale*, 84: 2–31.

Bourdieu, Pierre (1990c) *The Logic of Practice*. Cambridge: Polity Press.

Bourdieu, Pierre et al. (1999) *The Weight of the World: Social Suffering in Contemporary Society*. Cambridge: Polity Press.

Brown, Carol (1981) 'Mothers, Fathers and Children: From Private to Public Patriarchy', in L. Sargent (ed.) *Women and Revolution: A Discussion of the Unhappy Marriage of Marxism and Feminism* (pp. 239–68). London: Pluto Press.

Brown, Wendy (2004) 'At the Edge' in Stephen K. White and J. Donald Moon (eds) *What is Political Theory?* (pp. 103–23). London: Sage.

Brown, Wendy (2001) *Politics Out of History*. Princeton, NJ: Princeton University Press.

Brown, Wendy (1995) *States of Injury: Power and Freedom in Late Modernity*. Princeton, NJ: Princeton University Press.

Burkitt, Ian (1997) 'Social Relationships and Emotions', *Sociology*, 31, 1: 37–55.

Butler, Judith (2004) *Undoing Gender*. London: Routledge.

Butler, Judith (2000a) 'Restaging the Universal: Hegemony and the Limits of Formalism' in Judith Butler, Ernesto Laclau and Slavoj Žižek *Contingency, Hegemony, Universality* (pp. 11–43). London: Verso.

Butler, Judith (2000b) 'Competing Universalities' in Judith Butler, Ernesto Laclau and Slavoj Žižek *Contingency, Hegemony, Universality* (pp. 136–81). London: Verso.

Butler, Judith (2000c) 'Dynamic Conclusions' in Judith Butler, Ernesto Laclau and Slavoj Žižek *Contingency, Hegemony, Universality* (pp. 263–80). London: Verso.

Butler, Judith (1999) 'Performativity's Social Magic' in Richard Schusterman (ed.) *Bourdieu: A Critical Reader* (pp. 113–28). Oxford: Blackwell.

Butler, Judith (1998) 'Marxism and the Merely Cultural', *New Left Review*, 227: 33–44.

Butler, Judith (1997a) *Excitable Speech: A Politics of the Performative*. London: Routledge.

Butler, Judith (1997b) *The Psychic Life of Power: Theories in Subjection.*
Stanford, CA: Stanford University Press.

Butler, Judith (1995) 'Contingent Foundations' in Selya Benhabib,
Judith Butler, Drucilla Cornell and Nancy Fraser (eds) *Feminist
Contentions: A Philosophical Exchange* (pp. 35–57). London:
Routledge.

Butler, Judith (1990) *Gender Trouble: Feminism and the Subversion of
Identity.* London: Routledge.

Butler, Judith, Laclau, Ernesto and Žižek, Slavoj (2000) *Contingency,
Hegemony, Universality.* London: Verso.

Calhoun, Craig (1995) *Critical Social Theory: Culture, History and the
Challenge of Difference.* Oxford: Blackwell.

Castoriadis, Cornelius (1991) *Philosophy, Politics and Autonomy:
Essays in Political Philosophy.* Oxford: Oxford University Press.

Castoriadis, Cornelius (1987) *The Imaginary Institution of Society.*
Cambridge: Polity Press.

Castoriadis, Cornelius (1984) *Crossroads in the Labyrinth.* Brighton:
Harvester.

Cavarerro, Adrianna (2000) *Relating Narratives: Storytelling and
Selfhood.* London: Routledge.

Charlesworth, Simon (2000) *A Phenomenology of Working Class
Experience.* Cambridge: Cambridge University Press.

Chodorow, Nancy (1999) *The Power of Feelings: Personal Meaning in
Psychoanalysis, Gender and Culture.* New Haven: Yale University
Press.

Chodorow, Nancy (1995) 'Individuality and Difference in how
Women and Men Love' in Anthony Elliott and Stephen Frosh
(eds) *Psychoanalysis in Contexts: Paths Between Theory and Modern
Culture* (pp. 89–105). London: Routledge.

Chodorow, Nancy (1989) 'What is the Relation between
Psychoanalytic Feminism and the Psychoanalytic Psychology of
Women?' in Deborah L. Rhode (ed.) *Theoretical Perspectives on
Sexual Difference* (pp. 114–30). New Haven: Yale University
Press.

Coates, Jennifer (1993) *Women, Men and Language: A Sociolinguistic
Account of Gender Differences in Language.* Harlow: Pearson
Education.

Connell, Robert W. (1987) *Gender and Power: Society, the Person and
Sexual Politics.* Cambridge: Polity Press.

Coole, Diana (1996) 'Habermas and the Question of Alterity' in M.
Passerin D'Entreves and S. Benhabib (eds) *Habermas and the
Unfinished Project of Modernity: Critical Essays on the Philosophical
Discourse of Modernity* (pp. 221–44). Cambridge: Polity Press.

Culler, Jonathan (1985) 'Communicative Competence and Normative Force', *New German Critique*, 35: 133–4.

Dean, Jodi (1996) *Solidarity of Strangers: Feminism after Identity Politics*. London: University of California Press.

Dean, Jodi (1995) 'Discourse in Different Voices' in J. Meehan (ed.) *Feminists Read Habermas: Gendering the Subject of Discourse* (pp. 205–29). London: Routledge.

De Lauretis, Teresa (1987) *Technologies of Gender: Essays on Theory, Film and Fiction*. London: MacMillan.

De Lauretis, Teresa (1984) *Alice Doesn't: Feminism, Semiotics, Cinema*. London: MacMillan.

D'Emilio, John (1984) 'Capitalism and Gay Identity' in A. Snitow et al. (eds) *Powers of Desire: The Politics of Sexuality* (pp. 140–52). London: Virago.

Delphy, Christine (1984) *Close to Home: A Materialist Analysis of Women's Oppression*. London: Hutchinson.

Dietz, Mary (2002) *Turning Operations: Feminism, Arendt and Politics*. London: Routledge.

Donzelot, Jacques (1979) *The Policing of Families*. London: John Hopkins University Press.

Downs, Laura Lee (1993) 'If "Woman" is Just an Empty Category, Then Why Am I Afraid to Walk Alone at Night? Identity Politics Meets the Postmodern Subject', *Comparative Studies in Society and History*, 35, 2: 414–37.

Dreyfus, Hubert and Rabinow, Paul (1993) 'Can there be a Science of Existential Structure and Social Meaning?' in Craig Calhoun, Edward LiPuma and Moishe Postone (eds) *Bourdieu: Critical Perspectives* (pp. 35–44). Cambridge: Polity Press.

Dryzek, John (2005) 'Deliberative Democracy in Divided Societies: Alternatives to Agonism and Analgesia', *Political Theory*, 33, 2: 218–42.

Dryzek, John (2000) *Deliberative Democracy and Beyond: Liberals, Critics, Contestations*. Oxford: Oxford University Press.

Duttman, Alexander Garcia (2000) *Between Cultures: Tensions in the Struggle for Recognition*. London: Verso.

Emcke, Carolin (2000) 'Between Choice and Coercion: Identities, Injuries, and Different Forms of Recognition', *Constellations*, 7, 4: 483–94.

Fabian, Johannes (2002) *Time and the Other: How Anthropology Makes its Object*. New York: Columbia University Press.

Fanon, Frantz (1952) *Black Skin, White Masks*. London: Pluto.

Field, Nicola (1997) 'Identity and the Lifestyle Market' in Rosemary Hennessey and Chrys Ingraham (eds) *Materialist Feminism: A*

Reader in Class, Difference and Women's Lives (pp. 259–71). London: Routledge.

Flathmann, Richard (2003) *Freedom and Its Conditions: Discipline, Autonomy and Resistance.* London: Routledge.

Flax, Jane (1993) *Disputed Subjects: Essays on Psychoanalysis, Politics and Philosophy.* London: Routledge.

Foucault, Michel (1988) 'The Ethic of Care for the Self as a Practice of Freedom' in James Bernauer and David Rasmussen (eds) *The Final Foucault* (pp. 1–20). London, MIT Press.

Foucault, Michel (1980) *Power/Knowledge: Selected Interviews and Other Writings.* Brighton: Harvester.

Foucault, Michel (1978) *The History of Sexuality: An Introduction.* Harmondsworth: Penguin.

Franks, Suzanne (1999) *Having None of It: Women, Men and the Future of Work.* London: Granta Books.

Fraser, Nancy (2003) 'Rethinking Recognition: Overcoming Displacement and Reification in Cultural Politics' in Barbara Hobson (ed.) *Recognition Struggles and Social Movements: Contested Identities, Agency and Power* (pp. 21–32). Cambridge: Cambridge University Press.

Fraser, Nancy (2000) 'Rethinking Recognition', *New Left Review*, 3: 107–20.

Fraser, Nancy (1997) *Justice Interruptus: Critical Reflections on the Postsocialist Condition.* London: Routledge.

Fraser, Nancy (1995) 'Pragmatism, Feminism, and the Linguistic Turn' in Seyla Benhabib, Judith Butler, Drucilla Cornell and Nancy Fraser *Feminist Contentions: A Philosophical Exchange* (pp. 157–71). London: Routledge.

Fraser, Nancy (1989) *Unruly Practices: Power, Discourse and Gender in Contemporary Social Theory.* Cambridge: Polity Press.

Fraser, Nancy and Honneth, Axel (2003) *Redistribution or Recognition: A Political–Philosophical Exchange.* London: Verso.

Fraser, Nancy and Nicholson, Linda (eds) (1990) *Feminism/Postmodernism.* London: Routledge.

Frazer, Elizabeth and Lacey, Nicola (1993) *The Politics of Community: A Feminist Critique of the Liberal-Communitarian Debate.* London: Harvester.

Frosh, Stephen (1999) *The Politics of Psychoanalysis: An Introduction to Freudian and Post-Freudian Theory.* London: Macmillan.

Fox, Pamela (1994) *Class Fictions: Shame and Resistance in the British Working-Class Novel 1890–1945.* Durham, NC: Duke University Press.

Gal, Susan (2003) 'Movements of Feminism: The circulation of discourses about women' in Barbara Hobson (ed.) *Recognition*

Struggles and Social Movements: Contested Identities, Agency and Power (pp. 93–118). Cambridge: Cambridge University Press.

Gardiner, Judith Kegan (ed.) (1995) *Provoking Agents: Gender and Agency in Theory and Practice*. Chicago: University of Illinois Press.

German, Lindsey (1997) 'Theories of the Family' in R. Hennessey and C. Ingraham (eds) *Materialist Feminism: A Reader in Class, Difference and Women's Lives* (pp. 147–59). London: Routledge.

Paul Gilroy (2000) *Between Camps: Nations, Cultures and the Allure of Race*. Harmondsworth: Penguin.

Gilroy, Paul (1993) *The Black Atlantic: Modernity and Double Consciousness*. London: Verso.

Grosz, Elizabeth (1994) 'Refiguring Lesbian Desire' in L. Doan (ed.) *The Lesbian Postmodern* (pp. 67–84). New York: Columbia University Press.

Habermas, Jürgen (1998a) *On the Pragmatics of Communication*. Cambridge: Polity Press.

Habermas, Jürgen (1998b) 'Political Liberalism: A Debate with John Rawls' in J. Habermas *The Inclusion of the Other: Studies in Political Theory* (pp. 49–101). Cambridge: Polity Press.

Habermas, Jürgen (1996) *Between Facts and Norms: Contributions to a Discourse Theory of Law and Democracy*. Cambridge: Polity Press.

Habermas, Jürgen (1994) 'Struggles for Recognition in the Democratic Constitutional State' in Amy Gutmann (ed.) *Multiculturalism: Examining the Politics of Recognition* (pp. 107–48). Princeton, NJ: Princeton University Press/Oxford University Press.

Habermas, Jürgen (1992) *Postmetaphysical Thinking: Philosophical Essays*. Cambridge: Polity Press.

Habermas, Jürgen (1991) 'A Reply' in Axel Honneth and Hans Joas (eds) *Communicative Action: Essays on Jurgen Habermas's The Theory of Communicative Action* (pp. 214–64). Cambridge: Polity Press.

Habermas, Jürgen (1987) *The Theory of Communicative Action*. Cambridge: Polity Press.

Hall, Stuart (1997) 'Interview on Culture and Power', *Radical Philosophy*, 86: 24–41.

Harstock, Nancy (1990) 'Foucault on Power: A Theory for Women' in L. Nicholson (ed.) *Feminism/Postmodernism* (pp. 157–75). London: Routledge.

Harstock, Nancy (1985) *Money, Sex and Power: Toward a Feminist Historical Materialism*. Boston, MA: Northeastern University Press.

Hartmann, Martin and Honneth, Axel (2006) 'Paradoxes of Capitalism', *Constellations*, 13, 1: 41–58.

Hennessey, Rosemary (2000) *Profit and Pleasure: Sexual Identities in Late Capitalism*. London: Routledge.

Hennessey, Rosemary (1995) 'Subjects, Knowledges, . . . and All the Rest: Speaking for What?' in Judith Roof and Robyn Wiegman (eds) *Who Can Speak? Authority and Critical Identity* (pp. 137–50). Urbana, IL: University of Illinois Press.

Hobson, Barbara (ed.) (2003) *Recognition Struggles and Social Movements: Contested Identities, Agency and Power.* Cambridge: Cambridge University Press.

Hobson, Barbara and Lindholm, Marika (1997) 'Collective Identities, Women's Power Resources, and the Making of Welfare States', *Theory and Society* 26: 475–508.

Holloway, Wendy (1984) 'Gender Difference and the Production of Subjectivity' in J. Henriques et al. (eds) *Changing the Subject: Psychology, Social Regulation and Subjectivity* (pp. 227–63). London: Methuen.

Honneth, Axel (2004) 'Organized Self-Realization: Some Paradoxes of Individualization', *European Journal of Social Theory*, 7, 4: 463–78.

Honneth, Axel (1999) 'Postmodern Identity and Object-Relations Theory: On the Seeming Obsolescence of Psychoanalysis', *Philosophical Explorations*, 3: 225–42.

Honneth, Axel (1995) *The Struggle for Recognition: The Moral Grammar of Social Conflicts.* Cambridge: Polity Press.

Honneth, Axel (1994) 'The Social Dynamics of Disrespect: On the Location of Critical Theory Today', *Constellations*, 1, 2: 255–69.

Honig, Bonnie (1992) 'Towards an Agonistic Feminism: Hannah Arendt and the Politics of Identity' in J. Butler and J. Scott (eds) *Feminists Theorize the Political* (pp. 215–35). London: Routledge.

Jackson, Stevi (1999) *Heterosexuality in Question.* London: Sage.

Jamieson, Lynn (1998*) Intimacy: Personal Relationships in Modern Societies.* Cambridge: Polity Press.

Johnson, Miriam (1988) *Strong Mothers: Weak Wives: The Search for Gender Equality.* Berkeley, CA: University of California Press.

Kirmayer, Lawrence, J. (1996) 'Landscapes of Memory: Trauma, Narrative and Dissociation' in P. Antze and M. Lambek (eds) *Tense Past: Cultural Essays in Trauma and Memory* (pp. 173–98). London: Routledge.

Kogler, Hans (1997) 'Alienation as Epistemological Source: Reflexivity and Social Background after Mannheim and Bourdieu', *Social Epistemology*, 11, 2: 141–64.

Kruks, Sonia (2001) *Retrieving Experience: Subjectivity and Recognition in Feminist Politics.* Ithaca, NY: Cornell University Press.

Laclau, Ernesto (1989) 'Preface' in Slavoj Žižek *The Sublime Object of Ideology* (pp. ix–xv). London: Verso.

Laplanche, Jean (1999) *Essays On Otherness.* London: Routledge.

Lara, Maria Pia (1998) *Moral Textures: Feminist Narratives in the Public Sphere*. Cambridge: Polity Press.

Lawler, Steph (2000) *Mothering the Self: Mothers, Daughters, Subjectivities*. London: Routledge.

Lawler, Steph (1999) ' "Getting Out and Getting Away": Women's Narratives of Class Mobility', *Feminist Review*, 63: 3–24.

Lazreg, Marnia (1994) 'Women's Experience and Feminist Epistemology: A Critical Neo-rationalist Approach', in K. Lennon and M. Whitford (eds) *Knowing the Difference: Feminist Perspectives in Epistemology* (pp. 45–62). London: Routledge.

Lefebvre, Henri (1991) *The Production of Space*. Oxford: Blackwell.

Lewis, Jane (2001) *The End of Marriage: Individualism and Intimate Relations*. Cheltenham: Edward Elgar.

Lloyd, Moya (1999) 'Performativity, Parody, Politics' in *Theory, Culture and Society*, 16, 2: 195–213.

Lutz, Catherine (1990) 'Engendered Emotion: Gender, Power, and the Rhetoric of Emotional Control in American Discourse' in Catherine Lutz and Lila Abu-Lughod (eds) *Language and the Politics of Emotion* (pp. 69–91). Cambridge: Cambridge University Press.

Mansbridge, Jane and Morris, Aldon (eds) (2001) *Oppositional Consciousness: The Subjective Roots of Social Protest*. Chicago: Chicago University Press.

Markell, Patchen (2003) *Bound by Recognition*. Princeton, NJ: Princeton University Press.

McCarthy, Thomas (2004) 'Political Philosophy and Racial Injustice: From Normative to Critical Theory' in Selya Benhabib and Nancy Fraser (eds) *Pragmatism, Critique, Judgement: Essays for Richard J. Bernstein* (pp. 149–70). London: MIT Press.

McNay, Lois (2001) 'Meditations on *Pascalian Meditations*', *Economy and Society*, 30, 1: 139–54.

McNay, Lois (2000) *Gender and Agency: Reconfiguring the Subject in Feminist and Social Theory*. Cambridge: Polity Press.

McRobbie, Angela (2002) 'A Mixed Bag of Misfortunes: Bourdieu's Weight of the World', *Theory, Culture and Society*, 19, 3: 129–38.

Meehan, Johanna (ed.) (1995) *Feminists Read Habermas: Gendering the Subject of Discourse*. London: Routledge.

Miller, David and Dagger, Richard (2003) 'Utilitarianism and Beyond: Contemporary Analytical Political Theory' in T. Ball and R. Dagger (eds) *The Cambridge History of Twentieth Century Political Thought* (pp. 446–69). Cambridge: Cambridge University Press.

Moi, Toril (1999) *What is a Woman? And Other Essays*. Oxford: Oxford University Press.

Mulhall, Stephen and Swift, Adam (1992) *Liberals and Communitarians*. Oxford: Blackwell Publishers.

Newey, Glen (2001) *After Politics: The Rejection of Politics in Contemporary Liberal Philosophy*. Basingstoke: Palgrave.

Nielsen, Harriet Bjerrum (2004) 'Noisy Girls: New Subjectivities and Old Gender Discourses', *Young*, 12, 1: 9–30.

Nielsen, Harriet Bjerrum and Rudberg, Monica (1994) *Psychological Gender and Modernity*. Oslo: Scandinavian University Press.

Norval, Aletta J. (1998) 'Memory, Identity and the (Im)possibility of Reconciliation: The Work of the Truth and Reconciliation Commission in South Africa', *Constellations*, 5, 2: 250–64.

Novotony, Kristin (1998) ' "Taylor"-Made? Feminist Theory and the Politics of Identity', *Women and Politics*, 19, 3: 1–19.

Oliver, Kelly (2001) *Witnessing: Beyond Recognition*. Minneapolis, MN: University of Minnesota Press.

Ong, Aihwa (1991) 'The Gender and Labour Politics of Postmodernity', *Annual Review of Anthropology*, 20: 279–309.

Osborne, Peter (1995) *The Politics of Time: Modernity and Avant-Garde*. London: Verso.

Osborne, Peter and Segal, Lynne (1994) 'Gender as Performance: An Interview with Judith Butler', *Radical Philosophy*, 67: 32–9.

Phillips, Anne (2003) Recognition and the struggle for political voice' in Barbara Hobson (ed.) *Recognition Struggles and Social Movements: Contested Identities, Agency and Power* (pp. 263–73). Cambridge: Cambridge University Press.

Phillips, Anne (1997) 'From Inequality to Difference: A Severe Case of Displacement?', *New Left Review*, 224: 143–53.

Povinelli, Elizabeth (2002) *The Cunning of Recognition: Indigenous Alterities and the Making of Australian Multiculturalism*. Durham, NC: Duke University Press.

Probyn, Elspeth (2004) 'Shame in the Habitus' in Lisa Adkins and Beverley Skeggs (eds) *Feminism After Bourdieu* (pp. 224–48). Oxford: Blackwell.

Ray, Larry and Sayer, Andrew (1999) (eds) *Culture and Economy After the Cultural Turn*. London: Sage.

Reay, Diane (2000) 'A Useful Extension of Bourdieu's Conceptual Framework?: Emotional Capital as a Way of Understanding Mothers' Involvement in their Children's Education', *Sociological Review*, 48, 4: 568–85.

Reay, Dianne (1998) 'Rethinking Social Class: Qualitative Perspectives on Class and Gender', *Sociological Review*, 32, 2: 259–75.

Ricoeur, Paul (1998) *Critique and Conviction: Conversations with Francois Azouvi and Marc de Launay*. Cambridge: Polity Press.

Ricoeur, Paul (1992) *Oneself as Another*. London: Chicago University Press.

Ricoeur, Paul (1981) *Hermeneutics and the Human Sciences: Essays on Language, Action and Interpretation*. Cambridge: Cambridge University Press.

Riley, Denise (2000) *The Words of Selves: Identification, Solidarity, Irony*. Stanford, CA: Stanford University Press.

Rose, Jacqueline (1986) *Sexuality in the Field of Vision*. London: Verso.

Rose, Nikolas (1999) *Powers of Freedom: Reframing Political Thought*. Cambridge: Cambridge University Press.

Rudberg, Monica and Nielsen, Harriet Bjerrum (2005) 'Potential Spaces – Subjectivities and Gender in a Generational Perspective', *Feminism and Psychology*, 15, 2: 127–48.

Ruspini, Elisabetta and Dale, Angela (eds) (2002) *The Gender Dimension of Social Change: The Contribution of Dynamic Research to the Study of Women's Life Courses*. Bristol: Policy.

Rustin, Michael (1995) 'Lacan, Klein and Politics: The Positive and Negative in Psychoanalytic Thought' in Anthony Elliott and Stephen Frosh (eds) *Psychoanalysis in Contexts: Paths Between Theory and Modern Culture* (pp. 223–45). London: Routledge.

Saltzman Chafetz, Janet (1990) *Gender Equity: An Integrated Theory of Stability and Change*. London: Sage.

Sanders, Lynn (1997) 'Against Deliberation', *Political Theory*, 25, 3: 347–76.

Sayer, Andrew (2000) 'System, Lifeworld and Gender: Associational Versus Counterfactual Thinking', *Sociology*, 34, 4: 707–25.

Sayer, Andrew (1999) 'Valuing Culture and Economy' in Larry Ray and Andrew Sayer (eds) *Culture and Economy After the Cultural Turn* (pp. 53–75). London: Sage.

Schatzki, Theodore R. (2001) 'Introduction: Practice Theory' in Theodore R. Schatzki, Karin Knorr Cetina and Eike von Savigny (eds) *The Practice Turn in Contemporary Theory* (pp. 1–14). London: Routledge.

Scott, Joan (1993) 'The Tip of the Volcano', *Comparative Studies in Society and History*, 35, 2: 438–43.

Scott, Joan (1992) ' "Experience" ' in J. Butler and J. Scott (eds) *Feminists Theorize the Political* (pp. 22–40). London: Routledge.

Sedgwick, Eve Kosofsky (2003) *Touching Feeling: Affect, Pedagogy, Performativity*. Durham, NC: Duke University Press.

Seideman, Stephen (1993) 'Identity Politics in a "Postmodern" Gay Culture: Some Historical and Conceptual Notes' in M. Warner (ed.) *Fear of a Queer Planet: Queer Politics and Social Theory* (pp. 105–42). Minneapolis, MN: University of Minnesota Press.

Sennett, Richard and Cobb, Jonathan (1977) *The Hidden Injuries of Class*. Cambridge: Cambridge University Press.

Shapiro, Michael (2001) *For Moral Ambiguity: National Culture and the Politics of the Family*. Minneapolis, MN: University of Minnesota Press.

Skeggs, Beverley (2004a) 'Context and Background: Pierre Bourdieu's Analysis of Class, Gender and Sexuality' in Lisa Adkins and Beverley Skeggs (eds) *Feminism After Bourdieu* (pp. 19–33). Oxford: Blackwell.

Skeggs, Beverley (2004b) 'Exchange, Value and Affect: Bourdieu and the "Self"' in Lisa Adkins and Beverley Skeggs (eds) *Feminism After Bourdieu* (pp. 75–95). Oxford: Blackwell.

Skeggs, Beverley (2004c) *Class, Culture, Self*. London: Routledge.

Skeggs, Beverley (1997) *Formations of Class and Gender: Becoming Respectable*. London: Sage.

Skeggs, Beverley and Moran, Leslie (eds) (2004) *Sexuality and the Politics of Violence and Safety*. London: Routledge.

Skinner, Quentin (1991) ' "Who are We"? Ambiguities of the Modern Self', *Inquiry*, 34, 2: 133–53.

Smith, Dorothy (2005) *Institutional Ethnography: A Sociology for People*. Oxford: Altamira Press.

Smith, Dorothy (1999) *Writing the Social: Critique, Theory and Investigations*. Toronto: University of Toronto Press.

Spivak, Gayatri Chakravorty (1988) 'Can the Subaltern Speak?' in C. Nelson and L. Grossberg (eds), *Marxism and the Interpretation of Culture* (pp. 271–313). London: Macmillan.

Stacey, Judith (1988) 'Can There be a Feminist Ethnography?' *Women's Studies International Forum*, 11, 1: 21–7.

Steedman, Christina (1986) *Landscape for a Good Woman: A Story of Two Lives*. London: Virago.

Strawson, Galen (1997) ' "The Self".' *Journal of Consciousness Studies* 4: 405–28.

Sztompka, Piotr (1994) *Agency and Structure: Reorienting Social Theory*. Reading: Gordon and Breach Science Publishers.

Taylor, Charles (1999) 'To Follow a Rule . . .' in Richard Schusterman (ed.) *Bourdieu: A Critical Reader* (pp. 29–44). Oxford: Blackwell.

Taylor, Charles (1994a) 'The Politics of Recognition' in Amy Gutmann (ed.) *Multiculturalism: Examining the Politics of Recognition* (pp. 25–73). Princeton, NJ: Princeton University Press/Oxford University Press.

Taylor, Charles (1994b) 'Charles Taylor Replies' in James Tully (ed.) *Philosophy in the Age of Pluralism* (pp. 213–57). Cambridge: Cambridge University Press.

Taylor, Charles (1991) 'Language and Society' in Axel Honneth and Hans Joas (eds) *Communicative Action: Essays on Jurgen Habermas' The Theory of Communicative Action* (pp. 23–35). Cambridge: Polity Press.

Taylor, Charles (1989) *Sources of the Self: The Making of Modern Identity*. Cambridge: Cambridge University Press.

Taylor, Charles (1985) *Human Agency and Language: Philosophical Papers 1*. Cambridge: Cambridge University Press.

Tempelman, Sasja (1999) 'Constructions of Cultural Identity: Multiculturalism and Exclusion', *Political Studies*, XLVII: 17–31.

Terada, Rei (2001) *Feeling in Theory: Emotion after the Death of the Subject*. Cambridge, MA: Harvard University Press.

Thistle, Susan (2000) 'The Trouble with Modernity: Gender and the Remaking of Social Theory', *Sociological Theory* 18, 2: 275–88.

Thompson, Edward P. (1995) *The Poverty of Theory: Or an Orrery of Errors*. London: Merlin Press.

Thompson, John B. (1991) 'Editor's Introduction' in Pierre Bourdieu *Language and Symbolic Power* (pp. 1–31). Cambridge: Polity Press.

Thompson, John B. (1984) *Studies in the Theory of Ideology*. Cambridge: Polity Press.

Thompson, John B. and Held, David (eds) (1982) *Habermas: Critical Debates*. London: Macmillan.

Vandenberghe, Frederic (1999) ' "The Real is Relational": An Epistemological Analysis of Pierre Bourdieu's Generative Structuralism', *Sociological Theory*, 17, 1: 32–67.

VanEvery, Jo (1996) 'Heterosexuality and domestic life' in Diane Richardson (ed.) *Theorising Heterosexuality: Telling it Straight* (pp. 39–54). Oxford: Oxford University Press.

Wacquant, Loic (2005) (ed.) *Pierre Bourdieu and Democratic Politics: The Mystery of Ministry*. Cambridge: Polity Press.

Walby, Sylvia (1997) *Gender Transformations*. London: Routledge.

Walby, Sylvia (1990) *Theorizing Patriarchy*. Oxford: Basil Blackwell.

Walkerdine, Valerie, Lucey, Helen and Melody, June (2001) *Growing Up Girl: Psychosocial Explorations of Gender and Class*. New York: New York University Press.

Warner, Michael (1999) *The Trouble with Normal: Sex, Politics, and the Ethics of Queer Life*. Cambridge, MA: Harvard University Press.

Weberman, David (2000) 'Are Freedom and Anti-humanism Compatible? The Case of Foucault and Butler', *Constellations*, 7, 2: 255–71.

Weir, Allison (1996) *Sacrificial Logics: Feminist Theory and the Critique of Identity*. London: Routledge.

Wellmer, Albrecht (1991) *The Persistence of Modernity: Essays on Aesthetics, Ethics and Postmodernism*. London: MIT Press.

White, Stephen K. (2000) *Sustaining Affirmation: The Strengths of Weak Ontology in Political Theory*. Princeton, NJ: Princeton University Press.

Whitebook, Joel (1996) 'Intersubjectivity and the Monadic Core of the Psyche: Habermas and Castoriadis on the Unconscious' in M Passerin d'Entreves and S. Benhabib (eds) *Habermas and the Unfinished Project of Modernity: Critical Essays on the Philosophical Discourse of Modernity* (pp. 172–93). Cambridge: Polity Press.

Whitebook, Joel (1995) *Perversion and Utopia: A Study in Psychoanalysis and Critical Theory*. London: MIT Press.

Williams, Fiona (2003) 'Contesting "Race" and Gender in the European Union: A Multilayered Recognition Struggle for Voice and Visibility' in Barbara Hobson (ed.) *Recognition Struggles and Social Movements: Contested Identities, Agency and Power* (pp. 121–44). Cambridge: Cambridge University Press.

Williams, Melissa (1998) *Voice, Trust, and Memory: Marginalized Groups and the Failings of Liberal Representation*. Princeton, NJ: Princeton University Press.

Williams, Raymond (1977) *Marxism and Literature*. Oxford: Oxford University Press.

Williams, Simon (2001) *Emotions and Social Theory: Corporeal Reflections on the (Ir)Rational*. London: Sage.

Williams, Simon and Bendelow, Gillian (1998) *The Lived Body: Sociological Themes, Embodied Issues*. London: Routledge.

Willett, Cynthia (1995) *Maternal Ethics and Other Slave Moralities*. London: Routledge.

Wolf, Susan (1994) 'Comment' in Amy Gutmann (ed.) *Multiculturalism: Examining the Politics of Recognition* (pp. 75–85). Princeton, NJ: Princeton University Press/Oxford University Press.

Wood, Allen (1985) 'Habermas' Defense of Rationalism', *New German Critique*, 35: 145–64.

Wood, Ellen Meiskens (1995) *Democracy Against Capitalism: Renewing Historical Materialism*. Cambridge: Cambridge University Press.

Yar, Majid (2001) Beyond Nancy Fraser's "Perspectival Dualism'", *Economy and Society*, 30, 3: 288–303.

Young, Iris Marion (2000) *Inclusion and Democracy*. Oxford: Oxford University Press.

Young, Iris Marion (1997) 'Unruly Categories: A Critique of Nancy Fraser's Dual Systems Theory', *New Left Review*, 222: 147–60.

Young, Iris Marion (1996) ' "Communication and the Other": Beyond Deliberative Democracy' in Selya Benhabib (ed.) *Democracy and Difference: Contesting the Boundaries of the Political* (pp. 120–35). Princeton, NJ: Princeton University Press.

Young, Iris Marion (1994a) 'Comments on Selya Benhabib's Situating the Self', *New German Critique*, 62: 165–72.

Young, Iris Marion (1994b) 'Gender as Seriality: Thinking about Women as a Social Collective', *Signs* 19, 3: 713–38.

Young, Iris Marion (1990) *Justice and the Politics of Difference*. Princeton, NJ: Princeton University Press.

Zerilli, Linda (2005) *Feminism and the Abyss of Freedom*. Chicago: University of Chicago Press.

Žižek, Slavoj (2000) 'Da Capo senza Fine' in Judith Butler, Ernesto Laclau and Slavoj Žižek *Contingency, Hegemony, Universality* (pp. 213–62). London: Verso.

Žižek, Slavoj (1999a) *The Ticklish Subject: The Absent Centre of Political Ontology*. London: Verso.

Žižek, Slavoj (1999b) 'Preface: Burning the Bridges' in Elizabeth Wright and Edmond Wright (eds) *The Žižek Reader* (pp. vii–x). Oxford: Blackwell Publishers.

Žižek, Slavoj (1999c) 'Courtly Love, or Woman as Thing' in Elizabeth Wright and Edmond Wright (eds) *The Žižek Reader* (pp. 148–73). Oxford: Blackwell Publishers.

Žižek, Slavoj (1998) 'For a Leftist Appropriation of the European Legacy', *Journal of Political Ideologies*, 3: 63–78.

Žižek, Slavoj (ed.) (1994) *Mapping Ideology*. London: Verso.

Žižek, Slavoj (1991) *For They Know Not What They Do: Enjoyment as a Political Factor*. London: Verso.

Žižek, Slavoj (1989) *The Sublime Object of Ideology*. London: Verso.

Zurn, Christoper (2003) 'Identity or Status? Struggles over "Recognition" in Fraser, Honneth, and Taylor', *Constellations*, 10, 4: 519–37.

Zurn, Christopher (2000) 'Anthropology and Normativity: A Critique of Axel Honneth's "Formal Conception of Ethical Life"', *Philosophy and Social Criticism*, 26, 1: 115–24.

Index